HENRY JAMES

A Study of the Short Fiction

Also available in Twayne's Studies in Short Fiction Series

Twayne's Studies in Short Fiction

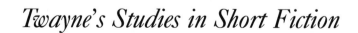

Gordon Weaver, General Editor
Oklahoma State University

HENRY JAMES

HENRY JAMES

A Study of the Short Fiction

Richard A. Hocks
University of Missouri, Columbia

TWAYNE PUBLISHERS • BOSTON
A Division of G. K. Hall & Co.

Copyright 1990 by G. K. Hall & Co.
All rights reserved.
Published by Twayne Publishers
A division of G. K. Hall & Co.
70 Lincoln Street
Boston, Massachusetts 02111

Twayne's Studies in Short Fiction Series, No. 17

Copyediting supervised by Barbara Sutton.
Book production by Gabrielle B. McDonald.
Book design by Janet Z. Reynolds.
Typeset in 10/12 Caslon
by Compset, Inc., Beverly, Massachusetts.

First published 1990.
10 9 8 7 6 5 4 3 2 1

The paper used in this publication meets the minimum requirements
of American National Standard for Information Sciences—Permanence
of Paper for Printed Library Materials, ANSI Z39.48-1984. ∞™

Printed and bound in the United States of America.

Library of Congress Cataloging-in-Publication Data

Hocks, Richard A., 1936–
    Henry James : a study of the short fiction / Richard A. Hocks.
        p.   cm. — (Twayne's studies in short fiction ; 17)
    Includes bibliographical references (p.   ).
    ISBN 0-8057-8328-8 (alk. paper)
    1. James, Henry, 1843–1916—Criticism and interpretation.
    2. Short story. I. Title. II. Series: Twayne's studies in short
    fiction ; no. 17.
    PS2124.H56   1990
    813′.4—dc20
                                            90-34509
                                            CIP

Contents

Preface

More than twenty-five years ago, in 1964, Krishna Baldev Vaid published the first major critical study of Henry James's short fiction, a traditional analysis of his formal technique focusing selectively on certain illustrative tales from James's large corpus. Several years later James Kraft examined James's earliest tales, but his brief study ends with 1880, well before James's great explosion of fine short fiction in the 1890s and long before the most powerful and important tales of his maturity. In 1984 Edward Wagenknecht published a helpful survey of James's tales, emphasizing sources and plot summary, though also including some analysis and evaluation. Finally, Richard Gage most recently has discussed the thematic unity found in James's metaphorically titled story sequences, a somewhat restricted but not unimportant portion of his total short fiction.[1] That one would find so few critical books since the 1950s on James's shorter fiction is very surprising, at least if one fully considers two facts: first, that Henry James is indisputably one of the greatest short fiction writers of all time, not just in America, the birthplace of the genre, but throughout the world; second, that James's fiction and nonfiction (if one can truly separate them these days) receive more academic analysis each year than any other American author save Faulkner, with whom he remains in a virtual tie.[2] Indeed, at a recent Modern Languages Association conference there were four separate sessions on Henry James, the most on any author other than Shakespeare and a remarkable occurrence in these days of poststructuralism, gender analysis, Marxism, and the like.

Something, as they say, has to give. How does one account for the disparity between so modest a number of books on James's short fiction, on the one hand, and his seismic importance to that genre, on the other, especially given the prolific amount of James scholarship in the past fifty years?

No small part of the answer is that James's short fiction is continuously interpreted and reinterpreted in academic journals, anthologies, or in books with broader topics. Another reason is that his canon of short fiction is so substantial, so distinguished, and of such variable length that the prospect of doing it justice between the covers of a single book seems daunting, especially when the task is further compounded by the perennially complex issue of James's textual revisions. Still a third vestigial reason of decreasing validity is that James's stature remains that of a great novelist for whom the short story was a lesser affair and primarily a way to make his living while composing artistically pristine novels. This assumption turns out to be wrong on both counts. We know now that James was passionately involved in the economics of his novels, not to mention his plays.[3] And we also know that James was a practitioner of the "poetics" of the short story and "beautiful and blest *nouvelle*" all his life, especially in his later period.

It remains true, however, that James has far less to say theoretically about the short story than the novel, perhaps because so many of his stories were not strictly short stories—what he calls "anecdotes"—but long tales. And, of course, we think he said so little only because, as the premier aesthetician of fiction, he had so much to say in general: if we compare his statements with those of his great predecessor in the genre, Nathaniel Hawthorne, his comments do not appear slim. More importantly, his copious critical commentary regarding the creative process applies equally to his short fiction as to the novel; otherwise he should not have written so much about both in his famous *Prefaces* to the New York Edition of his revised work. Admittedly, one can turn that argument around and argue that in enunciating his creative process for both novels and tales James had no distinct theory of the short story per se. But that view overlooks the powerful influence he has had on modern fiction and ignores what he does have to say in the *Prefaces*, his *Notebooks*, and other places, such as his critical essay on Maupassant. By analogy, one does not diminish the novels of Kate Chopin or Stephen Crane because they were quintessentially short story writers. James, for all his importance as a novelist, is "quintessentially" more a writer of tales than are Kate Chopin or Stephen Crane novelists. Indeed, one principal goal of this study will be to illustrate that James's shorter fiction became a genre with its own distinctive poetics and that his perennial influence on subsequent practitioners is the reverse of accidental.

The scope of my study includes representative work from all three major periods of his productive career, the early, middle, and later years, roughly from the early 1870s to 1910. Obviously a swift survey of all 112 short stories, nouvelles, and very long tales bordering on short novels by James would be tedious if not impossible, even a misrepresentation of what makes him a great artist to begin with. His powerful canon is hardly served by cramming this book with titles and tiny annotated summaries, feebly imitating Wagenknecht's far better handbook. At the same time, the massiveness and general high quality of James's canon cannot be disregarded, so I therefore must employ a "Lord Baconian" method: a few tales are "tasted," a good number "swallowed whole," and certain ones "chewed and digested." Freely translated, several tales are succinctly mentioned, a goodly number are analyzed with some depth, and a certain small group receive very lengthy and deliberately complex interpretations, a kind of analysis very seldom found in book-length surveys. These greatly elaborated readings include work from all three periods but deliberately exclude James's already most analyzed works, "The Turn of the Screw," "Daisy Miller," "The Beast in the Jungle," "The Aspern Papers," and "The Jolly Corner." Those works, I hasten to add, are not merely "tasted." While realizing there are several different hypothetical readers of this study, I think a "collective reader" is best served by being shown the same dense layering of meaning embedded in tales other than the most celebrated ones, which so many readers already know to be Dantesque or Joycean in depth and compression. My larger goal and sincere hope is that the reader of this study may emerge at its end with the intellectual tools to read any of James's finest tales the "chewed and digested" way.

These last comments identify my focus as well, which is to explore the interconnections among James's social, moral, psychological, and philosophical interests together with his experimental and technical innovations, ones by no means limited to narrative "point of view." The overriding theme of this study is that James's short fiction eventually achieves a poetic density that makes him the central bridge from nineteenth- to twentieth-century fiction at its peak. His craftmanship is never secondary to human issues, however, in the dominion of society and psychology, consciousness and philosophy. Vaid's 1964 study was appropriately preoccupied with isolating Jamesian technique, distinguishing among different types of tales, and in a general sense differentiating tales from novels. His governing classification and terminology—"omniscient narrator-tales" as essentially tragic versus biographical first-person tales as usually comic (Vaid, 259–60)—may perhaps now appear deficient in certain respects, yet it really is a good way of organizing and structuring a large complex body of material if one is primarily isolating distinctive types of Jamesian narrators.

Unlike either Vaid or Richard Gage, I have chosen to present James's work generally in chronological order rather than according to technical devices or thematic focus. This gives the reader an introduction to James's work, yet with an analysis intended otherwise to be critically advanced and sophisticated. Any survey or overview study is surely at some level derivative; over the years I have certainly benefited from the magnitude of James criticism more than I can pay adequate tribute—or probably even remember. At the same time, there is in addition to my own personal expression of the "cumulative wisdom" a reservoir of original thinking that I hope permeates and at its appointed times even percolates throughout this study. In any event, my chronological approach should aid the person not so familiar with James, while still challenging (or not disengaging) the reader who is already a seasoned Jamesian or teacher of American literature. The most obvious advantage, however, is that it allows the reader to assess James's development as artist and thinker from the social realism and internationalism of his first period through his aesthetic and moral preoccupations of the middle period toward the poetic expressionism and pioneering ghostly fiction of the late period. Chronological division by no means precludes the introduction of characteristically Jamesian themes as they constantly emerge both within and between successive tales.

In James studies, chronology intersects with the question of textual revision. Throughout his career James revised his tales greatly. Most appeared in English and American magazines and were revised when incorporated into book collections. But it is the important body of fiction chosen for The New York Edition that received the most extensive revision, revision often said to mirror features of the late convoluted prose style and thus alter most the idiom of the early and stylistically simpler stories. Scholar-critics remain sharply divided about this matter: if anything, we may be currently entering an early-text-preference period in line with "deconstructing" late James as mandarin master. Those who favor the earlier texts have always cited their greater simplicity and spontaneity in the rendering of human experience and motivation. And yet the actual studies of James's revision process reveal that, virtually without exception, his revision inevitably sharpens his earlier conception, most frequently through vivifying metaphor.[4]

One interesting feature of his late style unappreciated even now by many Jamesians is that, while his syntax certainly expands convolutely, he intentionally counteracts that process by introducing contractions and simplifying punctuation to enhance the vernacular quality of the prose. This is in line with his well-known practice, in later years, of dictating his first drafts to an amanuensis. Some scholars, however, prefer to cite James's unrevised texts simply to preserve the progression and development of his art. That always sounds reasonable, but in actual fact it overlooks two important points. First, any reader other than a text specialist has no notion whatever that the passage quoted contains prose later to be revised and so has no basis for comparison. Second, it is at least a moot point which citation *really* conveys James's development, since James himself contends in the Preface to *The Golden Bowl* that revision itself is the living, "poetic" principle of his development as an artist.[5] In some ways it would be easier never to cite his revised texts, for I could simplify my documentation by citing only the *Complete Tales* and avoid the volumes of the New York Edition entirely. But James's revisions are just too important and too good to ignore, even if most readers are unaware of them.

To give three intentionally "minor" examples: in "The Pupil," which I shall discuss at great length, James has Mrs. Moreen accuse the tutor Pemberton of walking and hurrying her son, Morgan Moreen, the pupil, too fast. The earlier text, both magazine and book, reads that Mrs. Moreen "tossed" this accusation at Pemberton over her shoulder. The revised New York Edition prints that she "hurled" it. At another point Pemberton reflects on his exploitation by the Moreens, that he "had simply given himself away to a band of adventurers. The idea, the word itself, had a sort of romantic horror for him—he had always lived on such safe lines." In the revision James writes "wore a sort of romantic horror," not merely to eliminate the proximity of several uses of the verb *had*. Finally, when confronted with the unforeseen prospect of taking young Morgan off his parents' hands for good, James changed the hesitant Pemberton's thought from "what could he do with Morgan's life?" to "what could he do with Morgan's dreadful little life?"[6]

All three are typical of the quiet revisions James made to his earlier tales in 1907–1909. None involves the more dramatic question of the early style versus the late prolix syntax, which scholars prefer to discuss. Yet all three bear on the interpretation of a great tale, and the cumulative effect of these and others like them may bear on it profoundly. Mrs. Moreen's "hurled" accusation sharpens her character and heightens the deep conflict between her and Pemberton. Morgan's "dreadful little life" in Pemberton's thought highlights the momentary repugnance he has at the prospect of being "stuck" with the boy just before Morgan's sudden tragic death. And Pemberton's notion that "the idea, the word itself, *wore* a romantic horror" buttresses an important point, that the tutor truly needs a rationale to disclaim his own complicity in the tragedy: to "wear" is to cover over or conceal something, in this instance, I believe, from Pemberton himself. In other words, he still wants to "live on safe lines."

Let me stress, however, that my lengthy analysis of "The Pupil" never cites any of this revision as evidence contributing to my reading of that tale, although it obviously affects my interpretation. To cite such evidence from "The Pupil" or the many other tales discussed in this volume would almost double the size of this book! Inasmuch as my emphasis is on James's poetic density I do believe it most important to cite his revised texts, although I shall not again stop and examine the revisions *as* evidence. I may now and then cite the earlier text for a special reason, but my preference is for the New York Edition—unless the tale under discussion was not included in that collection, as is sometimes the case.

Finally, a word should be said about basic nomenclature and terminology: "short fiction," "short story," "tale," "nouvelle," and the like. On this issue Vaid, who cautions, "There is no simple way out of the current confusion on this matter," nevertheless makes an excellent argument adequate for my purpose here. While he makes the right case for the subcategory termed "anecdote" by James (what we ordinarily mean by a short story), Vaid's principal points are these: first, that James preferred the term "tale" to "short story" (about which he was interested, however); second, that James never confused "his short novels with his long tales," and that "'Short novel' is a misleading equivalent for a James nouvelle." Therefore Vaid himself retains "both these terms (nouvelle and anecdote) and, following James's practice and preference, use[s] 'tale' as a general substitute for both." (Vaid, 4–7). With the confusing terminology fostered by various anthologies, I believe it is best and simplest to keep foremost in mind that *The Spoils of Poynton* and *The American* are novels, as much so as *The Portrait of a Lady*, *The Bostonians*, or *The Wings of the Dove*. *The Reverberator* is a bona fide "short novel." "The Aspern Papers," "The Turn of the Screw, and "In the Cage" are tales—albeit quite long tales—and as such are discussed in this volume. "Daisy Miller," "The Lesson of the Master," "The Pupil," "Glasses," "The Beast in the

Jungle," and "The Bench of Desolation" are in length ideal Jamesian nouvelles, all between 17,000 and 26,000 words—that is to say, they, too, are long tales, though shorter than the "Turn of the Screw" group. Finally, a quite respectable number of James's fine "anecdotes," usually between 7,000 and 11,000 words long, classify well enough as short stories. In sum, I believe *tale* is never inappropriate for any of James's fiction shorter than *The Reverberator*, which is approximately 53,000 words long and beyond the dividing line between tale and short novel.

Part 2 presents excerpts from James's *Notebooks, Letters, Prefaces*, and his essay on Maupassant, all of which record his views on his own short fiction and that of others. I do not, however, reprint "The Art of Fiction" or other classic documents by James so oft anthologized and easily available elsewhere, even though I certainly quote from such material now and then in Part 1. Part 3 is primarily a profile of critical essays on several major tales discussed in Part 1. These suggest the diversity of critical approaches possible to a given James tale and to a slight extent suggest why James today is the prism through which so much contemporary critical theory is refracted. To my knowledge, these essays have not been reprinted previously. The Bibliography includes the major collections of James's tales, including the pertinent volumes from the New York Edition, and also lists an inevitably abbreviated group of critical books and articles intended to augment the perspective defined by Part 3.

Richard A. Hocks

University of Missouri, Columbia

Notes

1. Krishna Baldev Vaid, *Technique in the Tales of Henry James* (Cambridge: Harvard University Press, 1964); James Kraft, *The Early Tales of Henry James* (Carbondale: Southern Illinois University Press, 1969); Edward Wagenknecht, *The Tales of Henry James* (New York: Ungar Publishing Co., 1984); Richard P. Gage, *Order and Design: Henry James' Titled Story Sequences* (New York: Peter Lang, 1988); hereafter cited in the text. S. Gorley Putt, *Henry James: A Reader's Guide* (Ithaca, N.Y.: Cornell University Press, 1966), also discusses a number of the tales. Opposing the view that James is technically original in his short fiction is John Gerlach, "Closure in Henry James's Short Fiction," *Journal of Narrative Technique* 14 (1984): 60–67.

2. The MLA International Bibliography lists over a hundred items for James and Faulkner each year, the most for any American writer.

3. For James's interest in the economics of his novels see Michael Anesko, *"Friction with the Market": Henry James and the Profession of Authorship* (New York: Oxford University Press, 1986); Marcia Jacobson, *Henry James and the Mass Market* (Tuscaloosa: University of Alabama Press, 1983); Anne T. Margolis, *Henry James and the Problem of Audience* (Ann Arbor, Mich.: UMI Research Press, 1985); and "Cash Accounts and Addresses" in *The Complete Notebooks of Henry James*, ed. Leon Edel and Lyall H. Powers (New York: Oxford University Press, 1986), 597–618.

4. See, for example, F. O. Matthiessen, "The Painter's Sponge and Varnish Bottle" in *Henry James: The Major Phase* (New York: Oxford University Press, 1944), 152–86; Anthony J. Mazzella, "The New Isabel" in *Henry James: The Portrait of a Lady*, Norton Critical Edition, ed. Robert D. Bamberg (New York: W. W. Norton, 1975), 597–619; for the same evidence when James revised a later text see J. Donald Crowley and Richard A. Hocks, "Notes on the Text," in *Henry James: The Wings of the Dove*, Norton Critical Edition, ed. J. Donald Crowley and Richard A. Hocks (New York: W. W. Norton, 1978), 407–21. A good case for the opposing view is Nina Baym, "Revision and Thematic Change in *The Portrait of a Lady*," *Modern Fiction Studies* 22 (1976), 183–200.

5. See *The Art of the Novel: Critical Prefaces*, ed. R.P. Blackmur (New York: Charles Scribner's Sons, 1934), 337–43.

6. *The Novels and Tales of Henry James*, vol. 11 (New York: Charles Scribner's Sons, 1908), 533–34, 572, 577. This is the New York Edition. The earlier readings can be found in *The Complete Tales of Henry James*, vol. 7, ed. Leon Edel (New York: J. B. Lippincott, 1963), 426, 456, 460.

Acknowledgments

I am very grateful to the Research Council of the University of Missouri for recommending to the Office of the Provost a semester's research leave, which greatly helped to advance this study toward completion. I am also thankful to Jane Smith for cheerfully typing the James selections in Part 2 as well as the Chronology and Selected Bibliography; I am likewise grateful to Kathie McCoy for cutting and pasting up the four critical articles in Part 3 as well as my "Maupassant" excerpts in Part 2. I appreciate furthermore Liz Traynor Fowler's help, suggestions, and support in turning my manuscript into this printed book. Finally, I am beholden once again to my wife, Elaine, this time especially for the innumerable delays of dinner plans so that I could work "just a little longer" on this study.

Part 1

THE SHORT FICTION

Introduction: James and the Art of Short Fiction

Although Henry James is routinely called the "novelist's novelist," his short fiction comprises twelve volumes, attesting to his productivity in the writing of tales and to their importance in his overall canon. Indeed, the New York Edition of his works, which bears his selection and careful revision of texts, is entitled, aptly, *The Novels and Tales of Henry James*. James was, of course, a prolific writer of novels and shorter fiction as well as the author of literary criticism, autobiographical volumes, travel literature, and even cultural analyses after the manner of Matthew Arnold, John Ruskin, and his friend Henry Adams. What should be stressed about his short fiction is that, like his work in general, it exhibits both high quantity and consistent quality. This sets him apart from the plight of the premodern American writer, voiced in the famous lament of Ernest Hemingway that our classic authors fail to exhibit a "third act" in their literary careers. Even cursory reflection on the work of Poe, Melville, Twain, Crane, and even Hawthorne will reveal that, although the absence of an extended proliferation of fine tales occurs for different reasons in their respective careers, each failed to produce short fiction with that combination of quantity, quality, and artistic development which marks James's and earns him the appellation of "master," although many feel that designation is now suspect for its disguise of James's artistic, personal, and professional economic anxieties. Poe pioneered the form, but his distinguished corpus remains small; Melville mastered it in a brief spurt in the early 1850s, but then left "Billy Budd" unfinished at his death almost forty years later; Twain, to be sure, wrote "shorter works" all his life, but the perennial question he poses is just how many of these qualify as short stories: if Melville, as Nina Baym once expressed it, had a "quarrel with fiction," Twain did not seem especially to like fiction, at least if judged by his own reading. Stephen Crane and Kate Chopin, in a sense like Poe at a later stage, perfected, refined, and advanced the short story as a work of art, but owing to early death and other factors their canons were somewhat stinted. And Howells, the author of "Editha" and the ally of James in the new post–Civil War realism, remained predominantly a novelist, critic, journalist, editor, and author of travel volumes rather than a writer of tales.

Only Hawthorne among James's predecessors and early contemporaries compares with or surpasses Poe as a significant composer of fine tales. Yet even Hawthorne, from whom James learned the "deeper psychology," cannot strictly be thought of as one whose work *evolved* artistically in any sense resembling James's: for example, the tale most consider his masterpiece, "My Kinsman Major Molineux," was written very early in Hawthorne's career; still, he did not deem it worthy of inclusion in either edition of *Twice-told Tales* or in *Mosses from an Old Manse*. One cannot imagine a similar occurrence in James's career, that he would have written his most profound tale so early; or, if he had, would then have overlooked it in putting together an important collection. Readers and critics, to be sure, are frequently discovering how strong a heretofore unanthologized story by James in fact is, but one never finds an opposing tendency to devalue stories that have been admired for some time. The early "Daisy Miller," the middle "Aspern Papers," and the late "Jolly Corner" remain as widely read as ever, regardless of the increasing interest in "The Great Good Place," "Glasses," "In the Cage," "The Tree of Knowledge," or "Maud-Evelyn." What this suggests is that James's contribution to both the canon and development of the American short story remains immense, perhaps the most important contribution of any American writer before the modern period. Historically speaking, he is our first poetic realist of prose.

Internationalism and the Quasi-Supernatural Realm

While James is most often celebrated for inventing "the international novel," the subject of which treats the conflict or confrontation of American characters with the labyrinth of European culture, his short stories exhibit a wider range of subject matter while by no means ignoring the so-called international theme, as evidenced by such early tales as "A Passionate Pilgrim," "Four Meetings," "Daisy Miller," "A Bundle of Letters," "Madame de Mauve," and "An International Episode." James's international fiction can be thought of as the "second frontier" in our literary history: at the time it sensed the completion of the westward settlement, the American psyche instinctively began to gravitate back toward its European "memory." The international theme—or, more accurately in James, the international subject—is prominent in his early period, tends to disappear in the middle period, and reappears with great complexity in his late period or major phase. That pattern, however, is somewhat truer for the novels than the tales, which follow the first two stages more closely than the third: those of the late period duplicate the complexity of the late novels but do not as a group exhibit the corresponding emphasis on internationalism, although both "A Round of Visits" and "The Jolly Corner" would qualify as "reverse international" (Americans returning home after long stays in Europe). In general, however, I believe James's international subject transposes imaginatively into the deep and archetypal paradigms of innocence and experience, nature and art, the ethical and aesthetic consciousness, freedom and determinism. James's international fiction, in short, often recapitulates the deep structure of universal polar or dialectical themes.

Some of his finest stories, however, are set in Europe, frequently England, and may just as often not even include American characters. Among the best that do not are "The Marriages," "The Bench of Desolation," and one of the most explicated tales in the language, "The Beast in the Jungle." Furthermore, his canon includes a very significant group of parable stories of artists and writers; these most frequently come from the 1890s and include such strong works as "The Lesson of the Master," "Greville Fane," "The Real Thing," and "The Figure in the Carpet."

Still another category of stories—in certain respects the most important—are James's "ghostly" or "quasi-supernatural" tales, the imaginative outgrowth of his preoccupation with the psychology of character. James's profound and abiding literary interest in normal psychology, so to speak, just kept deepening until eventually he began to probe the caverns and weirs of abnormal psychology, especially the condition of obsession. The best known of these tales is, of course, "The Turn of the Screw," the meaning of which has caused more debate than even Melville's "Billy Budd," yet unlike Melville's classic work, it does not derive its ambiguity primarily from its being unfinished and reconstructed from working manuscripts. But there are other ghostly tales in James's prolific canon, including "The Altar of the Dead," "The Friends of the Friends," "The Great Good Place," "The Real Right Thing," and the masterful "Jolly Corner," a work that at once reinvents the very genre of "double" literature and simultaneously condenses rich and multitudinous levels of meaning into an economy of form comparable to one of T. S. Eliot's *Four Quartets*, with which it also has thematic affinities. "The Beast in the Jungle," among its inexhaustible dimensions, is also one of James's ghostly tales. James's quasi-supernaturalism actually culminated in his 1910 essay "Is There a Life After Death?," the only spiritual document he ever wrote and the distillation of his preoccupation with abnormal psychology and the ghostly realm—a document, moreover, that corresponds closely to William James's psychological exploration of religious experience.[1]

Furthermore, there are tales that focus and depict the comedy or the tragedy of society, a thematic thread that also runs through the overwhelming majority of James's novels and is present in all three periods of his career independent of the international theme. In these, especially the tragedies, one often finds his abiding moral interest in human "cannibalism" or exploitation of one character by another. Although several tales are admixtures and classify uneasily, among the comedies are "An International Episode," "The Point of View," "The Liar," "Lady Barbarina," "Greville Fane," "Miss Gunton of Poughkeepsie," and "The Birthplace"; among the tragedies are "The Pupil," "Julia Bride," "Europe," "The Beast in the Jungle," "The Bench of Desolation," and "A Round of Visits." The well-executed "Aspern Papers," primarily a comedy, could, I suspect, also be grouped with most of the Jamesian classifications discussed hitherto, with the exception, perhaps, of the "ghostly" category—although Miss Tina's transformation at the end has for the unscrupulous narrator at least the effect of an "apparition," if not the tenor of it.

Jamesian Technique

In addition to James's wide range of subjects, his tales exhibit the distinctively Jamesian development of fiction as art and technical mastery for which the novels are famous. He was the first major critic and theoretician of fiction after Edgar Allan Poe, the author of innumerable essays on the writers of his time, and the composer of the definitive *Prefaces* to the New York Edition between 1907 and 1909, written with the same care and creativity he put into his best late fiction. Although he infrequently speaks there generically of the short story—far more often addressing the issue or challenge of a specific given tale—he does compare the short story to the "hard, shining sonnet, one of the most indestructible forms of composition," and acknowledges that "Great for me from far back had been the interest of the whole 'question' of the short story."[2] This view is greatly confirmed and amplified by his *Notebooks*.

In general, his experimentation in fiction makes one feel that, were it not demeaning to the genuine accomplishment of his great predecessors, we might say James delivers to us our native genre's "coming of age" in his mastery of the form and the articulation of its poetics. He is most conventionally associated with the development of "narrator point of view," or what he liked to call more fluidly and dramatically his various "registers" or "deputies"; chief among these is his creation of "the unreliable narrator" or, just as frequently, the specious third-person narrative "register." He is also associated with the doctrine of the author's originating "germ," which expands through the creative process into a living whole, often (but not always) endowing the finished work with a neo-Coleridgean unity or Goethean metamorphosis, though shorn of those writers' spiritual cosmology. Finally, James is associated with the brilliant alternation of what Percy Lubbock in one of the earliest and most important studies of prose fiction labeled "the panoramic" and "the dramatic."[3] James's own terms for these alternating structural elements in his fiction are "picture" (the rendering of interior thought) and "scene" (characters in action and speech)—the latter he also sometimes called "discriminated occasions." All such subtle narrative strategy, however, eventually conspires to intensify the condition of ambiguity and deception in a world where the simpler Cartesian division between mind and external phenomena no longer quite prevails, or at least provides us that consistent line of demarcation we might have wished.

Beyond "the Rise of Realism"

As already indicated, James's short fiction reflects his career phases, from the early, sharply delineated critiques of society to the late, rich, convoluted poetic prose, which conveys reality in its affective flux. Indeed, it is sometimes hard to decide which issue pertains to the development of James himself and which to the morphology of the American short story. James began his long career as an exponent of psychological realism. He collaborated with the other realists—William Dean Howells, Sarah Orne Jewett, Mary Wilkins Freeman, Hamlin Garland, Kate Chopin, and others—in formulating and practicing what is academically designated "the Rise of Realism," or what Vernon Louis Parrington called "the Beginnings of Critical Realism," a school of fiction that put a premium on the close notation of ordinary life, the rendition of a specific geographical region, the dramatization and criticism of social taboos, and the delineation of individual character. This post–Civil War movement flourished in the last three decades of the century and was greatly influenced by continental rather than English masters—especially Balzac, Flaubert, Turgenev, Maupassant, and, in the case of Howells, at least, Tolstoy. Also for later James, as for one of his successors, James Joyce, the name of Henrik Ibsen must be added, for the Danish writer's combination of poetic drama, social consciousness, technical innovation, and the study of individual psychology made his work consonant with James's fiction beginning in the 1890s and continuing through the first decade of the twentieth century.

James's special province within "the Rise of Realism" is increasingly the psychology of individual character. His early stories, to be sure, like Howells's fiction generally, exhibit social realism and what Howells liked to call a "scientific decorum," or what James called the "direct impression of life": they tend to subordinate the study of an individual's psyche to a conflict or misunderstanding that arises from social and cultural conditioning, as in "An International Episode," "A Bundle of Letters," "The Point of View," and "Daisy Miller." On the other hand, James's mature tales take their point of departure from the aspirations best voiced in his most famous critical essay, "The Art of Fiction" (1884), one of the most widely read and reprinted essays on prose fiction ever written by a practicing author. In the essay James not only establishes fiction as a fine art but continues to insist that its purpose is to "represent life," that all questions really come back to "execution," that fiction has a double heritage and analogy with both painting and history (thus fusing the realist program with high artistic composition), and finally, that the moral quality of a work of art resides not in any conscious moral purpose but rather in "the quality of the mind of the producer," that is, the aspiring author, who should "Try to be one of the people on whom nothing is lost."

In the same essay, however, he also makes a statement about the writer's experience that more than any other captures the heart of his doctrine and anticipates the ruling feature of his own short fiction from the late 1880s onward, well beyond his practice of anything like documentary realism. "Experience," he writes, is never limited and it is never complete; it is an immense sensibility, a kind of huge spider web of the finest silken threads suspended in the chamber of consciousness, and catching every air-borne particle in its tissue. It is the very atmosphere of the mind; and when the mind is imaginative—much more when it happens to be that of a man of genius—it takes to itself the faintest hints of life, it converts the very pulses of the air into revelations. . . . The power to guess the unseen from the seen, to trace the implication of things, to judge the whole piece by the pattern, the condition of feeling life in general so completely that you are well on your way to knowing any particular corner of it—this cluster of gifts may almost be said to constitute experience, and they occur in country and in town and in the most differing stages of education. If experience consists of impressions, it may be said that impressions *are* experience, just as (have we not seen it?) they are the very air we breathe.[4]

This famous statement promises us, among other things, that later the psychology of James's best and most mature work will render the drama of consciousness and convey for his characters and readers alike the moment-to-moment sense of human experience as bewilderment and discovery. Consciousness he conceives of as a field, in philosophical language what his brother William James, anticipating modern phenomenology, calls a "function" rather than an "entity," or, to adopt for a moment the terminology of contemporary thinker Owen Barfield, a "participating" rather than an isolated and onlooking faculty; that is to say, a mechanism not dichotomized from the phenomena of which it is conscious. James's late fiction suggests that reality itself is an affective flux corresponding to something like field theory. For this reason he came more and more to present subtle shades of human perception and intellectual nuance, to diminish physical action—or rather to present physical action as a living extension of consciousness—and to invent a prose style of elliptical syntax, periodic sentence, and capacious extended metaphor. His genius for linguistic experimentation began to simulate reality as a field even while he otherwise allied himself, precariously, to the assumptions of mimesis, his "direct impression of life." It is no accident therefore that his momentous influence on modern literature has become as strong on poetry as on fiction itself. It is also not surprising that scholars and critics of James's work today focus far less on his realism and more on his transcendence of the limitations of realism. Indeed, Sergio Perosa considers him the "great uncle of postmodernism," and John Carlos Rowe nothing less than the refracting prism for every major school of contemporary critical theory.[5] James has been regarded, then, for quite a long time as craftsman extraordinaire and innovator of fictive technique, but by now I believe more and more readers and scholars alike recognize that all such technique, at least in his later work, is but the avenue into the broader epistemological issues just sketched.

Female Consciousness

Finally, James is justly celebrated for the creation of great women characters in the novels. One thinks of them as a veritable gallery—Isabel Archer, Olive Chancellor, Fleda Vetch, Maisie Farange, Christina Light, Milly Theale, Kate Croy, Charlotte Stant, Maggie Verver. In his tales James does not, I believe, exhibit quite the comparable achievement. Inasmuch as his tales are obviously full of women, such a judgment is inevitably a matter of personal taste and interpretation, even perhaps of definition. I am thinking from the novels primarily of female protagonists and narrative "registers" along the lines of Isabel, Maisie, Fleda, Milly, and Maggie. The Governess in "The Turn of a Screw" is a great creation, to be sure, although a disturbing individual; the unnamed telegraphist of "In The Cage" is certainly an important figure whom I examine later in this study; I also explore closely the powerful, troubled spirit of Julia Bride. Yet even Daisy Miller, among the most unforgettable of James's women characters, is not the "register" of her tale. It is not that James fails to provide vivid female figures such as Caroline Spencer, Miranda Hope, Tina Bordereau, Lily Gunton, Mora Montravers, or Kate Cookham; it is only that male "registers" seem to predominate in the tales. It makes one wonder whether or not the more ample development possible in the novel better suited James's rendering of the internal working of female consciousness. At the very beginning of his *Prefaces* James defines the novel as "a long fiction with a 'complicated' subject" (*AN*, 4). Possibly he felt that, other things being equal, the "registering" of interior female consciousness was a "complicated subject" better suited to the novel.

One might counterclaim, however, that James's own narrative consciousness *within* the text of his fiction is as much female as male. I believe a glimpse at his "enabling androgyny"—to use a phrase from *Theoretical Dimensions* (Rowe, 91)—may be had in these reflections from his Preface to *The Princess Casamassima:*

My report of people's experience—my report as a 'story teller'—is essentially my appreciation of it, and there is no 'interest' for me in what my hero, my heroine or any one else does save through that admirable process. As soon as I begin to appreciate simplification is imperilled: the sharply distinguished parts of any adventure, any case of endurance and performance, melt together as an appeal. . . . I can't be intimate without that sense and taste, and I can't appreciate save by intimacy, any more than I can report save by a projected light. (*AN*, 65–66)

However we decide this question of James's "engendered" text, his best tales, whatever their length and the specific gender of their viewpoint characters, are inevitably marked by an imaginative concision not unlike the genius of Emily Dickinson and suggesting perhaps the aptness of James's comparison of the genre to the sonnet. From the period of his artistic maturity in the late 1880s and 1890s through his major phase after 1900, the tales exhibit increasingly subtle layers of meaning, stratification of irony and theme, integration of complex imagery, and, as always, psychology of character.

Early James: Social Realism and the International Scene

In James studies it is sometimes customary to cite "The Madonna of the Future" (1873) and "A Passionate Pilgrim" (1871) as early prototypes in James's evolution toward the international theme, yet many Jamesians would probably agree that both immature tales are uncertain in their focus. It is true that in "The Madonna" the artist-protagonist Theobald, an expatriate American and compatriot to the narrator, proclaims Americans "the disinherited of Art," and that the narrator himself admits to being of the "famished race";[6] yet the real center of the tale seems to be the ironic disparity between a pristine aesthetic idealism and artistic practice, and thus more generally between ideality and actuality. Theobald can boast that as an artist he has not yet "added a grain to the rubbish of the world" (13:444), but the ironic cash value of that proposition (as William James might say) turns out to be both the narrator and reader's eventual surprise discovery that the canvas of his Raphaelesque masterpiece, his "Madonna of the Future," has remained blank and unattempted through all his expatriate years in Florence due to his own paralyzing perfectionism.

James complicates this theme of Theobald's impotence-through-idealism, however, by providing some Melvillian "crosslights": a "productive" Italian artist who creates only crude figurines of cats and monkeys; the figure of Mrs. Coventry, an unpleasant American "social high-priestess of the arts" in Florence (13:458), who nonetheless predicts accurately Theobald's lack of any real accomplishment; and, finally, Theobald's "inspiration," the now stout model Serafina, hardly any longer the appropriate image for a "maiden mother," who carries on promiscuously with the Italian figurine maker. Only the narrator emerges intact, and even he must reckon with the knowledge that he himself has been the instrument of Theobald's disillusionment and eventual swift death. Indeed, this narrator is an early specimen of that frequent Jamesian unnamed narrator, a quasi-busybody whose curiosity is at once helpful and suspect: in later stories like "Four Meetings" and "Greville Fane" such curiosity is mostly helpful; in *The Sacred Fount* it is compulsive, obsessive, but also perhaps meta-artistic; and in "The Aspern Papers" it is self-deceptive, manipulative, and inhumane. "The Madonna of the Future" is really therefore neither a Jamesian art parable like his later tales of the 1890s nor an incisive exploration of the international theme. It is essentially an example of "negative realism," that is, a tale that exposes the flaws of a romantic or idealistic viewpoint, although it uses art and expatriation as its frame, background, and context.

"A Passionate Pilgrim" is perhaps more pointedly James's inchoate discovery of his international subject. Clement Searle, the expatriate American protagonist in England, is a dying man throughout the story. His "passionate" romanticizing of English life, culture, and countryside are checkmated thematically by two beggars, "immemorial vagrants," who appear in the tale and whom even Searle recognizes as his spiritual doppelgängers; also by the unpleasantness surrounding Searle's own abortive claim to an ancestral estate, which culminates in an ironic reversal when both Searle and his antagonistic cousin die at the same time. Most important, Searle's romanticizing is contradicted constantly by his very real dying condition, his "attenuated person" and the "spiritless droop of his head" (13:338). While such language clearly evokes Poe-like melancholy, James does not really affirm, as does Poe, its inevitable association with supreme beauty. Yet the American narrator, who remains Searle's confidant throughout the story, does respond like Searle time and again to the picturesque beauty of English life and landscape, evoking not a Poe but a Hawthornesque *Our Old Home* tenor, although the narrator himself intends from the start to return to America. The two characters taken together bespeak James's own ambivalence in the early 1870s to America and Europe, but what remains consistent, despite an authentic appreciation of English country life at times evocative of, say, Gray's "Elegy," is a similar strain of antiromanticism like that found in "The Madonna of the Future." Inasmuch as his illness is never specified, we cannot help but wonder whether Clement Searle's passionate-pilgrimage mindset is somehow destroying him, especially when we consider that at the end the accidental death of the hostile kinsman, coupled with the support and affection of his sister, which might have given Clement the estate after all, coincides with his own death: what he wants the most seals his demise, and the spirit behind that want, the passionate pilgrimage, has been killing him by inches.

Far more successful than either tale and indeed one of the truly significant works of James's immaturity is "Madame de Mauves" (1874), which Christof Wegelin says "points across the whole of [James's] career to his latest novels," in part because it "dramatizes the contrast between two visions of Europe—the romantic and the real, the sentimental and the objective," and partly because "we flounder in Jamesian ambiguity" at its end.[7] In the case of both the heroine, Euphemia de Mauves, victimized by an unfaithful French aristocrat husband, and the hero, Longmore, a young, ardent American timber merchant attracted to his abused compatriot, we get for the first time in Henry James the American innocent abroad in combination with his use of a central consciousness—in this case focused on Longmore—to render the narrative through a third-person "register"; in other words, the very ingredients found in James's classic international works, "Daisy Miller," *The Portrait of a Lady,* even *The Ambassadors.* All of this is accomplished within the familiar structure of James's longer tales, which are divided into several sections.

What is distinctive about "Madame de Mauves," however, is the skillful way it first enlists our sympathy for then gradually raises serious questions about the American idealism so deeply embedded in the two principal characters, Euphemia and Longmore. Euphemia's marriage to Richard de Mauves is greatly the result of her own youthful romantic delusions about European aristocracy, delusions enhanced by her convent reading (much like Emma Bovary's) but also seen in her obliviousness to the explicit warnings of old Madame de Mauves, her prospective grandmother. Warning signs abound, too, in the "pagan" lifestyle of her sister-in-law Madame Clairin, whose husband, a druggist and thus another outsider, "blew his brains out" after marrying into the high-born family (13:249). Just as important, perhaps, depending on one's reading of this tale, is the fact that Euphemia when young was placed in a European school by her rich mother to be educated and ends up through marriage coupling her American money to a French count. In any case, she is a deeply unhappy, long-suffering, pretty woman dressed in muslin and lace when Longmore first meets her through a mutual friend, Mrs. Draper, a bona fide early-Jamesian *ficelle,* that is, an indispensable auxiliary figure who imports necessary information to protagonist and reader alike.

One must stress that this is Longmore's story as much as, perhaps even more than, it is Euphemia's: for Longmore is a perfect match for her romantic nature, emblematized in her name Euphemia, or "euphemism." Longmore is a thoroughgoing restless idealist, as his name indicates (and only that surname is used); a man with a sense of "curiosity still unappeased," who "never chose the right-hand road without beginning to suspect after an hour's wayfaring that the left would have been the better" (13:215–16). As the two become close friends they share the American "Protestant" outrage at the infidelity of Richard de Mauves and a disgust at the conduct of his sister Madame Clairin, whose initial advances to Longmore—though as a widow she is free— are deeply repugnant to him. Once the situation is established, however, the center of the tale becomes Longmore's growing attraction for Madame de Mauves, an attraction fueled in part by his knowledge of her husband's neglect and misconduct but also by her beauty—of character, of body, and of something like moral compatibility.

It is precisely at this level that James introduces successfully a series of complications and irony of the sort that really do anticipate his later work. For one thing, Longmore fails to perceive the obvious parallel between his growing erotic love for a married woman and the rakish behavior of her husband, until the count finally proposes to his wife in front of his sister (who reports it all to Longmore) that he will encourage an affair between her and the attentive Longmore if only that the two may no longer bask in moral superiority like "a certain Wordsworth" Euphemia once tried to force him to read. James even gives an early hint of his patented operative irony when Mme. Clairin reports this episode to Longmore: "My *belle-soeur* sat silent a few moments, drawing her stitches, and then without a word, without a glance, walked out of the room. It was what she *should* have done!" And Longmore reiterates, "Yes, it was just what she should have done" (13:293–94). What is Jamesianly "operative" about that irony is that the two characters mean diametrically opposite things: Mme Clairin, in European fashion, means, yes, Euphemia reacted with appropriate discretion; Longmore, in American fashion, means, yes, she walked out of the room in the face of such an immoral proposition.

But the broader irony, of course, is that Longmore does court his countrywoman, who is also his neighbor's wife, and the count's suggestion externalizes the desires just beneath Longmore's own squeamishness. This becomes clear when in great frustration Longmore takes a sojourn into the French countryside and (amazingly like Lambert Strether at the other end of James's career in *The Ambassadors*) experiences a kind of "recognition" scene. He espies, admires, and idealizes a young picnicking French couple only to learn from the innkeeper that the two are not married, but that the woman is married. Following a countryside dream in which he and Euphemia appear on opposite shores of a river with de Mauves seated in a boat between them, the disillusioned Longmore now gives in to nature, embraces carpe diem, and comes to seek his prize, characteristically opting for the "left road," as it were, after previously choosing the right. At this point James manages a marvelous scene of re-reversal. When Longmore approaches Euphemia, never more desirable, dressed in white, standing in a "soft, warm wind," she confronts her would-be lover with the statement: *"Don't disappoint me."* Longmore must listen to a "marble statue," "a beautiful woman preaching reason with the most communicative and irresistible passion" (13:312). But with the appearance, one last time, of Mme Clairin and Euphemia's insistence that "If you should go away in anger this idea of mine about our parting would be but half-realised" (13:314), Longmore leaves and chooses, so to speak, the right road again.

James, however, is not yet finished. Longmore returns to America after both he and Euphemia successfully astound de Mauves by their mutual renunciation. Longmore reaffirms his moral idealism, that he "must assent to destiny," that "he must see everything from above" (13:318–19). And he does just that, even priggishly criticizing Mrs. Draper's simple reflection that "just a little folly's often very graceful" with a severe rejoinder: "Don't talk of grace till you've measured her reason!" (13:330). Longmore himself, however, has the opportunity to do such measuring after two years in America. He visits the returning Mrs. Draper and from her learns an astonishing sequel: that de Mauves, first frustrated and then smitten by his wife's moral courage, begged her forgiveness, changed his entire life, and on his knees beseeched to be readmitted to her favor. Euphemia, however, flatly refused him. Finally, like his own ex-brother-in-law, "they discovered he had blown out his brains." As for Longmore, he "was strongly moved, and his first impulse after he had recovered his composure was to return immediately to Europe. But several years have passed, and he still lingers at home. The truth is that, in the midst of all the ardent tenderness of his memory of Madame de Mauves, he has become conscious of a singular feeling—a feeling of wonder, of uncertainty, of awe" (13:331).

This ending (or re-reversal, if you will) is an important source of the ambiguity that Vaid, like Wegelin, sees in James's tale (Vaid, 144). But I really do not believe with Wegelin that we need "flounder" in such ambiguity to see that the tale does foreshadow the mature James. I think it fairly evident that Longmore at the end is not only divided characteristically between his "left and right roads"; he is downright afraid to go near her, or more accurately, he is on the threshold of discovering that she is "spooky" and that he wants no part of her. For what James really adumbrates in this early story is one of his great later themes, a character's "violation by an idea," the rapacious capacity to allow a tenacious prescriptive "idea" to take precedence over humanity and experience; the opposite, for example, of William James's counterbelief that *all* ideas must be subordinate to the ongoing stream of experience from which they arise in the first place.

This point can be far better appreciated as a whole in "Madame de Mauves" if we look at two features of the tale never discussed, yet both quite prominent. The first is James's ironic substructure of the whole medieval courtly love tradition. It runs from one end of the tale to the other, including even the "languid grey eyes" of the heroine, and "high-walled court" and "artificial garden" that form the principal meeting grounds of the two (13:217, 244). It is also inherent in the supernal devotion of the young man for the married woman: Longmore insists at one point that "if that in life from which you've hoped most has given you least, this devoted respect of mine will refuse no service and betray no trust" (13:276). The important Jamesian twist here is that the "mandatory" adultery of courtly love does not take place—not because, like Sir Gawain, Longmore must parry the sensuous advances of a Lady Bercilak, but because he must instead obey the strictures of someone more like Wallace Stevens's high-toned Christian woman. The real function of James's use of courtly love, however, is that it points up the great ironic disparity between these two American "Protestant" moralists and the age-old European tradition they unconsciously enact. But of course they *are* Americans and so do not, finally, consummate it. Like the artist James was to become, he is already having it both ways. Even Longmore's dream in the country, routinely dismissed as trite and simplistically allegorical, is not here, I believe, the clumsy device of a too-early Henry James; it is a variation of the dream vision associated with the literature James is in effect parodying: one need only recall a poem like *Pearl*, the other medieval masterpiece from the author of *Sir Gawain*, which culminates in a river scene dividing the lover from his beloved girl suspiciously like that presented as Longmore's dream. But again James has it both ways: on the one hand, Richard (as symbolized in Longmore's dream) does "come between" the two, when all is said and done, by his suicide and its sinister implications; on the other hand, the whole idea of Euphemia being on the opposing shore once Longmore reaches the other side—that is, on the shore he himself left to go to her—suggests that they are two sides of the same person, are, as it were, each other's alter-ego.[8] Longmore has good reason to pause in "awe" at the end.

The second feature of the tale is the motif James employs of the "secret." References to Euphemia's "secret" or its equivalent meaning occur nine times throughout the story, including even the old grandmother, who elaborates it as Euphemia's being "wound up by some key that isn't kept by your governess or your confessor or even your mother, but that you wear by a fine black ribbon round your own neck" (13:229). Longmore's "unappeased curiosity" is finally satisfied, he thinks, when he knows the source of Euphemia's sadness and tears: "He felt his heart beat hard—he seemed now to touch her secret" (13:275). He feels confirmed in this later when they speak openly of her abuse: "She had ceased to have what men call a secret for him, and this fact itself brought with it a sort of rapture" (13:296). There is here most certainly a sexual innuendo—also as old as medieval poetry—but the more critical level of meaning, I believe, is that this entire rhetorical motif of "secret" is a verbal artistic strategy that comes into its own with the end of the tale: Euphemia's "secret" is ironically reestablished with a vengeance at the conclusion, and Longmore is left in "awe." Even the sexual parallel functions ironically, for Euphemia's secret is not to be penetrated from the moment she asserts, *"Don't disappoint me."*

Ultimately, then, it really is legitimate to speak of Euphemia's "ambiguity" in the same respect that James's later fiction skillfully explores and affirms the ambiguity of a character or complexity of a situation—which I take to be different from the concept of our "floundering" in it. Euphemia's ambiguity and secret are both adroitly and subtly symbolized by her name. "Mauve" means a purple dye and refers to the first of the coal-tar dyes. She is literally named after an "odd compound" (Mme Clairin's characterization of her at one point), a phrase that works on two levels. First, since it is her married name it suggests initially the dark wickedness that surrounds her French family; this is exactly Longmore's idealistic assumption about her, that she is pure while the rest of them give him a "moral chill." Eventually, however, it points to her own capacity to give us—and even Longmore at the very end—a moral chill. In other words, the dual meaning of "mauve" parallels what is suggested by the multiple meanings of "secret." James seems to have wished us to grasp this, for he chose her name for his title. Further, by naming her Euphemia de Mauves, he combines and exhibits the terms of her ambiguity and our complex judgment of her— dreamy coal tar, an "odd compound." Thus, although it is quite common to cite "Madame de Mauves" for its renunciation theme, we must also recognize that renunciation is in the process of being redefined rather than simply affirmed, much less approved. Like the concept of "secret," we have with *renunciation* what William James would call a "transitional" term, one that undergoes new modification of meaning through successive experience and consequence. The opposing stance to *that* perspective is to be "violated by an idea," to make everything conform to it. This is Euphemia's principal flaw, one that Longmore probably has managed to escape. To discuss a very early James tale this way is to sense that Christof Wegelin is right—not about our "floundering" in its ambiguity but rather about its "point[ing] across the whole of his career to his latest novels."

Although "Four Meetings" (1877) may not be quite the remarkable anticipation of late James accorded "Madame de Mauves"—which is, after all, like no other tale written before it—it is every bit as valuable for my purpose here, since it is a fine representative short tale both in its realist theme and in its handling of the international theme, surely among the reasons for its traditional reappearance in anthologies. James's structure is relatively simple; in fact, the tale resembles a three-act play, two of the four meetings occurring consecutively at the same time period.[9] Although connoisseurs of late Jamesian complexity might think of it superficially as "four easy pieces," the story presents James's early technical mastery as well as a presage of certain important thematic preoccupations in his later work.

Caroline Spencer, a school teacher from North Verona in the depths of New England, has saved every penny to fulfill the great dream of her life, to visit Europe. The narrator of the tale, who like the majority of those in which James uses first-person narration remains unnamed, is a cosmopolitan European traveler from New York who befriends Caroline and takes an interest in her. At the first meeting they inspect a portfolio of European photographs, and he hears of her intense eagerness to go abroad. He warns her in a humorous vein that she must get abroad speedily because "Europe was getting sadly dis-Byronised" (16:271), and he also teases her that she possesses "the great American

19

disease" and has "got it 'bad'—the appetite, morbid and monstrous, for colour and form, for the picturesque and the romantic at any price" (16:274). Caroline is both shy and intense, yet single-mindedly interested in the narrator's travels and determined to experience for herself the adventure of Europe.

The second and third meetings take place several years later at the French port of Havre. Here he runs into Miss Spencer, who has just disembarked from the same ship as the narrator's own sister and brother-in-law. Her great enthusiasm on finally reaching Europe is immediately complicated, however, by her Europeanized American cousin, a Parisian art student, who arrives and asks for financial help in his courtship of a supposed noblewoman. Although the narrator warns Caroline that she is being fleeced, Caroline, empathetic and even intrigued by the "old-world romance," gives her money to the cousin and his young "Countess" wife, who has "written me the most beautiful letter" (16:291)—and departs for home. "The poor girl," the narrator tells us, "had been some thirteen hours in Europe" (16:294), never getting farther than the French seaport!

The final, fourth meeting occurs five years later back at North Verona, the scene of the initial meeting. The narrator, on a visit, discovers Caroline looking much older, haggard, "tired and wasted." In a Maupassant-like twist of irony, we learn that the "Countess," now a widow, has come over to live with Caroline and in fact treats her like her servant, a condition Miss Spencer accedes to. The narrator, even more impatient with her than at the previous meetings, tries to rekindle her interest in Europe, but Caroline says she doesn't "care for it now" (16:300). The worldly-wise narrator swiftly ascertains that the late art student's wife—if she ever was his wife—is anything but a countess; indeed, her speech and manner reveal to him someone of very low class and probably of questionable profession, since she seems to practice it with a young, rich Mr. Mixter to whom she presumably gives French lessons behind a "closed door." And yet his repeated attempts to show Caroline she is once again being cruelly exploited are, as before, to no avail. Sensing finally that she wants him to leave, he does so, leaving behind the young woman with "the great American disease." Although Caroline's long-cherished goal of going to Europe was stinted, Europe has come to her "to stay," while the cost of this trip is exacted in her constant servitude to her fraudulent guest.

Caroline's victimization is an early example in James of his lifelong theme of human exploitation, always the moral basis for his art. "Four

Meetings" also epitomizes James's theme of antiromanticism, or what I chose to designate earlier while discussing "The Madonna of the Future" his "negative realism"; that is, negative because the principal purpose is to show the destructive consequences of a romantic view, a realism found so frequently in Howells and Twain in stories like "Editha" or "The Private History of a Campaign That Failed." This is opposed to James's mastery of "positive realism," which is rather the attempt to render and poetize all the shades, nuances, and implications of ordinary everyday reality, especially the permutations of human consciousness. Like Poe's grotesque, arabesque, and ratiocinative elements, however, James's positive and negative realism are most frequently woven together in a given story and not simplistically divided. But they can be distinguished, however, for there are tales in James's canon in which either the negative or positive expression of his realist theme predominates. In general, one finds a predominance of negative realism in the earlier tales and of positive realism in the later ones.

"Four Meetings" also gives us an early taste of James's innocence-to-experience theme in the person of Caroline Spencer; we also find his trademark of some pivotal irony or "turn of the screw," a feature, again, very Maupassant-like, but one greatly embellished and complicated in his work much later. "Four Meetings" also points up another characteristic element in James's international theme, the fact that Caroline, the American, is exploited not only by a European (the "Countess") but first and foremost by a Europeanized American, her art-student, cousin who gives the narrator "a solemn wave, in the "'European' fashion," and who extracts "the stone from a plump apricot he had fondly retained" (16:284, 293). The morally flawed Europeanized American persists in Henry James's work and can be seen more individualized in such figures as Winterbourne in "Daisy Miller," Gilbert Osmond and Madame Merle in *The Portrait of the Lady*, and the Moreen family in "The Pupil." The exploitative European, like the "Countess" of "Four Meetings," is actually the rarer instance in James and found most prominently in his early novel, *The American*, in the personages of the Bellegardes and in Mlle Noemie. In *The American* the ambivalent Mrs. Tristram is the principal Europeanized American character; had she been more representative of Christopher Newman's moral hazards than the Bellegardes, the late James would likely have thought his early novel more realistic and less flawed by romance. Furthermore, for those (unlike the present writer) who may wish to read

"Four Meetings" in such fashion, James provides at least some slight possibility that the unnamed narrator is perhaps specious or slightly obtuse, if not unreliable—all trademarks of much of the late fiction.[10]

"Four Meetings" is in fact quite surprising in its subtle exhibition of poetic elements and metaphorical substructure, despite the fact that it remains an early piece and therefore would not be expected to have anything like the rich massive poetic texture of a late James tale. For example, at the conclusion of the first meeting, after Caroline and the narrator have finished speaking of Europe and of her firm intention to go, he tells us that "she left me, fluttering all expressively her little straw fan" (16:275). This figure is antiphonally answered and recalled at the conclusion of the second meeting, when the manipulative art-student cousin gestures "with his swaggering head-cover a great flourish that was like the wave of a banner over a conquered field" (16:286). These are, to be sure, instances of what James meant by "air of reality" and "solidity of specification" in "The Art of Fiction" (*PP*, 390), but it is interesting to note that with this pair of examples only one contains an overtly rhetorical metaphor (actually a simile), whereas both convey the *force* of imagery, especially when seen in relation to one another. Something of the same effect is also present when the narrator's brother-in-law tells him that during the trip over on the steamer Caroline "was never sick. She used to sit perpetually at the side of the vessel . . . looking at the eastward horizon" (16:277). This is the obvious attitude of Caroline portrayed in her emblematic "stance" facing Europe; but we have also the less obvious rhetorical and ironic point that the same woman who is about to be victimized by her European-ized relative has not been subject to the normal pitfalls of European travel, that is to say, seasickness, a point enforced by the fact that the narrator's own sister, unlike Caroline a frequent traveler, has had to retire to her room immediately upon landing because of seasickness.

James also employs direct metaphor to enrich his early tale. One example occurs when Caroline at the Havre informs him excitedly of her proposed plans of travel: "She had them on her fingers' ends and told over the names as solemnly as a daughter of another faith might have told over the beads of a rosary" (16:283). This is an excellent example from the early James of a "reflexive" image, that is, one whose content is not intended to lead the reader away from the character to the broader associations the image might otherwise denote but, as William James would say, circles back and "redirects itself" to its source, in this case the pious childlike character of Miss Spencer, whose plans will not materialize. The tenor of this metaphor consorts well with a subsequent one when Caroline, informed by the narrator that her cousin is about to swindle her, "asserted at this, her dignity— much as a small pink shorn lamb might have done. . . . 'I shan't be stripped. I shan't live any worse than I *have* lived, don't you see? And I'll come back before long to stay with them'" (16:292). This last declaration typifies the sort of anticipatory irony that permeates this tale, for it is ultimately the ersatz Countess who comes to stay with her. And the imagery of the innocent "small pink shorn lamb" asserting its dignity even echoes a detail from the first meeting at North Verona, when Caroline's fan is said to be "adorned with pink ribbon" (momentarily suggestive of Hawthorne's Goodman Brown's innocent wife Faith) and her attire "a scanty black silk dress" (16:269), suggesting fragility and vulnerability—someone who, as the narrator exclaims, eventually can be "stripped of every dollar" (16:292).

Another related technical achievement in this early story is the fluidity of what Mark Twain, in his praise of William Dean Howells, called a writer's "stage directions," those descriptive details accompanying dialogue that are in their quiet way touchstones for the kind of craftsmanship sought by the American realists beyond the technique of Poe, Hawthorne, or Melville.[11] Instead of the narrator's telling us he "said" or "cried" a statement, we hear such things as this: "'We *must* speak of it,' I declared as I dropped beside her again." Or Caroline, defending her cousin's young wife, whom she has yet to meet but who has written her "'asking me for confidence and sympathy'—Miss Spencer spoke now with spirit" (16:289, 291). James's early skill with such "stage directions," however, is most evident near the end of the tale when, during the fourth meeting, the bogus countess herself tells the narrator of her boredom away from Paris at such a place as North Verona. "'You may imagine what it is. These two years of my *epreuve*. . . . One gets used to things'—and she raised her shoulders to the highest shrug ever accomplished at North Verona" (16:309). This particularly fine "stage direction" seems to match up, if you will, with Twain's own unforgettable image of the Calevaras frog Dan'l Webster, who, full of shot and unable to jump, looks at his owner Jim Smiley and "hysted up his shoulder—so—like a Frenchman."[12] In general, James's "stage directions" in an early tale like "Four Meetings" also bespeak his ease in the strategic use of vernacular language, as when the narrator tries to warn Caroline not to be cheated "for such a rigmarole!" or when, on the lookout for the shifty art-student cousin, he tells us "There, sure enough," he was "at the end of a long table" (16:289, 292).

Still, the later James is at least tacitly embedded within the early James of "Four Meetings," for the character of Caroline Spencer at the end of the tale seems finally shrouded in ambiguity. Why does she allow herself to be so abused when the woman comes from Europe "to stay" with her and orders her to do all the work (the alleged noble-woman claiming exemption from "manual labor")? Why does the wasted, indeed, as it turns out, dying Caroline finally not see through the shabby charade? Does she remain a romantic even as her vision of old-world Europe ravages and brutalizes her? Neither the narrator nor the reader ever comes to know—at a certain level her psyche eludes us.

Nevertheless, James as potential master of the poetic novel and tale does create an acute "objective correlative" during the last awkward interview between Caroline and the narrator. First, when he arrives at her door unexpectedly Caroline unconsciously steps outside and closes the door before coming to herself again and inviting her old friend in; such "body language" hints that she knows the score at some deep recess of her being and prefers the narrator not to have access to that knowledge. Once inside, moreover, he persists in asking the now hag-gard young woman when she will finally make her European tour. Before answering him, Caroline "attached her eyes a moment to a small sun-spot on the carpet; then she got up and lowered the window-blind a little to obliterate it" (16:300). This literal act amounts on James's part to a fusion of metaphorical activity and landscape: that is to say, the image bespeaks her willful blindness; at the very same time, she herself is impenetrable. James clearly reinforces this tenor just after-ward when the "Comtesse" makes her first appearance and orders Caroline to fetch her coffee: "I looked at Miss Spencer, whose eyes never moved from the carpet" (16:303). She continues like a menial to do the Frenchwoman's bidding while young Mr. Mixter remains on the premises and pays for his questionable French lessons; but Caroline herself remains "impenetrable" (16:303) to both the narrator and to us. He finally tells us by way of sealing James's own extended conceit that "I couldn't let in, by the jog of a shutter, as it were, a hard informing ray and then, washing my hands of the business, turn my back forever" (16:311).[13]

That is, the narrator cannot, like his counterpart in "The Madonna of the Future," first undeceive Caroline and then simply walk away from the brutality attending her condition of knowledge. And yet it is all too clear that she does know, although apparently not yet consciously, while she continues in effect physically to obliterate the "sunspot." At this deeper level her character becomes ambiguous in a way that does adumbrate the later James. If there is any "hard informing ray" from the author himself on this score, it might lie in the references made at certain strategic moments in the story to Caroline's puritan sensibility. At one earlier point, for example, while she tells the narrator how she has "saved and saved up" for her trip, he tells us she "went on with suppressed eagerness, as if telling me the story were a rare, but possibly an impure satisfaction," and he even alludes to her as a "thin-stemmed, mild-hued flower of Puritanism" (16:273, 278). Moreover, at another early point, when the narrator quips in a humorous vein that she has wasted a great deal of time if she is to have all the "experience" she speaks of, she replies "Oh yes, that has been my great wickedness!" (16:275). Does Caroline, then, accept her intolerable situation cat the end because of some feeling of appropriate punishment, perhaps the "wickedness" of squandering her one opportunity? We cannot ever know, but we can see here again, especially in the final meeting, certain ingredients of James's later mode within the early tale. "Four Meetings" begins with the narrator learning of Caroline's death, after which he proceeds to narrate the story in retrospect, and it ends with the grim and ironic situation of the "Countess," that is to say, "Europe," coming to live with Caroline Spencer. And in between there is considerable humor that then turns to pathos, an interlocking substructure of poetic and metaphoric linkages, and, when one ponders it, a rather complicated view of the "international theme." And so although "Four Meetings" remains predominantly a piece aimed "negatively" at romanticism, it has significance beyond its salient ironic reversal in structure and theme. In it, James has already begun to master the short story form with an artistic compression not immediately obvious and has likewise insinuated a psychological complexity that emerges, as it were, when one takes a second look.

If "Four Meetings" culminates in pathos and a certain measure of psychological ambiguity, "An International Episode" (1878–79), "A Bundle of Letters" (1879), and "The Point of View" (1882) present a successful trio of early unabashed Jamesian international comedies of manners. The first is a long tale, longer than "Daisy Miller," its companion piece, and even a bit long for the nouvelle category or classification.[14] This allows James full development of the multiple biases and misunderstandings emanating from his symmetrical English and American cast of characters and played out structurally first in New York and Newport, then in London. This story has always escaped the prominence of "Daisy Miller," doubtless, as its different title suggests, because of the absence of the magnetic, almost lyric, central figure of Daisy herself. Nevertheless, as pure international comedy it is superb. "A Bundle of Letters" and "The Point of View" are thematically related, again through the comedy of internationalism, but they are most unusual on account of James's rare yet highly successful use of the epistolary form. He appropriately grouped them all together in one volume of the New York Edition with his international comedies, including "Lady Barbarina" (1884) and "The Pension Beaurepas" (1879), the latter a piece that overlaps characters with "The Point of View." Not reprinted in the New York Edition is James's fine work *The Europeans* (1878), which much resembles these international comedies yet inverts both *The American* and "Daisy Miller" by dramatizing the complications in New England arising from the "intrusion" from abroad of radically Europeanized Americans Eugenia Münster and Felix Young. The chemistry of defensiveness and circumspection that develops between Robert Acton and Eugenia is particularly well handled and worth exploring, but the book is too long to qualify as a tale and merit discussion here. What all of these stories illustrate best is James's objective or "perspectivist" stance on the international subject during this period of his work.

"An International Episode" abounds in hilarious crisscrossing cultural biases, foibles, and transcontinental suspicion. Englishmen Percy Beaumont and Lord Lambeth must deal with the stifling New York climate by taking epic baths, after first assuming quite wrongly that their hotel will not have sufficient showering facilities. Through a mutual friend they connect socially with Mr. Westgate, a lovely Jamesian profile of a downtown American businessman, who generously puts them up with his family in Newport and then, although continuously expected to arrive and join them, never appears again in the entire story, his absence a testimony to his total absorption in the financial enterprises that support his family's life-style and their trips abroad. The real complications arise between Beaumont and Lord Lambeth,

on the one hand, and Mrs. Westgate and her younger sister Bessie
Alden, on the other. Mrs. Westgate is a warm, pretty, stylishly dressed
woman of thirty who keeps a sort of open house in her Newport mansion and who chatters incessantly, beyond even the scope of Daisy
Miller; her verbal motif is that America is impoverished primarily by
having "no leisure class." Her sister, Bessie Alden, is a prepossessing
figure, a combination of Bostonian self-reliance, intellectual curiosity,
and romantic idealization of Europe—part Caroline Spencer, part
Euphemia de Mauves, and part Isabel Archer, of whom she is a prototype, strictly speaking, even more than is Daisy Miller. Lord Lambeth is wonderfully good natured and unpretentious, also very
handsome, yet totally inaccessible to ideas, reminiscent of Matthew
Arnold's concept of nobility as "barbarians" in *Culture and Anarchy*.
Percy Beaumont, his cousin, is continuously called by James's narrator
the more "clever" of the two, which indicates less his mental superiority than his constant suspicion of Americans. When Lambeth and
Bessie become attracted to each other in Newport, the vigilant Beaumont, despite his own pleasant diversion in Mrs. Westgate's company,
promptly alerts the Duchess of Bayswater, Lord Lambeth's mother,
who virtually dragoons her son back to England: both Beaumont and
the Duchess unquestionably assume that Bessie is out to hook Lord
Lambeth, an English marquis.

When Mrs. Westgate and Bessie arrive in England the following
May, some eight months after the two Englishmen's departure, James
beautifully complicates the cultural conflict. First of all, Mrs. Westgate
is entirely different in character and personality once away from her
native soil and Newport "turf": she arrives obsessively defensive, absolutely certain that the superior English society who accepted her
hospitality in America will snub her in England, and is therefore determined not to give them the chance. James diminishes the extent of
her chattering in line with her wariness, but now she continually introduces French phrases into her conversation (James's impartial narrator
never makes note of this; he just presents it dramatically). Moreover
Mrs. Westgate is now most proprietary about the "rules of conduct"
regarding her sister, Bessie, and at one point even announces that "For
me there are only two social positions worth speaking of—that of an
American lady and that of the Emperor of Russia" (14:357). Clearly
she has forgotten her earlier ubiquitous theme of "no leisure class" in
America! But of course Beaumont's continued suspicions regarding
Bessie's designs on Lambeth seem to justify Mrs. Westgate's defen-

siveness, and the two of them, once temporarily friendly while in Newport, now become outright verbal antagonists.

James's handling of the courtship in England between Bessie and Lambeth is wonderfully soft-toned and comic. Bessie constantly asks him about the great cultural artifacts in which he has no interest. About the Tower of London, for instance, she declares, "*You* have no right to be ignorant" of its history. "Why haven't I as good a right as anyone else?" he wonders. "Because you've lived in the midst of all these things," she argues with all her freedom, passion, and spirit. "What things do you mean?" he rejoins, "Axes and blocks and thumbscrews?" (14:361). Bessie is similarly frustrated in attempting to draw forth an expression of Lambeth's hereditary powers and obligations: when telling him she wishes to hear him speak in Parliament, he replies, "I never speak—except to young ladies," and when pressed as to why he doesn't address the House—"Because I've nothing to say" (14:351–52).

Nevertheless, Bessie remains attracted to the handsome and unpretentious Lambeth, and he becomes greatly enamored of her along with her iconoclastic American spirit. By now James has the "international episode" running at full tilt with its multiple agendas. Mrs. Westgate, assured that Bessie does not really love Lambeth, nonetheless yearns for the English nobility to be terrified at the prospect of the marriage so that she might rebuff their imperious assumptions. Percy Beaumont and the Duchess meanwhile are maneuvering to shame Bessie and get Lambeth to lose his interest; and Lambeth himself is asserting his preference and individuality independent of hereditary obligations by inviting Bessie to his castle at Branches to meet his mother and sister, which forces them (much to Mrs. Westgate's delight) to have to call first upon Mrs. Westgate and Bessie at their hotel in London. Finally, in a brilliant reversal, Bessie herself, after being looked over by both the Duchess and her daughter, puts an abrupt quietus to everything and everyone by refusing the invitation, and, in effect, rejecting the marriage proposal. This is wonderful Jamesian "operative irony" with respect to Mrs. Westgate: her very "plan" is achieved, yet she is just furious at the thought that the English noblewomen will believe that their hotel visit prevented and "saved" Lambeth from an inappropriate marriage. "But Bessie Alden," writes James, "strange and charming girl, seemed to regret nothing" (14:389).

Bessie does emerge as "very theoretic" and wishes from Lambeth "an ideal of conduct" to which he is unable to measure up. As James also expresses it, "she tried to adapt it to her friend's behaviour as you might attempt to fit a silhouette in cut paper over a shadow projected upon a wall. Bessie Alden's silhouette, however, refused to coincide at all points with his lordship's figure" (14:368). Critics understandably have long been interested in Bessie Alden as a prototype of the Jamesian independent American woman, sister to Daisy Miller and Isabel Archer. Yet to extrapolate her interesting figure from the various broader comic parameters of this long story, as is the temptation in James criticism, is to fail to appreciate the full "internationalism" of this tale and that of James's final witty stance of detachment.[15] If one laughs at Mrs. Westgate's turnabout of personality in England, for example, one must chuckle just as quickly, say, at the ingenuous, simple-minded Lambeth, who is named ironically for the great and historic councils of English ecclesiastical history.

James's objectivity is the key as well to his mastery of the epistolary form of "A Bundle of Letters" and "The Point of View." The first is set in a boarding house in Paris and comprises nine letters, four of which are written by Miranda Hope to her mother in Bangor, Maine. Miranda, a spontaneous young American woman traveling alone, combines the liveliness of a Daisy Miller with the culture-questing of a Bessie Alden. The second tale, "The Point of View," is set (if that is the right word for this second bundle of letters) in New York, Newport, Boston, and Washington; it comprises eight letters, two of which are by young Aurora Church, who has lived abroad with her mother but has persuaded her to spend several months in their native land—which Mrs. Church loathes—in search of a husband for Aurora. James's detachment, again, is the key to both these tales. His epistolary system allows for dramatizing the characters' opinionated ideas about the multitude of social data on which the tales collectively comment. Yet the two young American women, Miranda and Aurora, are, perhaps not surprisingly from James, the most attractive individuals. Still another American, Miss Violet Ray, a young society woman, is a snob who thinks Miranda the "most extraordinary specimen of self-complacent provinciality" (14:495)—an unwittingly self-reflexive proposition if ever there was one. Moreover, Louis Leverett, who appears in both tales, is an odious Boston aesthete; his letter from Paris is sprinkled with pompous allusions to Balzac, and his idiom is laced with affectations like "as they say here." In the second tale his corresponding letter from Boston is a shallow effete's lament at being severed from his beloved Paris. And so it goes. Young Evelyn Vane is probably a decent sort, yet her letter virtually glows with the narrowness of this English woman's horizon, as her mind inexhaustibly engages trivialities, and she totally misreads Miranda as "awfully vulgar" for "travelling about quite alone" (14:518). Leon Verdier is a French gallant whose immemorial and erroneous male presumptions about all young American women, especially Miranda, is a travesty and parody of Frederick Winterbourne's memorable questionings and doubts about Daisy Miller's "virtue" in James's tale the previous year. One gets the feeling at times that Miranda Hope, not unlike, say, Faulkner's Benjy in *The Sound and the Fury*, is in effect a sort of "moral mirror" that reflects and assesses the other figures. Dr. Rudolph Staub, who refers to the decline of English-speaking "specimens" and American "varieties," exhibits a contempt, superiority, and arrogance on behalf of the "conquest" and "incalculable expansion" of the "deep-lunged children of the Fatherland" that probably reflects James's own dislike of Germans, the one place his otherwise objective authorial stance may be transparent (14:531).

Characters in "The Point of View" besides Aurora Church and Louis Leverett, already mentioned, include Aurora's "Mamma," Mrs. Church, whose expatriate mind monotonously criticizes U.S. culture whatever topic she happens to land on. Equally mindless, perhaps, is the lawyer Marcellus Cockerel, whose chauvinistic Americanism negatizes both Mrs. Church and Louis Leverett. The dignified Honorable Edward Antrobus, M.P., is both priceless and meticulous in his elaborate discussion of American versus European train travel in his letter to his wife. Then there is M. Gustave Lejaune, of the French academy, who has such incalculable bias in his letter home as to permanently disqualify him to be "the first French writer of distinction who has been to America since De Tocqueville" (14:546)—so described by the generous Aurora in her letter. Only Miss Sturdy, a fifty-year-old spinster writing to her best friend in Florence, seems to give an intelligent, balanced mixture of pros and cons regarding America and Europe.

In these pieces James perforce ignores plot and concentrates on dramatizing character. As with "Four Meetings," most impressive is what James himself would in "The Art of Fiction" call "solidity of specification" in the cumulative effect of these letters and the collection of social data projected by the various figures—even though the later James would in his fiction intentionally prune such "solid specification" and subordinate it to the conceptualizing of language and the rendering of consciousness. The epistolary form and its effect as a whole in these pieces give further ample evidence of how much early James participated fully with Twain and Howells in post–Civil War American humor; one thinks of Twain's "Letters from Honolulu," for example, which have far less variety of character or "points of view." James at one point even goes out of his way to parody his own celebrated list of American cultural handicaps and "denudation" voiced in *Hawthorne* (1879)[16] in the mouth of M. Lejaune: "No salons, no society, no conversation." Indeed, "the country's a void—no features, no objects, no details, nothing to show you that you're in one place more than another. . . . Naturally, no architecture (they make houses of wood and of iron), no art, no literature, no theater. I've opened some of the books. . . . No form, no matter, no style, no general ideas: they seem to be written for children and young ladies" (14:589–90). All this, remember, comes supposedly from the first writer of distinction since De Tocqueville. But just in case we have missed James's parody and think for a second this really does reflect his own cultural critique from *Hawthorne*, James makes himself the butt of his own joke when Lejaune immediately declares: "They've a novelist with pretentions to literature who writes about the chase for the husband and the adventures of the rich Americans in our corrupt old Europe, where their primeval candor puts the Europeans to shame. *C'est proprement écrit;* but it's terribly pale" (14:590–91).

"A Bundle of Letters" and "The Point of View" as international social comedy are in fact mainly about provinciality in its inexhaustible variety. This holds true for everyone from Miranda Hope and Aurora Church on down to the far less attractive individuals. From the standpoint of subject matter the traits of American women and children probably predominate over any other single topic, but there are so many observations and topics as to give these papers a kind of comic miniature-encyclopedic tenor. James was not to cultivate the epistolary form as a major mode of fiction in his long career; and yet, if the following is not too preposterous a claim, it is not altogether impossible for the reader to think ahead to, say, *As I Lay Dying* when reading these virtual monologues and hearing these often free-associating voices commenting on the same experience and on one another.

Finally, the best known and perennial favorite among James's early stories is "Daisy Miller" (1878), a nouvelle that like "Madame de Mauves" employs third-person narration focused on a viewpoint character of "register." It occupies a special place in his canon for several reasons. First, its notoriety and popularity made James for a brief moment in his career a popular writer: Howells could have a character in *The Rise of Silas Lapham* refer casually to "Daisy Millerism"; society was even said by Howells to divide into "Daisy Millerites and anti-Daisy Millerites"; and James was frequently identified on the title pages of his later novels as the author of "Daisy Miller." The story, published in *Cornhill Magazine* by Leslie Stephen (Virginia Woolf's father), was pirated immediately, sold twenty thousand copies in pamphlet form in a few weeks, and spawned a play and even a Daisy Miller hat. The reason for this early and enduring interest is that James had fully identified and staked as his imaginative territory the plight of the international American woman whose free-spiritedness flouts European respectability. He also had focused swiftly on the antagonism between Daisy and the Europeanized "gang" abroad and had rendered convincingly the "moral muddlement" of the expatriate American Frederick Winterbourne, James's viewpoint character and a man attracted to Daisy's "natural elegance" (18:21), yet who eventually sides with her antagonists, Mrs. Walker and Mrs. Costello, both Europeanized Americans. Newly abroad from Schenectady, New York, Daisy's principal "crimes" are that she ignores class structures and customary behavior, whether at Vevey or in Rome, and both speaks and walks freely with whomever she likes, in essence treating all she meets as equal human beings. Eventually she dies of malarial or "Roman" fever after exposing herself through evening walks in the Colosseum with Mr. Giovanelli, a simple man disapproved of by the ardent American colony of matrons who assume custodial standing over Daisy and her family and who define expatriate morality. Daisy thus dies a sacrificial victim like the Christian martyrs who have preceded her.

To tell the story this way, however, is to fail to represent James's skillful complication of the conflict, his dialectical inquiry, or at least what has been called his "middle point of view" (Wegelin, 32). The key to any sophisticated reading along the line James intended is to focus as well on Winterbourne, since his is our point of view, whereas Daisy remains, as she should, the "phenomenon" into whose consciousness we are not permitted to enter, yet whose continual and insubstantial "chatter" and love of a "fuss" qualify her stature otherwise as free spirit and genuine expression of nature opposed to artificial forms of respectability. *Both* Winterbourne and Daisy are in James's language "queer mixtures" of contradictory elements and "booked to make a mistake" with each other (18:41, 93) because the reactions of each to the other are culturally and socially predetermined. He lives in Geneva and has lived in Europe since a boy of twelve, about the same age as Daisy's rambunctious brother, Randolph. Daisy's beauty and natural good taste in clothes no less than her enthusiasm and spontaneity do not change the fact that, like her mother and her absent, "downtown" father too busy working to come abroad, she inhabits an intellectual vacuum: mother and daughter in central and southern Europe can share as conversational topics only Randolph's antics and Schenectady's Dr. Davis, and Daisy believes Europe is "nothing but hotels" (18:15). Although much attracted to her, Winterbourne recognizes eventually that she is "nothing every way if not light" (18:75)—a "lightweight" in Jamesian lexicon usually meaning someone without sufficient consciousness. Daisy's own "queer mixture" incorporates her "natural elegance," commensurate with the flower for which she is named, and it includes her nighttime martyrdom symbolized by the same flower, the "day's eye," which is eclipsed at night; but it also comprises her "chatter," stubbornness, foolishness, and, on occasion, a sort of tactless crudity. The emphasis in "Daisy Miller" remains at the level of social determinism, and it is in that respect fundamentally what its companion tale immediately following it is called, "An International Episode," but with an extremely crucial difference necessary for grasping James's internationalism. In "Daisy Miller" he portrays the conflict and mutual misunderstanding that arises not between Americans and Europeans but between the "natural" American free spirit and the complicated response to that spirit by the Europeanized American, Winterbourne, who is at once attracted and repelled by it, as well as by the other Europeanized Americans who are merely repelled and think Daisy "of the last crudity" and a "little abomination" (18:23, 44).

In fact, Winterbourne's tale, if as James's "register" it is his tale—is really about the making of a Europeanized American, his ultimately siding with Mrs. Walker and Mrs. Costello against Daisy, his rejection of his own attraction to her "natural elegance" or what he earlier calls her "queer little native grace" (18:31). That sad and deleterious process of rejection completes itself by the very end, when he returns to Geneva and to a "very clever foreign lady" (18:94), the antithesis of a Daisy Miller. His name of course insinuates such moral culpability, for the chilly Winterbourne does in a real sense "kill" the innocent and vulnerable Daisy, especially when he espies her at the Colosseum with Giovanelli and turns against her: Daisy herself cries out, "Why it was

Mr. Winterbourne. He saw me and he cuts me dead!" (18:86)—her colloquialism doubling as James's metaphor for the death of a flower. Winterbourne's moral failure is underscored by James in numerous ways, including the young man's eventual reaction of "horror"—the very word used of Daisy by Mrs. Costello early on—and also his "relief" at finally deciding that Daisy "*had* no shades [and] was a mere black little blot" (18:86). Shades and nuances comprise a virtual microcosm of James's own epistemology and aesthetic practice, and therefore as "register" Winterbourne's relinquishing of "shades" at this critical moment in the story in effect pits him against everything James stands for as a writer and humanitarian sensibility.

There are very many other such instances where James's verbal patterns serve to indict Winterbourne. He himself admits that he has "lived too long in foreign parts" (18:93) when he realizes from the lips of Mr. Giovanelli, ironically the one *real* European of the story, that Daisy was "the most innocent" (18:92). One of the innumerable verbal signifiers for Winterbourne's flawed character occurs when James with exquisitely deceptive simplicity says of him that at the Colosseum he sought "a further reach of vision, intending the next moment a hasty retreat" (18:85). This is yet another instance in James of "reflexive" or "ricochet" language: for while the literal meaning is that Winterbourne intends to leave the monument quickly lest he become infected with the malarial disease, the deeper meaning, conveyed in subsidiary metaphor, is that in the course of his story Winterbourne first expands his "vision" by his positive response to Daisy and then "retreats" from his enlarged horizon by rejecting her. In point of fact, James drives home this kind of moral reflexivity when he writes of Winterbourne's Colosseum repudiation of Daisy's "shades," "He stood there looking at her, looking at her companion too, and not reflecting that though he saw them vaguely he himself must have been more brightly presented" (18:86). Any reader who assumes this is only a description of Winterbourne's visibility in moonlight simply does not comprehend James's Emily Dickinson–like layering of the figurative within the literal. Not only is the young man "shown" in the fullness of his own moral deformity, he even fails to realize that Daisy at that moment is visually enshrouded in the tenebrous "shades" he has just now abruptly denied to her character.

Although "Daisy Miller" remains a comedy of manners, James's later revisions coat it with a symbolic and poetic overlay, one that not only emphasizes her charm and spontaneity and the disagreeableness of her censors, but also stresses her obvious ties to nature, ties that, inevitably, also betoken her subjugation to its laws and processes. The "Roman fever" or "miasma" she catches in her innocence is worldly evil, which is pervasive, whether she knows it or not. Her instincts against conformity are most valid when she tried to coax Winterbourne out of his "stiffness," just as his are most valid when he senses that, with all her vibrant parts, she yet fails to "compose." It is not Daisy's directness, her fresh beauty, or obvious lack of ulterior design in her negotiations with people, any more than, say, Billy Budd's, that tell against her. Rather, she is unfortunately as devoid of a real inward life as she is of any guile. That void is filled up instead with capriciousness, chatter, and the unexamined desire for a "fuss." Daisy's will is at once strong and weak by virtue of the indistinctness of her aims and the absence of any critical reflection of them.

Thus the story remains a true dialectical inquiry from the early James and a penetrating examination of the internationalism that would be the hallmark of his finest novels throughout his career. Although it remains implicit, the iconography of this tale and of James's international theme tells us that nature requires art, activity and energy require meaning and consciousness, innocence requires experience, freedom demands an awareness of life's limitations, and spontaneity must always inhabit a world of history and custom. James's great early success in "Daisy Miller" with his distinctive social realism and his figure of the young American woman does not prevent our seeing in retrospect that we have also a case of quasi-tragedy through cultural implantation; or, to put it another way, a social comedy of errors with a darkening and lyric edge.[17] This retrospective view is also reinforced by our awareness that in *The Portrait of a Lady* Henry James was soon to deepen his generic Daisy Miller type into Isabel Archer and make *her*, rather than a male character, the reflecting consciousness of her own "history."

Middle James: Psychological, Moral, Aesthetic Explorations

With the exception of the "The Turn of the Screw," written in 1898, and several other proto-"ghostly" tales composed earlier in the 1890s, James's short fiction in the last twelve years of the nineteenth century tends to address moral and aesthetic questions, not so much to undermine his social realism as to enhance and complicate it by exploring the relation between moral and aesthetic experience. James provides a context for such experience by probing more deeply than before into the elusive psychological motivations of characters who reveal their interior consciousness through James's maturing prose idiom. Although James between 1880 and 1890 produced a number of important novels—*The Portrait of a Lady, Washington Square, The Bostonians, The Princess Casamassima, The Reverberator,* and the composition of *The Tragic Muse*—he published only ten tales between 1880 and 1888, the same number that appeared in the year 1900 alone. Some of his novels of the 1880s offered him a fuller and freer handling of social and political themes, which may well have preoccupied his mind and work. It was to be the last two years of the 1880s and then the 1890s that would bring forth a resurgence of some of James's finest short fiction; subsequently, in the period from 1900 to 1910, he was to extend the form still further and thereby become a major bridge in Anglo-American fiction from the nineteenth century to twentieth-century modernism. The 1880s also included the publication of his indispensable "Art of Fiction," and 1888 marked the publication of three important tales, "The Aspern Papers," "The Liar," and "The Lesson of the Master." Both "The Aspern Papers" and "The Liar" are unusually important specimens of unreliable narration, wherein the reader may expect to distrust or even reverse a protagonist's justification of his conduct and his overriding appraisal of others and of himself. This issue already surfaced, as we saw, with Winterbourne in "Daisy Miller," but Daisy's own counterdeficiencies qualify if not mitigate it. Reliability eventually reemerges as an issue with horrifying implications in "The Turn of the Screw." But even "The Lesson of the Master," as well as several other art parables, touch on this same question and will be examined in connection with it.

"The Aspern Papers" and "The Liar" are both not only tales of high merit—"The Aspern Papers" in particular has long been the recipient of considerable critical analysis—but both are usually cited, as I just mentioned, for James's handling of narrative unreliability, a truly major trademark of his originality and technique in the work of his maturity. In the case of "The Aspern Papers" we probably have the most pronounced instance in all James's fiction of the unreliable first-person narrator per se, the type of narrator whom we might associate later with, say, Ring Lardner's "Haircut." This narrator, an unnamed American publisher, will do anything to get his hands on the dead poet Jeffrey Aspern's papers, including outright deception of the Misses Bordereau in Venice and crass manipulation of Miss Tina Bordereau's affection. This "publishing scoundrel!" (12:118), as he is eventually denominated, nevertheless addresses the reader throughout the course of the story and tries (most unsuccessfully) to justify his villainous pursuit of legendary poet Jeffrey Aspern's papers and love letters written to his mistress, the ancient Juliana Bordereau. The narrator's attempts to track her and her niece to Venice, to pose as a lodger in their home, and even to feign a romantic interest in Miss Tina all hasten the death of aged Juliana, but result as well in thwarting the would-be duper himself: Miss Tina, in reaction to his rebuff of her incipient affection, both finds and burns the coveted Aspern papers—"It took a long time—there were so many" (12:143).

"The Aspern Papers" may, for James, appear to have a superficial technical simplicity just *because* of the clearcut unreliability of its narrator, and yet behind that device there is considerable complexity and virtuosity. To give one example: the narrator eventually reveals his "true name" to Miss Tina, a name *we* readers never know any more than its predecessor; and so of course he remains unnamed to us, is even, so to speak, "re-unnamed." Furthermore, the moral issues surrounding what is primarily a comic tale are anything but simple. The narrator's compulsive—nay, monomaniacal—quest for Jeffrey Aspern's papers recalls indirectly the destructive group of Hawthornian questers whose head has usurped their hearts: for example, Aylmer (of "The Birthmark"), Rappacini (whose Italian garden is recollected by this

Jamesian narrator's Venetian gardening), and of course Ethan Brand—all of whom, like James's narrator, in effect prey upon women. Indeed, one of the many satisfying elements of this long tale's conclusion with Miss Tina's burning of the coveted papers is that it seems almost as if the whole Hawthorne-James gallery of prying and preying men are finally repaid by the perennially exploited woman, yet one who does so without resorting to the narrator's own duplicitous tactics. Dame Juliana, by contrast, is more the narrator's adversarial alter ego—perhaps symbolized by her green eye shades in cat-and-mouse counterpoint to his "green thumb"—although she is obviously less culpable than he and acts primarily out of a wish to protect and provide for her niece. There is even some possibility that Tina is in fact her illegitimate daughter by Jeffrey Aspern.[18] In any case, a reader may feel with justification that by the end the obtuse narrator has lost the real prize in losing Tina Bordereau, not the Aspern papers.

Another dimension of the tale, one stressed by James himself in his later Preface to it, is the evocation of the past in the figure and associations of Aspern, an American poet who flourished at the beginning of the nineteenth century in culturally impoverished America—the same issue (as we have seen) that James addressed in his early study *Hawthorne* (1879) when he catalogues the cultural deprivations against which Hawthorne worked. This whole question, however, greatly complicates "The Aspern Papers," as Wayne Booth points out in *The Rhetoric of Fiction*'s much-cited analysis, "James and the Unreliable Narrator," a discussion focusing attention on both "The Aspern Papers" and "The Liar." The complicating factor, Booth contends, is that the narrator's evocation of the American past is never integrated rhetorically with his pernicious designs in the present.[19]

Booth notwithstanding, clearly the narrator's response to the past and James's in his Preface are not synonymous, but foils. The narrator's evocation is specious because he does not further but instead perverts cultural transmission through his pursuit of the letters; again, like Hawthorne's Aylmer, all that he touches, or tries to touch, ultimately dies: the papers, Aspern (through the papers), and Juliana—only Tina, whom he rejects, comes to life and thus reverses, as it were, the passive role of Georgiana in "The Birthmark." But in his Preface Henry James's own interest in the attenuated extension of the past away from the present is fostered precisely by the artist, not the deadly acquisitive collector. Hawthorne, for example, whose "past" is the subject of James's *Hawthorne* as is Aspern's the narrator's, surely "comes to life again" through James's reformulation of his tales by this one. The crucial difference between the *Aspern* narrator and James is reinforced by James's own magnificent metaphor—a bona fide "metaphysical conceit"—comparing the receding past to a baffling succession of walled English gardens viewed from a ladder (*AN*, 164), an extended figure wonderfully vivid and apt if one has ever visited or lived in England. The narrator, in short, belongs to that group of James characters—from Urbain de Bellegarde in *The American* to Gilbert Osmond in *The Portrait of a Lady* to Maud Lowder in *The Wings of the Dove*—who take, or would take, the veneer for the thing itself, the form for the substance, the walled barriers, if you will, for the gardens themselves. It is not so surprising, perhaps, that along with another publisher he is associated early in the tale with the devil. Short of that, he shares some of the inauthenticity of numerous Jamesian Europeanized Americans, although he is not one himself. Ultimately, however, he is again one of James's deeply flawed characters who are "violated by an idea." Against the Kantian dictum, he uses people as means rather than ends, but that is because he truly *is* violated by his idea. The retribution he receives at the conclusion by losing both the papers and Miss Tina signifies his willful blindness of precisely the kind of human love that produced both Aspern's letters and his poetry in the first place. Indeed, his relationship with Tina throughout the tale becomes an obvious parody of Aspern's with the youthful Juliana of the past. This parody is underscored by the language of the climactic scene, in Juliana's bedroom, when his clandestine search for the papers is expressed in such language as "the drawers of her tables gaping" and the "climax of my crisis" (12:116–17). Yet he fails in this scene, is unmasked by Juliana's finally unshaded "extraordinary eyes," and he fails once again with Tina herself when she later offers to become "a relation" (12:118, 133). With great success "The Aspern Papers" explores with its half-gothic narrative mode the life and death of creativity over time.

"The Liar," though perhaps not as highly regarded as "The Aspern Papers," is actually more complicated technically, at least in its use of unreliability. This is important because it is told in third person like "Daisy Miller" and "Madame de Mauve." "The Liar" turns on a Maupassant-like twist in which the putative liar of the story, Colonel Clemont Capadose, is juxtaposed to a protagonist narrative (James's "register") who emerges as the deeper, more profound liar—and is even named Lyon. A highly successful and gifted painter, Lyon re-meets Everina Brant, the woman who refused him long ago and is now the wife of Capadose, a man Lyon gradually discovers is a compulsive liar who "can't give you a straight answer" and possesses a "monstrous foible"—as his friends put it (12:343–44). Lyon gradually becomes obsessed by the thought that Everina, an unusually genuine and honest woman, can appear content in her marriage while presumably having to bear the shame and humiliation of her husband's "whoppers," which, typically, "shot up and bloomed" (12:368). Lyon's real motive, however, is the jealous "ache" he retains for Mrs. Capadose. He never sees, as will the attentive reader, that his own conduct and even his thinking are driven by jealousy and a desire for revenge or punishment for her choice of Capadose rather than him, and especially her absence of distress at that choice. He meditates thus, for example, on the couple's daughter, Amy: "The child was beautiful and had the prettiest eyes of innocence he had ever seen: which didn't prevent his wondering if she told horrid fibs. This idea much occupied and rather darkly amused him—the picture of the anxiety with which her mother would watch as she grew older for symptoms of the paternal strain" (12:354).

What in effect James exhibits here is the way Lyon's own evil has "shot up and bloomed," for indeed the crisis of the tale revolves around the juxtaposition of the Colonel's "genius" for lying with Lyon's own evil genius. Lyon's specialty is portraiture, and he persuades the couple to let him paint Capadose's portrait, in which he conveys by caricature the full, ugly monstrosity of a person's massive dishonesty. When Everina comes with her husband to view it, she breaks down for the only time in the tale and cries, "It's cruel—oh it's too cruel!" (12:374). Ostensibly absent when the couple comes to see the painting, Lyon is, significantly, there; he hides and watches the entire episode. Capadose, apparently not comprehending the meaning of his own portrait yet responding emotionally to his wife's horror and distress, slashes the picture with a knife and hacks it to pieces, causing the unseen Lyon immediately to feel "success"—in breaking down the veneer, as he interprets it, of the happy pair. Yet later, at the story's end, both Capadose and Everina feign no knowledge whatever of the painting's destruction, alleging it to be the act of a disgruntled drunken model seen near the premises. Lyon thus assures himself that the hitherto forthright Everina has herself finally lied for her husband in a crisis, although James provides a lovely little narrative "swerve" in the fact that Everina left the studio in tears ("Come away—come away," she repeats) *before* her husband actually slashed the painting: hence Lyon can never know for certain that *she* lies at the end, although he assuredly persuades himself she has done so.

The central moral insight of "The Liar" is that Capadose's lies are never malicious, never self-serving, never harm humanity, whereas Lyon's conduct is deceptive and egotistical through and through. Lyon's first name, Oliver, is not introduced by James until well into the tale, and I feel that James thereby emblematizes his "twistedness" with a kind of Dickensian pun. Moreover, Lyon steps back and hides when he sees the Capadoses arrive at his studio to view the picture, an act insinuating his own wrongdoing and even evoking obliquely the image of someone like, say, Hawthorne's psychically troubled Ruben Bourne in "Roger Malvin's Burial." The truth is, the portrait Lyon paints is, like his twisted thinking, self-reflexive; he has projected his own insidious deception into it. As a portrait of the Colonel the painting would be a moral lie. Therefore, Colonel Capadose's slashing act is symbolically appropriate, for the picture, which Lyon would like to send to the Academy entitled "The Liar," is at the core a self-portrait. Likewise the "hypocrisy" Lyon attributes to Everina at the end—for never acknowledging the disfigurement—is reflexive of Lyon himself throughout the narrative. There is even considerable Jamesian indication that the Colonel's habitual lying is correlative to artistry, to fabulation and storytelling, an idea James developed again in "The Birthplace" (1903), where Morris Gedge's inventive lies to tourists about Shakespeare's childhood not only save his job but delight his visitors. The falsifications of Capadose are at times called alchemy, "an incalculable law," even "the muse of improvisation" and the "laying on" of "colour" (12:350–51). As such they strongly contrast with Lyon's own use of art for morally distorted ends. Wayne Booth's criticism that this story, like "The Aspern Papers," suffers from "double focus" and is "still partially unrealized" and "only half-developed" thus seems less valid the more one studies the tale—even if one considers Jamesian ambiguity a defect! (Booth, 352–54). Lyon's sinister psychic projection is simply everywhere, including even his creative activity while painting the portrait: Capadose "had his intermissions, his hours of sterility, and then Lyon knew that the picture also drooped. The higher his companion soared, the more he circled and sang in the blue, the better he felt himself paint" (12:362). This is also a kind of "early draft" of Jamesian quasi-supernaturalism, a feature we shall see more of in his late fiction; but here it is primarily one more instance of Lyon living up to his name and projecting himself onto the canvas of his rival.

James's handling of third-person unreliability in "The Liar" at times recollects Winterbourne and even prefigures John Marcher in "The Beast in the Jungle." But it resembles more immediately Adela Chart of "The Marriages" (1891), whose antagonism to her widowed father's prospective marriage to Mrs. Churchley and equally harsh opposition to her brother Godfrey's marriage are gradually shown, despite Adela's own bewilderment and rationalizing, to be motivated by her pathological devotion to her mother's sacred memory and thus her barely subconscious wish to replace her mother as her father's lifelong companion—a wish she achieves with "success" at the ironic conclusion of the tale. Indeed, that is one of the several "marriages" radiating thematically from James's story.

"Greville Fane" (1892), a superbly compressed tale, designated in its New York Edition volume as one of the "hard shining sonnet[s]," is superlatively representative of the convergent strands of James's middle period, in that respect very like "Four Meetings" in relation to the early period. Though not concerned with specious or unreliable narration, it is a magnificently witty tale that qualifies at one level with James's art parables. More deeply, however, it exhibits his moral preoccupation with internecine human relationships. Greville Fane is a pen name for the prolific Mrs. Stormer, a widow who writes potboiler romances and adventure dramas along the lines, let us say, of *The Prisoner of Zenda, The Prince of Foxes,* or, in more recent years, the Harlequin romances. James's story is narrated by a young unnamed journalist, a friend of Mrs. Stormer's. This narrator functions much like his early predecessor in "Four Meetings," that is, as the narrative agent for another's story. In fact, both tales begin with the announced death of the woman protagonist and then evolve into a retrospective of her life or some particular aspect of it. "Greville Fane," however, introduces a most important element not found in "Four Meetings": the journalist-narrator is himself also an artist, an unsuccessful novelist who, unlike Mrs. Stormer, tries "in my clumsy way, to be in some direct relation to life" (16:116). This extra dimension accounts for some striking features of the tale, most notably the narrator's crisp prose style with which James endows it from beginning to end—one of the more decisive proofs anywhere in his entire corpus that the convoluted prose idiom of a few years later was fully thought out and intentional. The narrator's razor-sharp burlesque of Greville Fane's literary productions and vogue constitutes a satire that somehow manages miraculously to remain affectionate. "Oh bother your direct relation to life!" replies Greville Fane, for she was "always annoyed by the phrase—which wouldn't in the least prevent her using it as a note of elegance. With no more prejudices than an old sausage-mill, she would give forth again with patient punctuality any poor verbal scrap that had been dropped into her" (16:116).

As this language suggests, our gifted narrator offers a devastating critique of Mrs. Stormer's fiction that far exceeds anything James himself, writing likewise from the realist's standpoint, says about comparable work of the costume-romance variety in "The Art of Fiction." Yet it is clear enough that James would endorse the narrator's assessment of Greville Fane's work. "She wrote only from the elbows down," he tells us; "She could invent stories by the yard, but couldn't write a page of English. She went down to her grave without suspecting that though she had contributed volumes to the diversion of her contemporaries she hadn't contributed a sentence to the language" (16:111, 113). And again: "She turned off plots by the hundred and—so far as her flying quill could convey her—was perpetually going abroad. Her types, her illustrations, her tone were nothing if not cosmopolitan. She recognised nothing less provincial than European society, and her fine folk knew each other and made love to each other from Doncaster to Bucharest" (16:114). In what is virtually a metaphysical conceit, this narrator even tells us that Greville Fane "had an unequalled gift, especially pen in hand, of squeezing big mistakes into small opportunities" (16:122–23). Indeed, a large segment of this story seems to consist of nothing but a cascade of beautifully memorable locutions by James's narrator at the expense of Greville Fane's mode of fiction. "She carried about her box of properties, tumbling out promptly the familiar tarnished old puppets. She believed in them when others couldn't, and as they were like nothing that was to be seen under the sun it was impossible to prove by comparison that they were wrong. You can't compare birds and fishes; you could only feel that, as Greville Fane's characters had the fine plumage of the former species, human beings must be of the latter" (16:121).

If this were the extent of James's story, it would qualify as a memorable burlesque, not unlike Mark Twain's parody of Fenimore Cooper's literary offenses. But in fact the tale itself (somewhat like a figure skater or a fine football running back) "changes direction" on us. Most

all of James's short stories, even the later philosophical ones so different from this one, usually turn on a Maupassant-like twist, even when
they proceed to explore entirely different issues, like the nature of the
unknown, bewildering, attenuated "field" of phenomenal reality itself. In this case, however, the twist, while obviously less philosophical, is hardly less engaging and interesting: it consists in the irony that
behind her novels of romance, forbidden passion, and high adventure
we discover a woman whose main, indeed whose only, activity when
not writing is that of doting on her two children. "The immoral and
the maternal lived together," we are told, "on the most comfortable
terms, and she stopped curling the moustaches of her Guardsmen to
pat the heads of her babes" (16:122). Not only does she trace "the
loves of the duchesses beside the innocent cribs of her children," but
for fans who seek her out she is inevitably "disappointing to most of
these pilgrims, who hadn't expected to find a shy stout ruddy lady in
a cap like a crumbled pyramid" (16:122); moreover, she may write
about "the affections and the impossibility of controlling them, but she
talked of the price of pension and the convenience of an English chem-
ist" (16:122).

If this seems not so much a change in the story's direction as merely
added content for the journalist-narrator's wit, that is only because it
does not yet tell of the real implication and consequence of Mrs.
Stormer's maternal devotion. Her two children, Ethel and Leolin,
grow up to become parasites and manipulative snobs, and the narrator
chronicles the way they proceed to destroy their doting and eventually
bewildered mother. In other words, Mrs. Stormer, like Caroline Spencer, is victimized, not by an art-student cousin, but by her own off-
spring. She spends great sums of money educating her daughter "at a
very superior school" at Dresden, and the result is that the pompous
girl, according to Mrs. Stormer herself (sounding a little like the vulnerable and perplexed Edith Bunker of "All in the Family"), "can't
read me . . . I offend her taste. She tells me that at Dresden—at
school—I was never allowed" (16:123). The narrator's portrayal, however, of this daughter is annihilating. Ethel, the snob who is perfectly
willing to milk her mother for every penny, is herself "singularly col-
ourless . . . only long, very long, like an undecipherable letter"
(16:118). Eventually she produces "the effect, large and stiff and
afterwards eminent in her, of a certain kind of resolution, something
as public and important as if a meeting and a chairman had passed it"
(16:118). At an earlier time our narrator had never seen "sweet sev-

enteen in a form so hard and high and dry . . . and she carried an eyeglass with a long handle, which she put up whenever she wanted not to see" (16:118). Eventually Ethel secures Sir Baldwin Luard, who, as a "joyless, jokeless young man," is a perfect match for her, and so becomes Lady Luard; but she remains for the narrator a person "surrounded" as if "with a spiked iron railing" (16:118).

Greville Fane's son, Leolin, is just as repugnant, although in an entirely different way. Encouraged by his mother to become a novelist like her, Leolin proceeds to adopt every conceivable affectation of an avant-garde "form-tormented" artist, while in fact he, like his sister, is a parasite, eventually being paid by his mother to provide "all sorts of telling, technical things, happy touches about hunting and yachting and cigars and wine, about City slang and the way men talk at clubs—that she couldn't be expected to get very straight" (16:125). The dubious formation of Leolin's character is crisply summarized by the narrator at one point. With his mother's hope that he would become a novelist, Leolin

> was eager to qualify himself and took to cigarettes at ten on the highest literary grounds. His fond mother gazed at him with extravagant envy and, like Desdemona, wished heaven had made *her* such a man. She explained to me more than once that in her profession she had found her sex a dreadful drawback. She loved the story of Madame George Sand's early rebellion against this hindrance, and believed that if she had worn trousers she could have written as well as that lady. Leolin had for the career at least the qualification of trousers, and as he grew older he recognised its importance by laying in ever so many pair. (16:120–21)

Of course, this passage is admittedly almost as telling on Greville Fane herself as on Leolin. Already lacking the critical faculty in art, she lacks it as well in life. Nevertheless, Leolin's exploitation of his mother is especially odious, even while he engages in psuedo-artistic posture—he "*felt* life so, in all its misery and mystery," he "goes beneath the surface . . . he *forces* himself to look at things from which he'd rather turn away" (16:132). This, to be sure, is from his deceived mother. We even learn through her that "in addition to his salary he was paid by the piece: he got so much for a striking character, so much for a pretty name, so much for a plot, so much for an incident, and had so much promised him if he would invent a new crime" (16:133). The narrator tries to point out that Leolin already *has* invented a new crime and is paid everyday for it! But Mrs. Stormer fails to understand. Whenever Leolin visits the narrator he monotonously and pretentiously intones about Balzac, Dickens, Flaubert, and Thackeray, and earnestly enquires "how far . . . in the English novel, one really might venture 'to go.'" The narrator explains that if on such occasions he did not "kick [Leolin] downstairs it was because he would have landed on her at the bottom" (16:129–30).

This last statement reminds us that, with all the satiric punch at our narrator's disposal, his view is ultimately sympathetic of Greville Fane's humanity. And the tale corroborates this, because eventually she herself does land at the bottom. As time goes on she burns herself out, taking less and less for her work while sucked more and more dry by her two children. "She was weary and spent at last, but confided to me that she couldn't afford to pause" (16:127). Ethel, Lady Luard, continues to possess a smile "the dimmest thing in nature, diluted, unsweetened, inexpensive lemonade" (16:126), and even though she despises the execrable Leolin, "it didn't save her after all from the mute agreement with him to go halves" (16:129). The narrator calls on Mrs. Stormer at Primrose Hill, her final residence after the earlier sprightly years traveling abroad, and finds her "wasted and wan"—in other words, reminiscent of Caroline Spencer at the end of "Four Meetings." Unlike Caroline, however, Mrs. Stormer eventually begins to cry as she explains to the narrator that, on the one hand, her daughter and son-in-law are ashamed and embarrassed by her in their society, while, on the other, Ethel is upset with her mother for letting her "pieces go down" in price, even though the daughter's marriage alone cost her three novels. "I had never seen her break down," the narrator informs us, "and I was proportionately moved; she sobbed like a frightened child over the extinction of her vogue and the exhaustion of her vein" (16:131). She dies soon afterward, and the two devouring children publish "every scrap of scribbled paper that could be extracted from her table-drawers," then quarrel "mortally about the proceeds" (16:133–34).

What is most remarkable about "Greville Fane," apart from the deft acute wit and dissecting prose of its proficient narrator, is the way that James, at least by the conclusion of the tale, turns what looks like one of his art parables inside out and makes it instead an acute moral tale preoccupied with the theme of human cannibalism and exploitation, in this case of the parent by the children. It is a most skillful performance, especially when one thinks back to the opening of the short story, an apparently simple device by which James provides his lead into the narrative proper. The journalist receives a telegram from his editor that reads: "Mrs. Stormer dying; can you give us half a column for tomorrow evening? Let her down easily, but not too easily" (16:109). The narrator has never "admired" Greville Fane, but has "liked" her so long that his difficulty is not "in letting her down easily but in qualifying that indulgence"; he initially tells himself, "So I simply won't qualify it" (16:109). But a female companion that evening has never heard of Greville Fane, and another neighbor pronounces her books "too vile." The narrator, who is obviously preoccupied with his assignment, ruminates that "I had never thought [her books] very good, but I should let her down more easily than that" (16:109).

The column he writes is not, of course, the story itself, and yet James clearly invites the reader to evaluate the one in terms of the other. After his thoroughgoing, pungent analysis of Greville Fane's romantic, passionate potboilers—"To myself literature was an irritation, a torment: but Greville Fane slumbered in the intellectual part of it even as a cat on a hearthrug or a Creole in a hammock" (16:113)—the tale, as we have already seen extensively, goes "behind" her fiction and sympathetically engages the decency and eventually the desperate plight of the woman herself. In fact, it is the meretricious Leolin who, even more often than the narrator, bespeaks the artistic preoccupations we would normally associate with James himself: the concern with form, the necessity to represent life, the need for experimentation in the genre. Greville Fane writes the sort of trivial and artificial work James alludes to early in "The Art of Fiction"; yet, by engaging her character and probing her domestic situation, he makes her one of the long line of figures in his work for whom the romantic is not just wrong, it is also "real"—that is to say, an example of James's pole of "positive" realism in counterpoise to his pole of "negative" realism. Like Caroline Spencer, Isabel Archer, and other romantic individuals, she is ultimately victimized by others in a way that renders the consequences of her romanticism with acute realism.

Indeed, when one ponders this tale, it inevitably dawns on the reader that, finally, it is precisely her uncritical, "fairy-land" view of life (as the narrator once calls it) manifest in her writing that is the true source of her destruction. Leolin in particular acts out her wishes: as the narrator says at one point, "If she had imposed a profession on him from his tenderest years it was exactly a profession that he followed" (16:128). And although she breaks down and cries, as we have seen, she never does understand the reason for what has happened to her: "she never saw; she had never seen anything, and she passed away with her fine blindness unimpaired" (16:133)—a true mother of the daughter with the long-handled eyeglasses. There is again a resemblance to Caroline Spencer, although James has clearly sharpened the criticism by making the character's fiction the correlative of her own victimization. Greville Fane's work "from the elbow down," her "squeezing of large mistakes into small opportunities," the absence of any "direct relation to life"—these are the ingredients that, Count Frankenstein-like, seem to eventually take fruit and hideously mirror themselves in the two parasitical children, who, after the fashion of self-mirroring monsters, then turn and devour their progenitor. So that although we could say that our narrator tried "to let her down easily," James himself, by fusing inextricably the artistic issue with the moral exploitation theme, cannot, as the narrator tries to do, "let her down too easily." Or if we prefer, we can even hypothesize that the narrator of this retrospective tale is now sufficiently the writer he once hoped to be that in the tale itself he approximates something like James's full understanding of the issues. There is in fact more than a hint of this. Late in the story when Mrs. Stormer explains that Leolin is additionally paid if he invents a new crime and the narrator insists he already has invented one, Mrs. Stormer, "looking hard at the picture of the year, 'Baby's Tub,'" asks what the crime is; the narrator hesitates a moment: "I myself will write a little story about it, and then you'll see" (16:133). If, then, he is really the putative author as well as Jamesian narrative "witness" of her story, he could not let Greville Fane down quite as easily as he probably tried to do in his column.

Although they are not always recognized as such, James's art parables, like "Greville Fane," are usually inquiries as well into matters over and above aesthetic ones, most often human relationships and gradations of moral behavior, primarily because James saw such issues, as he saw fiction, as interconnected elements of an organic whole, a "living thing, all one and continuous, like any other organism"—as he expressed it in "The Art of Fiction" (*PP*, 392). The best parable stories also examine the disparity as well as the connection between appearance and reality. In "The Real Thing" (1892), "The Lesson of the Master" (1888), and "The Figure in the Carpet" (1896), for example, we find as many human questions raised as aesthetic tenets presumably proposed; and we are often as not dealt a kind of Jamesian sleight-of-hand when it comes to determining what is real and what is illusion.

In "The Real Thing" an unnamed narrator-artist attempts unsuccessfully to use a lady and a gentleman, Major and Mrs. Monarch, as his models in doing professional illustrations of ladies and gentlemen for magazines, for "story-books, for sketches of contemporary life" (18:309), including book illustrations for contemporary novelists. Instead he finds that professional models like Miss Churm or a young impoverished Italian named Oronte, both lower class, can pose more successfully for the drawings of ladies and gentlemen, even, when need be, of Russian aristocracy. Thus in addition to the Maupassant-like ironic twist we have come to expect from James, the tale also "unstiffens," in William James's language, the issue of what is most real, especially when involving the "alchemy of art." The theme seems in short to be one of distinguishing literal or "photographic" realism from a more valid rendering that allows the artist sufficient freedom to transform his or her material in order truly to represent it. The "stiff" Monarchs constantly prevent this process because, although they are "the real thing" they are always "the same thing," looking "like a photograph or a copy of a photograph" (18:326).

And yet if one reads the story differently, one can perceive that James superimposes a reverse meaning and theme atop his ostensible one in a way that cancels neither reading but allows for both, depending upon the starting point. The narrator has always wanted to be "a great painter of portraits," his illustrations only "my pot-boilers" (18:310). We know from "The Art of Fiction" and elsewhere that James analogizes fiction and painting, but the painting is portraiture, never illustration; nor would he ever have thought to call Isabel Archer's history "The 'Illustration' of a Lady."[20] Could it not be that the reason Major and Mrs. Monarch keep coming out as "brawny giants" and keep looking like themselves is that they represent the distorted attempt by the narrator to express his deeper aspiration for portraiture? His imagination is as free and authentic when reconstructing their touching social history and financial reversals as it seems locked and paralyzed when he actually tries to draw them. Furthermore, his sympathetic understanding of their *characters* and of their situation as misplaced members of the human community is akin to his portraitist's imagination rather than his more superficial illustrator's imagination:

he is responding to their humanity as ideally as he would were he to paint them—or were James to write about them.

This second reading broadens the tale, makes it more resonant, and illuminates innumerable suggestive details from the text. It also gains support from the fact that, like so many of James's stories, this too is a retrospective telling, as if the narrator wishes us to understand what caused the earlier psychological "crisis" in his life. He is far more than mere *ficelle*, also more than a device for expounding an aesthetic. And the Monarchs themselves gain stature in this alternate reading. Instead of merely being incompetent and clumsy creatures who can look good but not do anything, they instead unfold in the story and take on humanity, thus transforming from lowly "type" to regal "character" in a way commensurate with the butterfly for which they are named.[21]

James's imaginative elasticity is admittedly exceptional in "The Real Thing," but both "The Lesson of the Master" and "The Figure in the Carpet" exhibit it, too, in quite different ways. In "The Lesson of the Master" Henry St. George, a highly successful and respected novelist experiencing a decline in the quality of his work, convinces Paul Overt, a young writer and ardent admirer whose own first book shows considerable promise, that the responsibilities and pleasures of marriage and family exert too high a price for the true artist. Although good in themselves, they nevertheless compete with the creative process and eventually force the serious writer to do inferior work in order to make money. "Don't become in your old age what I have in mine— the depressing, the deplorable illustration of the worship of false gods!" (15:36). Since it is well known that Henry James dedicated his life to his art and never married, this tale is frequently cited as his manifesto in favor of a strict monastic pursuit of the muse of fiction.[22] But again, the story itself greatly "unstiffens" such a thesis.

Paul, the point-of-view character or "register," is much attracted to Marian Fancourt, a young disciple of letters whose enthusiasm is associated by both St. George and Overt with vitality. Under the influence of St. George's precept, however, Paul leaves London and Miss Fancourt and goes abroad to write his second novel. When he returns, he is astonished to discover that St. George, a recent widower, is about to marry Miss Fancourt! Paul has indeed written a fine book while gone, but feels that he has been "sold" by St. George, whom he now senses had his eye on Miss Fancourt even while his own poor wife was dying. St. George, however, insists "warmly" that he is now finished with writing, and that the proof of the validity of his earlier advice lies both in that fact and in Paul's artistic success with his new book. The tale ends, however, with Paul's lingering suspicion that perhaps St. George, regenerated by the vitality of Miss Fancourt as his companion for life, may surprise them all by producing a book of high quality such as his earlier *Shadowmere,* or even something "finer than his finest." Should this occur, the lesson of the master would indeed be different from what it seemed, although James as narrator "admits" that Paul would be the first to appreciate the accomplishment—"which is perhaps a proof that the Master was essentially right and that Nature had dedicated him to intellectual, not to personal passion" (15:96). The softly humorous vein of much of this tale, which includes the universal case of the rookie who is outfoxed by the veteran, does not alter the important point that James is once again complicating the vexing question of the mutual demands of art and life, not just issuing forth through the "Master" an artistic dictum.

"The Figure in the Carpet" brings back to us another of James's first-person narrators, although this man, unlike the narrator of "The Real Thing," is a writer and literary reviewer rather than painter. The story revolves entirely around the quest by the narrator and his colleague George Corvick to discover the secret meaning or "exquisite scheme" that informs the work of an exceptional novelist, Hugh Vereker. As Vereker himself explains, it is "the particular thing I've written my books most *for.* . . . an idea in my work without which I wouldn't have given a straw for the whole job. . . . It stretches . . . from book to book, and everything else, comparatively, plays over the surface of it. The order, the form, the texture of my books will perhaps some day constitute for the initiated a complete representation of it. So it's naturally the thing for the critic to look for" (15:230–31). Vereker tells all of this to the narrator in an unguarded moment, the narrator tells George Corvick, and Corvick tells his fiance, Gwendolen Erme. What interests James here is not only the questionable preoccupations of criticism and interpretation but the psychology of obsession, an issue that becomes central in his ghostly tales. Here the treatment is lighter but no less pertinent. The narrator, for example, rereads all of Vereker's books in search of the secret "spring," but discovers that "my new intelligence and vain preoccupation damaged my liking. I not only failed to run a general intention to earth, I found myself missing the subordinate intentions I had formerly enjoyed" (15:236). Vereker regrets having told the narrator about the informing idea, but he still insists that it is for his books the very "organ of life," that it "governs every line, it chooses every word, it dots every i, it places every comma" (15:233–34). He also approves of the narrator's comparing it to a complex figure in a Persian carpet, and even adds a figure of his own: "the very string that my pearls are strung on!" (15:241).

The narrator himself cannot break the code; Corvick, however, after first estranging himself from Gwendolen, actually leaves for India, where in apparent contemplation of Vereker's "buried treasure" he manages to penetrate the novelist's secret. Corvick writes the narrator and Gwendolen—who have begun to spend time together in his absence—of his momentous discovery: "When once it came out it came out, was there with a splendour that made you ashamed; and there hadn't been, save in the bottomless vulgarity of the age . . . the smallest reason why it should have been overlooked. It was great, yet so simple, was simple, yet so great, and the final knowledge of it was an experience quite apart" (15:256–57). First Corvick corroborates his discovery with Vereker himself and is assured he has "not a note wrong" (15:255). Then Corvick does two things: first, he virtually makes marriage the condition of his telling Gwendolen the secret; second, he plans a major critical project "for one of the quarterlies, a last great word on Vereker's writings," an "exhaustive study . . . to trace the figure in the carpet through every convolution, to reproduce it in every tint" (15:260). But before he starts he dies in a bizarre accident while on his honeymoon. Gwendolen later admits to the narrator that *she* was told the secret by Corvick but has determined to keep it to herself. The frustrated narrator thereupon begins to contemplate the "price" of marriage with Gwendolen for "the blessing of her knowledge," while she persists that she is not "the right person" to "break the silence" (15:265–66). Vereker himself (like Daisy Miller) dies of malarial fever in Rome, and eventually Mrs. Corvick does remarry another literary man, Drayton Deane, a man in the narrator's view far less perceptive than himself. Somewhat reminiscent of Paul Overt at the end of "The Lesson of the Master," the narrator begins "with due promptness to look for the fruit of the affair" (15:271)—not the couple's children, of course, but some sign that Drayton Deane now knows the great secret from his wife. Deane, however, writes nothing on Vereker. Finally, Gwendolen herself dies in childbirth, and the narrator eventually cannot refrain from interrogating Deane to learn if *he* was told Vereker's secret meaning by his late wife. Deane knows nothing about it whatever. The final ironic twist, however, is that once the narrator explains to Deane the entire chain of events Deane himself over a sufficient period of time similarly becomes so obsessed with "unappeased desire" to know the Vereker secret that today "there isn't a pin to choose" between him and the narrator. Indeed, "The poor man's state is almost my consolation; there are really moments when I feel it to be quite my revenge" (15:277).

James's tale, like the two previously discussed, thoroughly eludes any simple "aesthetic" interpretation, for the center of this tale is surely not just the recurrent theme in a given author's corpus but, as with "The Real Thing" and "The Lesson of the Master," more a dialectical inquiry into art and human relationships; in this case also the potentially destructive fascination with and obsession for something rare and special. Corvick's triumphant discovery of the figure in Vereker's carpet seems emblematically to have cost him his life and marriage. Gwendolen's silence both to the narrator and to her second husband, Drayton Deane, seems to me motivated by the perceptive realization on her part—perhaps after losing Corvick and then examining honestly her own reasons for marrying him—that the obsession with Vereker's secret meaning is what really destroys the "organ of life." Although she dies in delivery of her second child, Gwendolen does give birth to two children while married to Deane rather than pass on the almighty secret. Even the narrator, while filled with avidity, realizes momentarily, as if it were somehow peculiar, that Gwendolen "had married [Deane] for something else" (15:276): Why not for once as a loving companion and fellow member of the human community, not as a special seeker of the secret? But the narrator himself by the conclusion seems totally myopic, and his pleasure, "consolation," and "revenge" at having infected Deane with the virulent desire for the figure in the carpet stamps him as a deeply flawed human being. At the same time, the great fecundity with which the "figure," or the desire for it, passes from one character to another all but inverts the ostensible theme of the tale, much as the unread and ultimately destroyed Aspern papers are in a sense the primary "text" of that story.

Indeed, the narrator's obsession does not really differ in kind from that of James's "publishing scoundrel" in "The Aspern Papers." The principal difference between the two men is that the "The Aspern Papers" narrator intentionally sets out to defraud Dame Juliana and her niece, Miss Tina, although he constantly tries to rationalize his devious tactics to the reader by proclaiming his devotion to Jeffrey Aspern's memory as well as by his romantic response to Venice. The narrator of

"The Figure in the Carpet," on the other hand, is the unexpected recipient of the knowledge that there is a special discovery to be unearthed. But both narrators are, by the end, foiled and, in a sense, convicted by and therefore frustrated in their goals. What interests James in both stories—for the most part wonderfully humorous stories—are the psychology of obsession and the other issue of utmost importance for some of his greatest fiction, the potentially sinister capacity of a person to be "violated by an idea," a theme stretching all the way back, we recall, to "Madame de Mauves" and forward to "The Beast in the Jungle."

A compressed "anecdote" tale, to use James's own terminology, that could likewise be considered with his art parables and is also from the volume of "hard, shining sonnet[s]" in the New York Edition is "The Middle Years" (1893).[23] This tale has for some readers (including this one) a deeply affecting and personal aura that distinguishes it from the parable tales of the 1880s and 1890s such as those discussed above or others like "The Author of Beltraffio," "The Death of the Lion," or "The Next Time." Dencombe, the protagonist and viewpoint character, is a dying author who at first is desperate for "another go," a chance at a "splendid 'last manner,'" a last "extension" for the slow developer who had "ripened too late" (16:95, 98). While sojourning at a health resort in Bournemouth he makes two unforeseen discoveries, equally important. The first is young Dr. Hugh, who in all likelihood is "the greatest admirer in the new generation of whom it was supposable [Dencombe] might boast" (16:87). Dr. Hugh's devotion is tested and validated by his willing renunciation of a handsome inheritance from a coercive aristocratic patroness and her companion, Miss Vernham. He chooses instead to remain with Dencombe until his death at the end, a sacrifice reminiscent in miniature of Lambert Strether's in *The Ambassadors*, except that Dr. Hugh is here the son figure, the reverse of Strether, and as such is the true and appropriate "extension" of Dencombe's art through his appreciation as a reader. In fact, the two men really "discover" each other as readers responding differently to the same book, Dencombe's novel *The Middle Years*.

Dencombe's second discovery is precisely that "the madness of art" operates independently of one's designs or one's regrets, however multitudinous either may be. This comes home to him when he discovers with surprise that in his "latest"—and last—novel, *The Middle Years*, he has "forgotten what his book was about," then upon reading it discovers that "Everything came back to him, but came back with a

wonder, came back above all with a high and magnificent beauty"
(16:80–81). Indeed, Dencombe "recognised his motive and surren-
dered to his talent. Never probably had that talent, such as it was, been
so fine. His difficulties were still there, but what was also there . . .
was the art that in most cases had surmounted them" (16:81).

The irony and pathos of this tale is that Dencombe's surprise at the
achieved art of *The Middle Years*, reinforced by his metonymic "public"
in the person of Dr. Hugh, causes him only ache and regret at the lost
opportunity for his second chance. Yet this same experience proves
that artistic creation is an ultimate mystery whose essence is in effect
its own timetable. It is a case of Jamesian operative irony in a softened
key. Less "operatively" ironic (but just as ironic in traditional terms) is
the fact that Dr. Hugh, who prefers literature to medicine, cannot min-
ister to Dencombe's dying body but can to his soul and understanding.
The title of both Dencombe's book and James's story suggests that
one can never prescribe the "beginnings and ends" of an artistic career
any more than of life itself. Dencombe, also reminiscent of *The Ambassadors*'s Lambert Strether, has already lost a wife and son (although Dr.
Hugh brings sonship back) and is now dying himself at much too young
an age—his middle years. And yet the "weary man of letters" comes
at his death to see in the veneration of his newfound disciple the unanticipated power of his last novel and even signs of some burgeoning
public recognition that art and life always have their own plan and providence independent of one's wishes or designs. This epiphany is expressed in Dencombe's dying words: "We work in the dark—we do
what we can—we give what we have. Our doubt is our passion and our
passion is our task. The rest is the madness of art" (16:105). Earlier
the protagonist had lamented that it had "taken too much of his life to
produce too little of his art. The art had come, but it had come after
everything else" (16:82). Dencombe's deeper discoveries, however,
contradict this regret, inasmuch as both life and art somehow work
together alchemically in their own fashion.[24]

James also chose *The Middle Years* as the title for his own unfinished
autobiographical volume, a hint of his rare personal identification with
both this tale and this character. Furthermore, Dencombe's aim at a
"rare compression" in his fiction (16:80) and his being a "passionate
corrector" and "fingerer of style" (16:90) are all unmistakable charac-
teristics of James himself and details virtually unique in his fiction. At
the same time, such details probe deeply into the complex meaning of
the tale, for constant "correcting" or revision requires and signifies ex-

tended time, precisely what Dencombe regrets not having until Dr. Hugh's devotion, sacrifice, and sonship "revise" this regret by providing paradoxically "another go" in a different sphere. Moreover, the unquestionable "reliability" of Dencombe's final epiphany at his death also supports the unusual sense of spiritual oneness between author and character. Even Bournemouth, the setting, was one of James's favorite places. Apart from all such personal elements, however (or perhaps partly because of them), "The Middle Years" is a powerful and strangely affecting tale that combines strands as diverse as those found in Hawthorne's "Artist of the Beautiful," Tolstoy's "Death of Ivan Ilych," and Emily Dickinson's "Pain—Has an Element of Blank."

Very shortly after James wrote his art parables, his powerful criticism of English society flourished in such novels as *What Maisie Knew*, *The Spoils of Poynton*, and *The Awkward Age*, all published in the late 1890s. Out of the well of this same imaginative vision is distilled "In the Cage" (1898), a long tale that has begun to come into its own in recent years and shows promise of becoming a minor classic. What gives the tale its distinction is James's complex and sympathetic portrayal of its unnamed protagonist "register," the young female telegraphist who works at the post office enclosed within a grocery store suggestively named "Cocker's." Given the length of this tale, some thirty-three thousand words, and the fact that the telegraphist is not a first-person narrator like that of "The Aspern Papers," *The Sacred Fount*, or the Governess of "The Turn of the Screw," it is astonishing that James manages successfully to tell her story without ever once naming her, especially since we share her interior life and observe her in conversation with several friends and characters, all of whom are named. This helps impart or augment the "sociological" dimension already present in the situation of a young woman who is a mere functionary, an "obscure little public servant" (11:377). She could be any young woman of the lower class in Victorian society and, as such, a figure of interest today, especially to a Marxist or feminist critic-historian, for by 1898 the great transformation of clerical workers from men to women had swiftly taken place; Melville's Bartleby, so to speak, had turned into James's telegraphist.

What puts James ahead of his time in this tale is that he explores the mystification and technology of communication—including even "the sounder . . . being the innermost cell of activity, a cage within a cage, fenced off from the rest by a frame of ground glass" (11:376)—and renders his analysis at once elliptical and multidimensional. Many of the specifics and details of the story are never entirely clear, yet the larger issues come across as important and resonant, as if the "vehicle," were actually somewhat less comprehendible than its "tenor." "In the Cage" is nonetheless acute social commentary, for the telegraphist's story consists essentially in her fleeting involvement with her "betters," the gentry, especially her vicarious infatuation with Captain Philip Everard and his intrigue with Lady Bradeen, only to result in her decisive choice at the end to forget such people and immediately marry Mr. Mudge, a grocer on his way up, to whom she has been engaged but has hitherto postponed marriage. Furthermore, it is an epistemological story with its heroine a kind of psychic detective like Maisie Farange, a person whose encaged existence galvanizes her free-floating divination of the romance, excitement, and inside knowledge of upper-class life, where people like Everard and Bradeen have money, unlike herself and her impoverished family. She knows that "her imaginative life was the life in which she spent most of her time" (11:373), and she believes she "had seen all sorts of things and pieced together all sorts of mysteries" (11:376). But again, she discovers at the end the severe limits of her knowledge and in deciding swiftly to marry Mr. Mudge erects a kind of new psychic cage against her sense of possibility even as she paradoxically must quit Cocker's—where such imaginative possibilities have been bred—to marry him.

"In the Cage" is also a hermeneutical tale, for the entire springboard to her inner life lies in the telegraph codes and interpretive skills acquired and fostered at Cocker's to penetrate the secret lives of the rich and important, although, once again, she is ultimately disillusioned by the fruits of such messages and in effect gives up her hermeneutics at the end. Finally, it is a sexual tale inasmuch as she is fascinated by Everard, whose clandestine affair with Lady Bradeen she has decoded through their secret messages and false names; also, however, because she herself defers (even while she sublimates) her own loss of virginity by marriage with Mr. Mudge. She wishes to aid Everard in all the difficulties of his forbidden romantic love, for "He himself, absent as well as present, was all" (11:384). Of course, all the levels of this tale intersect with and permeate one another. For example, the epistemological level absorbs all the others when the caged young woman thinks: "With Captain Everard she had simply the margin of the universe" (11:414). Nevertheless, she decides instead at the conclusion just how severely marginalized she herself is, even though she no longer uses that terminology as such.

In one sense, to be sure, this tale can be read in a more traditional way as another case of Jamesian "negative" realism, the unmasking and discovery of romantic illusion, or more generically the loss of innocence. There is nothing wrong with such a reading, but what makes "In the Cage" at once more supple and differently focused is the whole class and gender system that impinges on the heroine's interior life and then, inexorably, on her external life as well.[25] James has, after all, chosen the rich conceit of the cage to open up the various inversions and dualities of the tale, the idea, for example, that the "transparent screen fenced out or fenced in" (11:367) depending on one's perspective; or the idea that "to be in the cage had suddenly become her safety, and she was literally afraid of the alternate self who might be waiting outside. *He* might be waiting; it was he who was her alternate self, and of him she was afraid" (11:469). *"He"* in this instance is Everard, whose sexual knowledge represents the possibility of her own, the "alternate self" she both desires and fears.

Her inner life thrives, however, just because of the "meanness of her function" and the fact that she must "count words as numberless as the sand of the sea" (11:367). If James were a lesser artist, he might have spun a light Disneyesque or even whimsical Irvingesque piece wherein the heroine's flights of imagination compensate for her prosaic external station in life, her Mudge-life, as it were. But both the integrity and suggestiveness of the tale lie precisely in his doing something at once more ambitious, oblique, and implicitly subversive. The telegraphist must come to her painful knowledge of the "system" through a set of educative experiences. First, her friend Mrs. Jordan, who has carved out a small but unsustainable business doing floral arrangements in the homes of the wealthy, decides to marry Mr. Drake, who has now hired on as butler to Lady Bradeen. This means the telegraphist and Mrs. Jordan can no longer be "sisters," but henceforth can "now after all only look at each other across the social gulf" (11:500). Furthermore, Mr. Mudge, who suffers no ambiguity about his class status, is nevertheless someone with stability and even heroism, a man who can come to her rescue and "collar a drunken soldier, a big violent man" (11:404). More than that, he accepts her confidences about Everard and is also willing to provide for her alcoholic mother in their new house when they marry. As the heroine has sensed all along, "Mr. Mudge was distinctly her fate" (11:455).

Most important of all her discoveries, however, is that the mystifying and exciting Captain Everard, the "alternate self" and Jamesian "germ" of her whole fantasy life, turns out to be a man of anything but heroic stature and thus inferior to Mudge. The telegraphist learns this through Mrs. Jordan, whose information comes from her own betrothed, Mr. Drake, the new butler to Lady Bradeen. Everard, she discovers, has no money whatsoever and, with the sudden death of Lord Bradeen, is about to marry the widow—his own paramour—out of economic necessity, not even genuine affection. Inasmuch as the telegraphist feels she has aided and at one point even "saved" the affair from exposure out of loyalty to Everard, she now feels implicated in the relationship that leads, ironically, to a loveless marriage. And she must face up again to the grim dominance of the economic principle: she herself has never had a penny, and now, she learns, neither has Everard; in fact, he has nothing but debts. The telegraphist thus decides that her own deferred marriage must take place immediately. She wishes no longer to learn about sexuality through Everard and his telegrams, but prefers, presumably, to learn it—if she must—directly from unromantic but also undeceptive Mr. Mudge. Yet this likewise means the end of her "deciphering" of the "mysteries" and the mastery of "the sounder"; and so her marriage, while a deliberate act of choice, is also the disappointing acceptance of denial.

Since throughout the tale she is both enticed by yet feels vestigial hatred for the upper class, her criticism is as acute as her fascination. She thinks of Everard's "class that wired everything, even their expensive feelings" (11:382). She also opines suspiciously that "when people had awfully good manners—people of that class—you couldn't tell" (11:384–85). But she expresses the full anger of her lowly station in the cage when she ruminates thus: "What twisted the knife in her vitals was the way the profligate rich scattered about them, in extravagant chatter over their extravagant pleasures and sins, an amount of money that would have held the stricken household of her frightened childhood, her poor pinched mother and tormented father and lost brother and sister, together for a lifetime" (11:386–87).

Both behind and in front of this anger, however, are the questions that torment her like "the sound of the splash of water that haunts the traveller in the desert" (11:428). Preeminent among such questions is this one: "how could she also know where a poor girl in the P.O. might really stand?" (11:471–72). That same generic question is most fully particularized and articulated on the one evening she has a confidential meeting—outside the cage—with Philip Everard in Mayfair Park:

> This was one of the questions he was to leave her to deal with—the question whether people of his sort still asked girls up to their rooms when they were so awfully in love with other women. Could people of his sort do that without what people of *her* sort would call being "false to their love"? She had already a vision of how the true answer was that people of her sort didn't, in such cases, matter—didn't count as infidelity, counted only as something else: she might have been curious, since it came to that, to see exactly as what. (11:434–35)

Her entire "matter" is in fact only settled because of inside knowledge provided by a butler who is soon to be her friend Mrs. Jordan's husband, both of whom are henceforth "superior" to herself simply by virtue of being connected in a menial way to Lady Bradeen. She has, in short, discovered in the course of her story that she does not really "matter" at all to such people as Everard or Lady Bradeen. Her epiphany at the conclusion is that all her efforts to aid and "save" Everard have been expended on behalf of someone without honor, without his own money, and, apparently, without even romantic passion. Lady Bradeen has "nailed" him after he had earlier "compromised" her. The telegraphist walks into the fog of London and prepares to take her restricted place in a social system that has no place for her imagination: she deliberately denies any hermeneutics to her future. James conveys all of this elliptically and aslant, yet also with an almost astringent succinctness. In fact, part of what makes "In the Cage" difficult to read and understand is that James constructs it with a kind of shorthand idiom that is itself suggestive of a telegram. Most of what I have just been elaborating as the heroine's final epiphany is not really "there" in the text; it is only my attempt, as it were, to decipher James's code. However we understand the sociocultural vision of this tale, we can all agree that it does not partake one iota of the sentimental. "In the Cage" will no doubt continue to engage the next generation of interpreters; it is one of James's tales for the future.

Finally, "The Pupil" (1891) is one of the truly great nouvelles not only from James's middle period but from his oeuvre. It makes an interesting thematic contrast with the exploitation theme of "Greville Fane," for in this tale it is the youngest child of an itinerant American family traveling in Europe, Morgan Moreen, who is exploited by his parents. But "The Pupil," like James's other famous tale of child victimization, "The Turn of the Screw," introduces new elements that complicate it beyond either "Four Meetings" or "Greville Fane." In part this may result, of course, from James's more ample treatment in the nouvelle form, yet we have seen by now that at times James can, Keats-like, "load his rift with ore" in his compressed "sonnets." The greater complexity of "The Pupil" lies instead in its preoccupation with epistemological bewilderment, a feature that adumbrates the central questions and themes in many of the great novels and tales after 1900. Thus his title "The Pupil," with its associations of discovery or learning, refers first to Morgan Moreen (the pupil in the story), but eventually as well to Pemberton, the young boy's tutor, who is also the third-person viewpoint character, the Jamesian "deputy" or "register" by way of which the story is told; it refers also, I would add, to the reader, whose process of discovery must mirror that of the two principal personages in the story.[26] At the same time, "The Pupil" is also among the most searching moral tales James has written, and so the challenging process is one of our trying to discover just where, in Pemberton's own words (or thoughts) at one point, "it pointed a moral" (11:534). The tale, as one critic has said, "is one of James's most concise and delicate studies of the difficulties of moral choice; so it is a good story for demonstrating the difficulties and possibilities of moral criticism."[27]

The most overt arena of human manipulation is that practiced by the shabby Moreen family on both the tutor Pemberton and their son Morgan. The Moreens are a group of showy adventurers, "toadies and snobs," who are driven by a "fifth-rate social ideal" (11:534, 553). This takes the form of their moving from city to city throughout Europe, taking rooms at hotels they cannot afford and employing every stratagem possible to elbow their way into society in order to bring off a lucrative marriage for one of their three older children, Ulick, Amy, and Paula; and then always, without paying, abruptly quitting the premises and moving on, usually on the pretext that "they couldn't get the rooms they wanted" (11:536). As their name suggests, the Moreens are all outward show. Mr. Moreen wears medals and decorations of an all too mysterious origin; Mrs. Moreen, the real driving force of the family, pinches pennies like a miser when the family is not entertaining or otherwise on display. One of the ironies of the tale, however, is that, despite their univocally concentrated effort, they are never able to pull off the match that might establish them socially or financially, and the time finally arrives when every hotel proprietor and social establishment in Western Europe is on to their routine, and they eventually collapse.

Morgan, however, although "wandering about Europe at the tail of his migratory tribe," displays a "whole range of refinement and perception" (11:523). He is so utterly different from the rest of the Moreens that Pemberton the tutor is "moved to speculate on the mysteries of transmission, the far jumps of heredity" (11:522). Morgan, whose eyes give off the "glimpse of a far-off appeal" (11:515), is a truly appealing character on several grounds: first of all, he is prodigious in his perception and awareness beyond his years (the story chronicles roughly the period from his eleventh to his fifteenth year); second, he is a stoical, plucky little person who suffers from a congenital "weakness" somewhere in "the region of the heart" (11:512). Finally, he is morally repelled and ashamed by his family's scheming and subterfuge; though he wishes to get away from them, he also, like any young boy, feels the deep emotional blood ties to his own kin, especially his parents. For their part, the Moreens know him to be a "special case" and contribute to his conflicting emotions by both keeping him out of their way and reacting toward him as their most priceless possession, someone who should have "something really superior in the way of a resident tutor" (11:512).

The "resident tutor" in this case is of course Pemberton. The foreground as well as early dramatic focus is the way the Moreens first engage Pemberton and then, once they have perceived his great interest and concern for the child, fail to pay him his wages. This ploy and injustice duplicate the way the Moreens operate in every facet of life. But it raises an important ethical question for Pemberton, for he feels that, however much the Moreens exploit him, he "must never abuse his parents" to Morgan: "Hang it, I can't complain of them to the child!" (11:526–27). Yet this is precisely the point at which James complicates the tutor's moral and ethical code, for it is the precocious Morgan himself, not Pemberton, who begins to bring up the whole issue of his parents' mistreatment of Pemberton; and although Pemberton keeps fending him off, Morgan counters by calling him a "jolly old humbug" and then, repeatedly, "a hero" (11:525, 545–46). So the next moral conflict in "The Pupil" is between Pemberton's righteous indignation stemming from the Moreen's manipulative abuse of him and his own ethical imperative not to speak of the parents to young Morgan, despite the fact that Morgan, who at one point even calls the family's language "Ultramoreen," insists, "I'm not afraid of the stern reality" and knows all too well of Pemberton's victimization—indeed, he keeps bringing the matter up (11:520, 537).

If this moral conflict does not exactly come to a head, it does reach a certain plateau when Mrs. Moreen, the principal spokeswoman of her clan, arrives one evening at Pemberton's room with a token fifty francs in hand—nowhere near what is owed him. She compounds her duplicity by urging "ardently" that Pemberton is already amply "paid above all by the sweet relation he had established with Morgan—quite ideal as from master to pupil—and by the simple privilege of knowing and living with so amazingly gifted a child" (11:540). There is, of course, sufficient truth to this to make her ulterior motive effective, for she now wants to put their relations on a regular "comfortable footing." Pemberton, furious at her emotional blackmail, counters with this proposal: "If I stay on longer it must be on one condition—that Morgan shall know distinctly on what footing I am." Mrs. Moreen pockets the francs and says, "You may tell him any horror you like!" (11:543) The two make this exchange in their dressing gowns, emblematic, perhaps, of a moment both of complicity and the absence of the usual outward show or "velveteen" associated with the family surname.

It is really from this point on that James begins subtly to explore, as in an intricate athletic counterplay, the potential moral complicity of Pemberton himself, and to introduce along with that issue his chiaroscuro-like system of epistemological illumination and bewilderment exhibited in the fiction after "The Pupil," especially by 1900 with *The Sacred Fount* and the novels of the major phase. Morgan asks Pemberton the quintessential question about his parents: "They're so beastly worldly. . . . All they care about is to make an appearance and pass for something or other. What the dickens do they want to pass for? What *do* they, Mr. Pemberton?" "You pause for a reply," replies Pemberton, trying very hard to treat "the question as a joke, yet wondering too and greatly struck with his mate's intense if imperfect vision. 'I haven't the least idea'" (11:549). Morgan's question essentially stays unanswered throughout the story, and his vision remains "imperfect" only in the sense that such people, in art as in life, are, finally, impenetrable. Still,

Pemberton holds back even yet from speaking openly to Morgan, although Morgan, now getting older and "already flushing faintly into knowledge" (11:547), insists, "We must be frank, at the last; we *must* come to an understanding" (11:548). This language is deeply ironic in its evocation of Pemberton's earlier encounter with Mrs. Moreen, but more extraordinary still as foreshadowing the tale's own eventual climax, "at the last," although no reader is likely to pick this up the first time through the story. Pemberton merely parries with him: "I want to turn you out—I want you to do me credit," and, "You had better let me finish you" (11:550). Yet Morgan, while closer to Pemberton than to anyone by now, feels his tutor should leave if his parents continue to exploit him. Moreover, the young pupil in reaction to Pemberton's frivolity also kiddingly says he only hangs around because he knows that he, Morgan, being congenitally sick, will probably not "make old—make older—bones." The two engage in a witty exchange but with a deep Jamesian edge: "You *are* too clever to live!" agrees Pemberton. "But I shall punish you by the way I hang on," retorts the boy. "Look out or I'll poison you!" counters Pemberton. And Morgan concludes this scene of simultaneous tension, humor, and ambiguity with "a sigh of mingled weariness and relief. 'Ah now that we look at the facts it's all right!'" (11:551). It is a Jamesian false resolution.

Their mutual understanding establishes the next plateau in James's ethical landscape, the stage at which Pemberton and Morgan freely discuss the parents. What happens is that "the pair had such perceptions in common it was useless for them to pretend they didn't judge such people; but the very judgement and the exchange of perceptions created another tie" (11:552)—that is, an even greater emotional intimacy between the two, which gradually takes the form of a plan someday to go away and live together. It is clear by now that Morgan has shifted his allegiance to Pemberton, for the pair are now telepathic: "It was really by wise looks—they knew each other so well now" (11:560). Morgan seems to be beating the odds of his illness, for he is now "mainly conscious of growing taller and stronger and indeed of being in his fifteenth year," and that "in a little while he should stand on his own feet. . . . that in short he should be 'finished'" (11:556–57). A telegram from a London friend gives Pemberton the opportunity to coach an "opulent youth" on favorable terms. "I'll make a tremendous charge," he and Morgan together decide. "I'll earn a lot of money in a short time, and we'll live on it" (11:560). Here again the tone, if not the intent (at least consciously) is strained and ambiguous.

After Pemberton leaves the Moreens for an unspecified period of time and coaches the "opulent youth" (who does not pass his exam, but whose parents wish Pemberton "to renew the siege"), he receives from Mrs. Moreen, to whom *he* has now lent some money, a frantic communique that Morgan is "dreadfully ill" (11:564). Pemberton, having received a number of "charming young letters" from Morgan, tries to write him, but receives no answer. And so he takes "abrupt leave of the opulent youth" and goes to Paris, where the Moreens are, typically, "on the rebound" (11:564–65). He soon learns it was a ruse to get him back of which Morgan himself is innocent. Yet he also discovers eventually that the Moreen game is over; they have used up all their "retreats" and are on the verge of collapse. "Take me away—take me away" (11:567), the boy implores, and indeed for once this is the self-same wish of the Moreens themselves. In their desperate straits and now definitive "social failure," they have determined to send Morgan away with Pemberton while they attend "to the readjustment of their affairs" (11:576). James's ending after such deliberate complication and reformulation of issues is powerful, unexpected, and concise. Morgan, surprised and seemingly delighted, asks his parents, "Do you mean he may take me to live with him for ever and ever?"; and then "looking at Pemberton with a light in his face" and with "boyish joy" asks him, "My dear fellow, what do you say to *that?*" Then suddenly, "He had turned quite livid and had raised his hand to his left side." Mrs. Moreen breaks out, "Ah his darling little heart!" and the pupil, suffering a stroke or heart attack, dies in front of them (11:576–77).

Morgan's sudden death might be accounted for by his excitement and excess of joy at finally being free to leave and live with his tutor, but such a reading lacks a certain internal consistency, for Morgan has already become stronger and healthier during the time of Pemberton's tutorial, a period of about four years. Another explanation is that, despite his apparent disaffection from his family, he exhibits, at bottom, his deepest psychological blood ties, the "mysteries of transmission," and so is crushed at heart when his parents actually do choose to abandon him. The rhetoric of this tale's fiction at its conclusion does proffer that explanation: "But I thought he *wanted* to go to you!" wails Mrs. Moreen. "I *told* you he didn't, my dear." James concedes that "Mr. Moreen was trembling all over and was in his way as deeply affected as his wife. But after the very first he took his bereavement as a man of the world" (11:557).

This concluding language is most telling, not only in its immediate pungent irony but in exhibiting a patented type of verbal strategy present in a number of James's later nouvelles and in at least one novel, *The Ambassadors*. That is, the concluding line—that Mr. Moreen took his bereavement "as a man of the world"—is also the last in a series of identical reiterative phrases designating Mr. Moreen throughout the tale, and thus conveys a cumulative irony. At the same time, the statement that he "was in his way as deeply affected as his wife" is also cutting, for we sense only too well James's overall assessment of Mrs. Moreen. Hence whatever genuine emotion Morgan may have felt in his dying moment for his family, it cannot alter our view of them throughout the tale as a band of "pickpockets or strolling players" (11:520). The Moreens take their place with the numerous morally flawed Europeanized Americans in Henry James—Winterbourne, Mrs. Costello and Mrs. Walker in "Daisy Miller"; Madame Merle and Gilbert Osmond in *The Portrait of a Lady;* the art-student cousin in "Four Meetings"; Louis Leverett in "The Point of View" and "A Bundle of Letters," to name but a few—who are seeking to substitute veneer for substance, outward form for intrinsicality, social gloss for moral imagination. Pemberton, too, has an American background, for we are told only once and briefly that before his Oxford years no such note as the Moreens' had been "struck to his younger American ear during the four years at Yale in which he had richly supposed himself to be reacting against a Puritan strain" (11:519). So Pemberton also qualifies as a Europeanized American in James's international schema.

Yet this is finally not an international tale as such but a searching examination of moral complexity and epistemological bewilderment. Hence the most Jamesian reading of its abrupt ending is, I believe, that Morgan, in perhaps the most painful of James's handling of the innocence-to-experience theme, dies because at the precise instant he learns his parents do not want him he simultaneously discovers Pemberton does not really want him either. In order to appreciate this reading of the ending—in my judgment the core one—we must first recognize the emerging extent to which Pemberton already has begun inwardly to regret the prospect of living with the young boy once they have become close and articulated the getaway scheme. Shortly before the arrival of the telegram requesting him to coach the "opulent youth," Pemberton feels most apprehensive about the boy's unrealistic notion of attending with the tutor's companionship and help Pemberton's own college at Oxford: "How could [Morgan] live without an allowance, and where was the allowance to come from? He, Pemberton, might live on Morgan; but how could Morgan live on *him?* What was to become of him anyhow? Somehow the fact that he was a big boy now, with better prospects of health, made the question of his future more difficult" (11:557). Difficult, that is to say, for Pemberton, who is experiencing the Jamesian "germ" of his own doubt. James picks up this issue again: when returning after Mrs. Moreen's frantic communiqué and implored by Morgan to "take me away," Pemberton stammers, "Where shall I take you, and how—oh *how*, my boy?" He can only think of the "rude way in which his friends in London held that, for his convenience, with no assurance of prompt return, he had thrown them over; of the just resentment with which they would already have called in a successor, and of the scant help to finding fresh employment that resided for him in the grossness of having failed to pass his pupil" (11:567).

One can hardly blame Pemberton for such worries at this moment, but later on while back again with the Moreens he starts to think of the boy as a kind of millstone: "He had spent all his money accruing to him in England, and he saw his youth going and that he was getting nothing back for it. It was all very well of Morgan to count it for reparation that he should now settle on him permanently—there was an irritating flaw in such a view. He saw what the boy had in his mind. . . . But [Pemberton] didn't desire the gift—what could he do with Morgan's dreadful little life?" (11:572). Therefore Pemberton is *not* elated at the conclusion of the tale when the Moreens actually offer him their son. So when Morgan looks at him in "boyish joy" and exclaims, "My dear fellow, what do you say to *that?*" Pemberton can only think to himself reluctantly, "how could one not say something enthusiastic?" (11:577).

But the key point here is that Morgan himself, precocious and by now so attuned to Pemberton that, as we earlier learned, the two have "such perceptions in common" and fully communicate by such "wise looks" as to be virtually telepathic, *knows* on the spot he is not wanted by Pemberton any more than by his own family. This double awareness ruptures the boy's heart. The whole reversal of the pupil-tutor role, so prominent and engaging throughout the tale, takes its ironic, unexpected, and devastating toll. It is also for this reason, I believe, that at the very moment Morgan expires James writes that Pemberton "pulled him half out of his mother's hands, and for a moment, while they held him together, they looked all their dismay into each other's eyes" (11:577). For if we recall the earlier episode when Mrs. Moreen and

Pemberton collaborated in putting things on a regular "footing," we see now the same two "go halves" as James symbolically reenacts their collaboration while holding the dying boy. Pemberton's complicity, I further believe, is also expressed emblematically when Mrs. Moreen "hurled over her shoulder," at him, "You walked him too far, you hurried him too fast!" (11:577). Although she means their just-completed walk outside before entering and hearing the grim news and the new plan, James intimates figuratively through the accusation the whole process of bringing Morgan along emotionally too fast and of making quick ties with him that Pemberton is unwilling or simply unable to follow through; indeed the metaphorical force of hurrying Morgan too fast recalls those many times, precariously humorous, when Pemberton spoke of wanting to "finish" Morgan (or even "poison" him)—James playing enigmatically with the common meaning of "finish" in tutorial parlance as preparing the student successfully for examination. The "opulent youth" in that context is never "finished"; Morgan, one might say, learns too much and is "finished" too soon.

And yet it is not, surely, that Pemberton is some treacherous villain. His flaws are those with which every one of us must all profoundly identify, and his own misuse by the Moreens has made whatever he did or feel all the more understandable. That is the distinctive genius of Henry James in this as well as his finest moral tales. "The Pupil" is a work of layers. Pemberton's measure of culpability, for instance, is well prepared by James much earlier when Mrs. Moreen, on the occasion of their "understanding," rightly reproaches Pemberton in not succeeding at his writing and sketches of "pretend[ing] to abilities you're sacrificing for our sake" (11:542). It is just that at that time in the tale, the reader is inevitably so preoccupied with her exploitation of him that her otherwise "nailing" a particular fissure in Pemberton's character goes by undetected. But James has *all* his layers in mind at once, for it is precisely in response to this comment by her that Pemberton insists on the one crucial condition of his staying on, the openness with Morgan—and she complies.

Still another layer, perhaps the final one, relates to the reader's sense at certain times early in the story that the entire work is another of James's retrospective or memory tales like "The Real Thing," "Greville Fane," or "Four Meetings," even though unlike them the narration of "The Pupil" is never in the first person. Consider this after-the-fact passage, for example: "Today, after a considerable interval, there is something phantasmagoric, like a prismatic reflexion or a serial novel, in Pemberton's memory of the queerness of the Moreens. If it were not for a few tangible tokens—a lock of Morgan's hair cut by his own hand, and the half-dozen letters received from him when they were disjoined—the whole episode and the figures peopling it would seem too inconsequent for anything but dreamland" (11:518–19). One of the ways this Jamesian insertion makes sense and functions dramatically is to conjecture that in time present, "today," if you will, Pemberton still cannot see his own possible contribution to the boy's eventual death.

This can be seen again in another retrospective passage: "He had simply given himself away to a band of adventurers. The idea, the word itself, wore a romantic horror for him—he had always lived on such safe lines. Later it assumed a more interesting, almost a soothing sense: it pointed a moral, and Pemberton could enjoy a moral" (11:533–534).[28] Later on, that is to say, his remembered "horror" of the Moreens becomes a "soothing" rationale for Pemberton: it intercedes, thankfully, between his psyche and his own possible culpability, and therefore the "moral it points" for him keeps, so to speak, the disquietingly fuller Jamesian moral away from him. In the story itself Pemberton had reflected rightly that "the real problem" was "how far it was excusable to discuss the turpitude of parents with a child of twelve, of thirteen, of fourteen"; also how it "wasn't decent to abuse to one's pupil the family of one's pupil" (11:535, 537). James's nouvelle in exploring that question reveals bewildering implications, possibilities, and consequences that penetrate deeply into the moral landscape of the soul. This may be analogous to Pemberton's admission at one point that to have called the Moreens "cosmopolite," while it impressed him as "very sharp that first day," ultimately seemed "confessedly helplessly provisional" (11:519). Nor could he possibly realize when he took Morgan's arm "tenderly" and asserted "*I'm* your doctor" (11:551) that he was speaking tragic and unwitting irony, an issue we shall meet again more fully in James's last published tale, "A Round of Visits." "The Pupil" is thus very aptly named, for there is always much left to learn in the obscure moral universe of a truly great James tale.

Late James: Consciousness, Ghostly Reality, Poetic Expressionism

In a very early letter to Charles Eliot Norton, James once remarked, "To write a series of good little tales I deem ample work for a lifetime."[29] As the reader of this study will already surmise, in James's lifetime his 112 short fictions are generally very good indeed, but most of them, including many of his most famous and enduring, are hardly little; yet, interestingly, a surprising number of those that are little are admirably "foreshortened"—James's own most recurrent aim in his short fiction—and comprise the "hard, shining sonnet" variety, such as "Four Meetings," "Greville Fane," "The Middle Years," "The Marriages," and some others, yet to be examined in this study, of his major phase. James's short fiction after 1900 is discussed briefly in the first chapter of *The American Short Story: 1900–1945*. Ellen Kimbel, the author of that chapter, comments on "The Great Good Place" (1900), "The Beast in the Jungle" (1903), and "The Jolly Corner" (1909), summarizing very well the overall development of James's late short fiction:

> By the turn of the century, [James's] richly textured social world and its interest in the subtleties of ethical behavior and the difficulties of interpersonal relations gives way to more philosophical considerations at once more mystical, more meditative, and more sombre. Now his stories are relatively unpeopled; often two characters dominate, sometimes only one, in the interests of exploring the problems of the solitary soul. . . . No less successful as pure fiction than the stories of his earlier periods, these tales function additionally as speculations on the nature of the unknown, the unlived life, and the might-have-been. One sees in them the gradual movement away from the social realism and irony of his first and middle phases and the emergence of themes increasingly abstract, contemplative, and philosophical.[30]

Kimbel's characterization fits best the three stories she addresses; many of James's twenty-five tales from 1900 to 1910 are simply not as philosophical and speculative as are the "The Beast in the Jungle" and

"The Jolly Corner." Nevertheless, Kimbel's account is most acute in designating the distinctive new element that suffuses both the great novels of the major phase—*The Ambassadors, The Wings of the Dove,* and *The Golden Bowl*—and the finest stories of that period.

If we remember that for James the nature of an "adventure" transposes more and more into the drama of consciousness itself, a doctrine enunciated earlier in the famous "spiderweb" passage in "The Art of Fiction," it may not seem so surprising that his fiction evolved along the lines Kimbel describes above. Furthermore, by the beginning of the new century Henry James, though never a formal philosopher, seemed to grasp intuitively the broad development and trajectory in Western thought concerning mankind's inner and outer worlds in the twin areas of psychology and physical science—the profound importance of the unconscious realm, on the one hand, and the non-Cartesian awareness of external reality as a phenomenal field, on the other. Moreover, he sensed that human consciousness, his quintessential preoccupation, was all the more pivotal in both dominions, for its drama provides the arena through which the unconscious must express its drives and forces, and yet it also structures and organizes the external world itself, transforming particles and waves into phenomenal representations, imposing the categories of time, space, extension, number—in short, those elements that before modern science had once been thought to be "primary qualities," whose existence was entirely independent of the percipient mind. Inasmuch as James intuited this matrix of modern thought, we find, among other things, that in his late work the mind's subconscious powers replace Poe's, Hawthorne's, and Melville's gothic imaginations, while his prose, so unlike that of his realist-ally Howells's, for instance, projects in its subtlety, elliptical syntax, and prolixity the external world as an extension and reciprocal twin of consciousness—a viewpoint first hypothesized and later increasingly confirmed in the mainstream of twentieth-century physical science.[31]

The year 1900 was something of an annus mirabilis for James's short fiction. He published ten tales in addition to his novel *The Sacred Fount.* Three of the stories, "Miss Gunton of Poughkeepsie," "The Two Faces," and "The Great Good Place" show certain elements of the late James emerging from the earlier James in interestingly different ways, although only "The Great Good Place" exhibits the new philosophical or stylistic expressionism of the late period.

"Miss Gunton," perhaps unfairly, is occasionally regarded as a slighter work, one that "did not tempt James into 'developments.'"[32] Lily Gunton, a young American woman with great riches, that is, immense "drafts," as well as stubborn independence, unexpectedly and carelessly quells her betrothal to a young Roman prince from a "very great house, of tremendous antiquity, fairly groaning under the weight of ancient honours" (16:383), even though he has already bent to Lily's will and coerced his proud mother to put aside ceremonial protocol and write the first letter of invitation. An additional irony is that the bewildered and abashed prince not only loses the impatient Miss Gunton but is henceforth obviously in bad straits with his humiliated mother, since she most unwillingly wrote the letter.

James, in his Preface to the *Daisy Miller* volume of the New York Edition, frequently speaks of Miss Gunton as one of a group with Daisy and Julie Bride, thus identifying the young, independent American women who constitute a signal component of the fame of his fiction. It is intriguing and not inaccurate, I think, to see Lily Gunton as the intermediate stage in James's transformation of the early, innocent Daisy Miller type into the late, morally disfigured example of Julie Bride, whose story I shall later examine at greater length.[33] Lily Gunton, unlike Julia, has great wealth, far more, one realizes, than Daisy Miller. But she has none of Daisy's affecting vulnerability; although "lovely and candid," like Daisy, she also possesses "disparities—the juxtaposition in her of beautiful sun-flushed heights and deep dark holes" (16:376, 375). In contrast to the young prince's imposing blood line, Miss Gunton "was not great in any particular save one. She was great when she 'drew'" (16:378). One cannot conceive of Daisy Miller so described, nor would she ever address her would-be fiance as "My dear boy" or "My dear child" (16:381)—even though the prince most frequently appears naive and emasculated. Lily Gunton thus marks a stage in James's revisionist view of the Daisy Miller/Bessie Alden/Isabel Archer figure into that of Julia Bride, who lacks the money, or perhaps even of Maggie Verver, in *The Golden Bowl*, who certainly has the money and who in fact does buy her Italian prince in James's last and most massive complex novel. The emerging later James, then, is found here in his reconsideration of the free American woman and, implicitly, in his recomplication of the international theme by focusing on the enigma of what really constitutes and drives Lily's Americanism, those "disparities" expressed in the passage above. The *mode* of the story is not particularly late-Jamesian, however, and it remains a comedy of manners vestigially reminiscent of "An International Episode." Finally, the point-of-view character, Lady Champer, recalls the author's middle period, for he reveals her English imperiousness when she claims at first to have analyzed Lily's abrupt withdrawal from the engagement only to contradict herself. So she can only conclude, "With Americans one's lost!" (16:392). This may be true—indeed, it reinforces the whole enigma-theme of Lily's Americanism—but it does not in any way infuse the reader with confidence in Lady Champer. The two letters "crossing" in the mail—Lily's recantation and the elder princess's reluctant overture—symbolize both the tale's international dissonance of manners and its Maupassant-like juxtaposition, a reversal not further complicated, however, by additional Jamesian "developments."

"The Two Faces," on the other hand, while just as concise, just as Maupassant-like, nevertheless achieves an effect of greater moral complexity, although without the rich elaboration, for example, of a nouvelle like "The Pupil." The two faces belong, first of all, to Mrs. Grantham, a handsomely beautiful impresario of sophisticated English society, and to the simple Lady Gwyther, an innocent young woman newly married and brought from rural Germany by Lord Gwyther despite his previous "understanding" with Mrs. Grantham. Lord Gwyther takes the bold step of asking Mrs. Grantham—as an appeal to her honor and generosity—to take hold of his untutored wife, dress her up, help her, and then introduce her into London society. The Jamesian "register" of the tale is Mr. Shirley Sutton, another suitor and confidant of Mrs. Grantham, most particularly since Lord Gwyther's surprise marriage. It is principally Sutton who conveys and reacts to the sudden climax of the tale: Mrs. Grantham's introduction of shy "Valda" Gwyther at Burbeck, dressed monstrously like a monkey with "feathers, frills, excrescences of silk and lace—massed together and conflicting" and "decked . . . for the sacrifice with ribbons and flowers" (12:410, 408). Mrs. Grantham's pleased expression is like "that of the artist confronted with her work and interested, even to impatience, in the judgement of others" (12:410). Everyone agrees that "the poor creature's lost" to society, a "Roman mob at the circus [awaiting] the next Christian maiden brought out to the tigers" (12:411, 407).

Ironies abound in this condensed tale. Gwyther gave his wife over to Mrs. Grantham's revenge in the naive hope that she would be "a real friend" to the young woman "for the great labyrinth" of London

(12:396). Yet by disgracing Valda Mrs. Grantham reveals something new, for Shirley Sutton at least, in her *own* face; and this is the real epiphany of the story and its double-focused title (which James changed in its second printing from simply "The Faces," surely to isolate and emphasize his multiple thematics of duality). Sutton's attraction for Mrs. Grantham all along has been that he "was at the mercy of her face" (12:399), but he detects that "Something new had quickly come into her beauty; he couldn't as yet have said what nor whether on the whole to its advantage or its loss" (12:398). He eventually learns the answer when watching her contentment in Lady Gwyther's grotesque entrance. "The face—the face!" he keeps repeating (12:412). "It was as if something had happened in consequence of which she had changed." That is, "She had a perfection resplendent, but what in the world had it done, this perfection, to her beauty?" (12:409).

James provides us, then, with a "double-layered" effect characteristic of his later method. The two faces, on the one hand, signify that face which has hitherto captivated Sutton exhibiting the revelation of its new monstrous design, and the result is to make Sutton recoil as he witnesses Mrs. Grantham's fatal beauty borne of revenge. On the other hand, Sutton perceives in young artless Valda's facial distortion and disfigurement a humanity that, as he says, "goes to the heart," a case of "unimaginable pathos," a dim discovery of the knowledge of what has been done to her "glimmer[ing] upon her innocence" (12:412). This discovery imparts to the young woman's disgrace a beauty, even while the charmingly dressed and tailored Mrs. Grantham becomes, in Sutton's eyes, hideous. The multiple meaning compressed into James's revised title informs the tale, a compression that pleased James himself in his New York Edition Preface for its "neat evolution, as I call it, the example of the turn of the *whole* coach and pair in the contracted court, without the 'spill' of a single passenger or the derangement of a single parcel" (12:xxiv). Another aspect of this same economy, concision, and duality is the reader's gradual realization that triumphant Mrs. Grantham has ultimately lost two different suitors to the same artless woman. As Wagenknecht has put it, "There was never a better illustration of the truth that for James the world of 'high society' was only a theater to be used to test and to reveal moral values" (Wagenknecht, 129). Through Mrs. Grantham's act James presents a critique of the corridors of social forces wherein such cultivated cruelty as hers can occur, while yet allowing ultimately its victims, as in his large novels like *The Wings of the Dove* and *The Golden Bowl*, to possess somehow the final superior power. Mrs. Grantham herself unwittingly expounds the very feature of the story, in which she herself emerges ugly while bedecking Lady Gwyther in ugliness, when she remarks archly at one point, "What profundities indeed then over the simplest of matters!" (12:402)

The third tale from 1900, "The Great Good Place," is utterly different from either "Miss Gunton" or "The Two Faces." Like "Maud-Evelyn," also of that same year, we find James experimenting with the bizarre and the ghostly. The very odd story of "Maud-Evelyn"—a wealthy couple's long-dead daughter "courted" and "wedded" by a sympathetic young man who later dies and wills his inheritance to his former fiancée—is quite an expansion of the Jamesian oxymoron of the unlived life or the absent-present. "Maud-Evelyn" even evokes James's affinity with Poe's beloved and deceased heroines, in poetry and fiction alike, who function as inspiration and obsession, the major difference lying in James "nesting" his narrative totally with the interesting narrative "witness" of Lady Emma, who orates the whole peculiar story to a listening group, much like Conrad's Marlow. "The Great Good Place," while equally concerned with presenting a particular conception of "positive" death or "plenitude" of absence, is otherwise entirely different. Alone of all ten tales published in 1900, it exhibits the rich abstractionism that begins to dominate in James's post-1900 fiction taken as a whole.

"The Great Good Place" is at once a modern dream narrative and, not unlike "The Altar of the Dead" and "The Turn of the Screw," two immediate predecessors, a type of the fantastic—more extended than the first, less extensive than the second. More than either story, however, it is an especially modern parable: for the protagonist, successful writer George Dane, is suffused with anxiety, harassed by life's constant "series of decapitations," and "wearily, helplessly" mired in "books from authors, books from friends, books from enemies, books from his own bookseller" (16:225–26). He turns a "heavy eye" on his smothering world and longs for escape. This deep psychic wish miraculously comes to pass in the form of a forgotten "appointment with the young man" (16:232), an admirer of Dane's who by merely taking his hand precipitates a momentous transformation: Dane reawakens in a kind of secular monastery, a "great cloister," and converses with companions known only as "Brothers," all part of "The Great Want Met" (16:235, 238), all exquisitely without the "complication of an identity" (16:250). He and his "conversers" exist in an "abyss of negatives," an "absence of positives" (16:234). Dane feels deeply that "This key, pure gold, was simply the cancelled list. Slowly and blissfully he read into the general wealth of his comfort all the particular absences of which it was composed. One by one, he touched as it were, all the things it was such rapture to be without" (16:252).

Some scholars over the years have read this story as ironic, as a kind of criticism of escapism, but the language of the tale itself with its "postmodern" tenor, as in the passage just cited, constantly insinuates the opposite of such ironic interpretation. So does the structure. With each succeeding section of its five parts Dane moves inexorably toward his total rejuvenation, his rebaptism, his allotted moment to "return" to his apartment, whence he sleeps or has been transported. When he does reawaken, he finds that the young man has taken care of all his responsibilities that day, has eliminated the asphyxiating clutter. "I've been so happy!" declares Dane. "So have I," responds the nameless young man (16:263).

"The Great Good Place" conveys the aura of late James in a way vastly different from a comedy of manners like "Miss Gunton" or a less comedic analysis of society like "The Two Faces." The parabolic quality is part of it, the rich abstractionism a greater part and often found in prolonged elliptical conversations between Dane and the two principal "Brothers" at the Place. Another aspect, a very important one, is the rich introduction of Jamesian alter egos. The "forgotten" young man who comes and "exchanges places" with Dane is one; the "Brothers" with whom he converses are others. James even signals the alter-ego condition when he has Dane emphasize the "back of a person writing at his study-table," and again notes "the mere sight of his back" (16:261, 247). Henry James uses the back of a person as a kind of musical key signature denoting the alter ego in such works as *The Sense of the Past* and "A Round of Visits"—the latter story to be examined at great length at the conclusion of this study. Dane himself even thinks at the end that "Every one was a little someone else" (16:263), and earlier at the Place itself: "It's charming how when we speak for ourselves we speak for each other" (16:240).

James also reinforces his theme of temporary flight as refreshment-rebirth by his extensive symbolic use of rain. It is raining when Dane experiences the great wish to escape his angst; "I do love the rain," he declares. "Perhaps, better still, it will snow" (16:231). At the Place itself he experiences "the deep deep bath, the soft cool plash in the stillness!" (16:251). And the final section, which treats the completion of his restorative process, begins, "Why it's raining!" (16:256)—thus returning us symbolically as well as narratively to where we began. Indeed, the whole meaning of this remarkable story is that one's experience of death and rebirth is a psychic matter and an affair of consciousness, the same thematic concept explored in James's celebrated late tale, "The Jolly Corner." Here the concept of psychic transformation is articulated by such passages as the following: "It was part of the whole impression that, by some extraordinary law, one's vision seemed less from the facts than the facts from one's vision"; and also, "What he had felt the first time recurred: the friend was always new and yet at the same time—it was amusing, not disturbing—suggested the possibility that he might be but an old one altered" (16:254).

Such language helps to confirm what the attentive reader of this tale must sense, that there are really no other "characters" than that of George Dane in the various guises of his psychic self. Entirely unlike "Miss Gunton" or "The Two Faces" in its mode, "The Great Good Place" is not only a parable about modern "distraction" of the sort commemorated later by T. S. Eliot but also, without its being a ghost story like "The Turn of the Screw" or "The Jolly Corner," a Jamesian foray into the quasi-supernatural, more so than even "Maud-Evelyn." As such it signals the central stream within his late period. Any potential allegorical element is attenuated into the fantastic, allowing us a type of work that actually duplicates what is said of the Place itself: "The thing's so perfect that it's open to as many interpretations as any other great work—a poem of Goethe, a dialogue of Plato, a symphony of Beethoven" (16:257). Verily, the only final explanation of what the Great Good Place may really be is "the thing for instance we love it most for being" (16:238).

It is certainly appropriate to cite, as Kimbel and other scholars do, "The Beast in the Jungle" (1903) and "The Jolly Corner" (1908) as two masterpieces of the first decade of this century. These two stories bring to fruition James's important development of the ghostly tale, the power of human obsession to bring into being the occult life upon which it fastens, whether John Marcher's presentiment of his special fate, which stalks and awaits him, crouching like a beast in the jungle, or Spencer Brydon's compulsive pursuit within his ancestral home of his own lurking alter ego, the man he might have become had he remained in America and developed the abilities, latent in his "organism," for business and enterprise. As ghost stories dealing with the abnormal psychology of obsession, "The Beast in the Jungle" and "The Jolly Corner" extend and refine the kind of eerie and destructive experience commemorated in what still remains James's best known and most widely read ghost story, "The Turn of the Screw" (1898). The Governess's need to "protect" young Miles and Flora from the bestial "horrors" of the deceased lovers Peter Quint and Miss Jessel seems to emanate from conflicts within the deep well of her own subconscious life, yet it also seems to draw forth the malevolent powers she challenges with disastrous results, particularly the death of young Miles apparently from sheer fright at the end, a death reminiscent in certain ways of Morgan Moreen's in "The Pupil." "The Turn of the Screw," to be sure, remains one of the most widely discussed and controversial stories ever written, but the massive scholarship it receives seems weighted more and more against the Governess's reliability, at least in her claim that the ghosts of Peter Quint and Miss Jessel have possessed the children at Bly independently of any act on her part. The interpretive literature on this one story can fill a not-so-modest library; it probably exceeds in quantity James's entire corpus, as far as I know, an unprecedented situation in academic scholarship, at least for a single tale. Part of the cause for this phenomenal growth is that "Turn of the Screw" studies are well into a "second wave" of critical theory, which uses the debate to explore broader hermeneutical questions; that is, the criticism has begun to "displace" the text and become its own evidence for further analysis.[34] Even so, it will be helpful here to touch on what have always seemed to me the key points in the controversy, although such points are in turn themselves the subject of controversy many times over.

Those who support the governess' veracity have, I believe, three basic arguments: first, the man she sees on the tower and outside the window and whose face and hair she describes in considerable physical detail is identified immediately by Mrs. Grose as Peter Quint, a man the Governess has never seen before. Second, the story's introduction and frame indicate through the character of Douglas that the Governess's record of service *after* the horrific events at Bly was exemplary. Third, the sudden death of an otherwise healthy ten-year-old boy from heart failure at the end seems on the face of it physically unlikely, if not impossible, unless he were possessed; or rather, through the Governess's heroic efforts at exorcism finally "dispossessed."

Over against this view are what might best be called clusters of counterevidence. First, there is simply yet pervasively the Governess's own increasing language of obsession as the tale unfolds and she defines her mission as her "joy" and "passion," her "extraordinary flight of heroism," the "chain of my logic," the "long halter of my boldness," the "particular way strength came to me," the "success of my rigid will," or "Proofs, I say, yes—from the moment I really took hold" and similar expressions (12:194, 199, 228, 275, 295). Like Conrad's *Heart of Darkness*, published the very next year, this tale too is a "nested narrative" whose primary text is given in first person; but Marlow's expressions of self-skepticism, doubts, or self-contempt are entirely absent from the Governess, even though her language both of "possession" and "dispossession" resonates symbolic meaning beyond the facts of the case she intends to make, doubtless due to James's "Central Intelligence," as he liked to call his omniscient narrative consciousness in the *Prefaces*.

Furthermore, the reactions by the other characters to the governess' claims fail to corroborate her view; Mrs. Grose is unconvinced, Flora accuses her of inflicting fright, and Miles, after first attempting to put up a brave front, finds her terrifying. Mrs. Grose does in a sense "convert" to the Governess's position after she hears Flora utter what seem to be obscenities, but these occur only after the Governess herself has relentlessly raked them up from the child's repressed memory. In some respects the most damaging evidence, however, consists in the many times James has the Governess in effect "replace" or visually substitute for one of her alleged demons—a rather clear case of his rhetorical and imaginative shaping, again his "Central Intelligence." The first time is when she stands at the window precisely where she has just seen Quint, and her image turns Mrs. Grose "white" as the older woman comes into the dining room. This early pattern repeats itself throughout the tale: the Governess sits on the very step where she has seen Miss Jessel; she espies Miss Jessel sitting in her chair in the little schoolroom; she herself stands on the bank of the lake where earlier she claims to have seen Miss Jessel; she even observes Miles and Flora out on the lawn the evening of their "prank" from the very tower section of Bly where she first saw Quint, while assuming *they* are the ones communing with the nefarious deceased pair. Other evidence could include the final scene, when the horrified Miles gasps in response to the Governess's goadings to utter Quint's name, "Peter Quint—you devil!" That she should be called a "devil" in the very scene and very moment when she last sees Quint and calls him the "hideous author of our woe" (12:308, 309) can hardly be accidental: James surely knew well that phrasing from the opening of Milton's *Paradise Lost* and its traditional reference to the devil. One might even follow this vein of thought back to the episode when the Governess walks toward the church but cannot enter it. But we need only recollect the final scene with Miles: his fright before her accusations in no way resembles demonic possession, and the subsequent figure of Quint at the same dining room window cannot fail to remind the reader of the earlier episode—as if Quint and the Governess are finally revealed in the fullness of their "collaboration," much as both were placed entirely in charge by the children's neglectful uncle, the irresponsible but charming Harley Street master who so conspicuously infatuates the young woman.

While admittedly I have elaborated far more of an anti-Governess reading, my principal suggestion is not that we casually substitute Freudian projections for any supernatural elements but that we should at least recognize that, whatever the malevolent agency let loose, it has been accomplished only with her deep complicity. And we should keep in mind that by 1898 James, as we have seen, was already preoccupied in his nonghostly tales with the psychology of obsession and would become even more so in the great quasi-supernatural tales after 1900. Although conceived differently by James in each case, the ghostly realm deepens and in fact parallels the deepening psychological obsession of the protagonist in all three classic ghostly tales, "The Turn of the Screw," "The Beast in the Jungle," and "The Jolly Corner."

In the two latter works, John Marcher's and Spencer Brydon's very different obsessions seem, no less than the Governess's, to emanate from their subconscious life and conflicts. May Bartram's victimization by Marcher in "The Beast in the Jungle" is fortunately avoided and counteracted in "The Jolly Corner," however, precisely because Spencer Brydon confronts his subliminal self with the active help of Alice Staverton—unlike May Bartram, an American woman who, though considerably older, still belongs to the tribe of Daisy Miller and Isabel Archer. Brydon is therefore saved by the regenerative power of love; in more psychoanalytic terms, his divided self is reintegrated with her help. It is important to point out here that, although most English-speaking psychologists were unaware of Freud's ideas until the end of the first decade of this century, a rare exception was F. W. H. Meyers, whose writings on "the subliminal consciousness" were immediately cited by William James in his 1896 essay "What Psychical Research Has Accomplished." Henry James therefore did have some access to early Freud, but that very access was indirectly by way of his brother William James, a pre-twentieth century psychologist.[35]

In addition to exhibiting a modern view of the psyche and its sub-conscious realm, "The Beast in the Jungle" and "The Jolly Corner" are also modern parables of isolation, angst, inward journeys, and, in the case especially of John Marcher, Prufrockian paralysis. Indeed, like Eliot's Prufrock, John Marcher seems to anticipate the sterility of the modern world revealed more extensively in *The Waste Land*. He is also, however, the quintessential specimen of the specious third-person nar-rative's "deputy" or "register" in all of James's fiction, a counterpart to the unreliable first-person narrator of "The Aspern Papers." He is furthermore the supreme embodiment of Jamesian "operative irony": that is, his celebrated "special fate," so "rare and distinguished" (17:108), which lies in wait for him like the beast in the jungle, his "mysterious fate" that "he had been marked for" turns out to have been "the man of his time, *the* man, to whom nothing on earth was to have happened" and therefore the "sounded void of his life" (17:77, 125). And since he is always obsessed, as he puts it, with his mysterious fate in "the lap of the gods" (17:85), he is therefore the perfect ex-emplum in late James of the inseverable oneness of character and fate, and of the self-fulfilling prophecy. Moreover, by continuously rejecting May Bartram as a potential lover while instead exploiting her as fellow "watcher" of his fate, Marcher evades the possibilities inherent in the present. It is doubtless for this reason that the tale is also the surpassing instance in James of his mastery in the late style of the "iterative mode," or constant compression of several similar occurrences into one narrative event, so that time itself becomes amorphous and approxi-mates internal experience.[36] This tale conveys the sense of immense duration, and the avoided present is ever-present—still another haunt-ing and supernal dimension of James's operative irony.

Marcher is likewise the epitome in all Henry James of a "man vio-lated by an idea." Throughout this study, beginning with "Madame de Mauves," I have made frequent mention of the specious or morally destructive character in James who is violated (that is, raped) by an idea at the expense of humanity, whether the violating character's own potential or another's actual humanity. My text for this interpretive perspective is T. S. Eliot's early essay on James, wherein he proclaims admiringly (in a routinely misunderstood locution) that James "had a mind so fine that no idea could violate it."[37] In "The Beast in the Jungle" everything is brutally sacrificed to Marcher's violating idea: he thus articulates as well as embodies the full implication of James's interest in the psychology of obsession present in stories otherwise as different as, say, "The Figure in the Carpet" and "The Turn of the Screw." Lastly, John Marcher's cannibalistic misuse of May Bartram is perhaps signified most powerfully by his noxious conception that he discovers "too late" his alleged love for her once she is entombed, like a Poe heroine, and thus must be receding into the past away from the living present.

Spencer Brydon's life history in "The Jolly Corner" seems, at least, to have a redemptive outcome denied to Marcher. Nevertheless, he invokes in his spectral alter ego the ravages of modern life in its economic sphere, a parallel to the grotesque American culture portrayed by Thorstein Veblen, which James himself encountered at his return after twenty-two years and which, like his friend Henry Adams in *The Education of Henry Adams*, he chronicled in *The American Scene*. On one level, Brydon's two American properties—the one he is converting into apartment houses and the other his ancestral home on the Jolly Corner—signify the deep split in his psyche. But the Jolly Corner house itself more deeply recapitulates that same split, for it represents his innocent beginnings where "he had first seen the light" (17:437). It is also the home he left to become one of James's Europeanized Americans. More fundamentally it is the home that houses his alter ego, the hideously maimed yet successful American robber-baron capitalist, the "other" Brydon had he stayed and developed the entrepreneurial "capacity for business and a sense for construction . . . dormant in his own organism" (17:438).

"The Jolly Corner" is assuredly among the most remarkable "double" stories ever composed, for it is the only one in which the reader can ultimately track what the hunted ghost has done or decided to do in no other way than by carefully following the unfolding thought processes of Brydon himself—Brydon and his double are that psychically and profoundly tethered to each other. And since the night-stalking of the alter ego becomes for the obsessed Brydon "the real, the waiting life" (17:455) in contrast to his trivial outward social life, the house on the Jolly Corner is not entirely unlike James's own famous "house of fiction," depicted in his *Prefaces*, signifying here the intensely private, refracted experience of the modern world so soon prominent in Eliot, Conrad, Woolf, and elsewhere. However, since it is likewise the habitation of the defiled and blighted "downtown" American businessman Brydon might have been, the house finally represents the gilded edifice and residential corridors of power in modern American industrial society: so that what symbolizes, so to speak, the farthest reach of the inner life is also the emblem of the external, cultural life, the one addressed by James in *The American Scene*. There is always, of course, immeasurably more to be said about "The Jolly Corner" no less than "The Beast in the Jungle," both great and classic works. But I shall let go of them here, having already had my extended say of them elsewhere.[38]

Three tales from his last phase, "Julia Bride" (1908), "The Bench of Desolation" (1909–10), and "A Round of Visits" (1910), are profound reworkings of James's earlier social realism, which by now achieves a kind of fictive metamorphosis into the poetic extravagance of James's last work. Although "The Bench of Desolation," unlike the other two, concerns penurious English working (if not quite working-class) people, all three tales contain protagonists as fully rendered as John Marcher or Spencer Brydon. Furthermore, "Julia Bride" and "A Round of Visits" both treat small groups of leisured, social climbing, often desperate people whose interactions reveal, as with so many of James's tales, the ironic disparity between social pretention and moral truth, or else the profound cleft by which appearance and reality by turn separate and exchange places. All three tales exhibit the same restricted third-person or "deputy" point of view long since mastered by James and by now preferred over his first-person narrators, reliable or otherwise—a device that opens up the amplitude necessary for James's layering of meaning and also makes possible the drama of individual consciousness.

"Julia Bride" presents a dark, grim, ironic vision of New York society and of the way people scramble and connive to work their way up by using other people, the perennial James moral issue. Julia is, among other things, a reformulation of Daisy Miller, the independent American woman now anything but innocent, but whose desperation is somehow both touching and gritty. Her mother has been thrice divorced, and Julia herself, though still young, has already been through six engagements; although remarkably pretty, she has not been a bride. "Since when hadn't she been passing for the prettiest girl any one had ever seen?" she thinks. "She had lived in that, from far back, from year to year, from day to day and from hour to hour—she had lived for it and literally *by* it, as who should say" (17:493). Julia's immediate crisis is that although she has been fortunate enough recently to keep company with Basil French, a wealthy, attractive young man from the most respectable of New York families, she is certain he will never marry her unless she can convince him, and through him his family, that her own family history is somehow less tawdry than in reality it has been: "Such were the data Basil French's inquiry would elicit: her own six engagements and her mother's three nullified marriages—nine nice, distinct little horrors in all. What on earth was to be done about them?" (17:502).

In desperation she arranges a meeting at the new Metropolitan Museum with Mr. Pitman, the second of her mother's ex-husbands and a man with whom, from her twelfth to seventeenth year, she "had got on with . . . , perversely, much better than her mother had" (17:491). She "needed some one to lie for her—ah she so needed some one to lie!" (17:495). That is, she needs Pitman, a nice man of forty-two (five years younger than Julia's perennially young-looking mother) to be her character witness and assure Basil French he himself was "even a worse fiend than you were shown up for; to having made it impossible mother should *not* take proceedings." Pitman replies, "Lordy, lordy!": the very reason *he* has sought out Julia is to ask her to inform a widow, Mrs. David E. Drack, whom *he* hopes to marry, "the truth for me—as you only can. I want you to say I was really all right—as right as you know; and that I simply acted like an angel in a story-book, gave myself away to have it over" (17:504). Partly from unexplained magnanimity, partly because Mrs. Drack shows up even while they speak, and partly because Mr. Pitman persuades Julia that Murray Brush, a man to whom Julia was once attached, has returned from Europe and is a better witness for her ("*He's* your man!"), Julia Bride impetuously "saves" Pitman with the truth, using the full effectiveness of her youth and beauty on Mrs. Drack.

James's description of Mrs. Drack, however, evokes a kind of dehumanized blob through a virtually surrealistic conceit suggesting the degradation of the respectable monied society of New York to which Julia and the other characters of this story are indissolubly "wedded." Mrs. Drack presents

> a huge hideous pleasant face, a featureless desert in a remote quarter
> of which the disproportionately small eyes might have figured a pair
> of rash adventurers all but buried in the sand. They reduced them-
> selves when she smiled to barely discernible points—a couple of
> mere tiny emergent heads—though the foreground of the scene, as

if to make up for it, gaped with a vast benevolence. In a word Julia saw—and as if she had needed nothing more; saw Mr. Pitman's opportunity, saw her own, saw the exact nature both of Mrs. Drack's circumspection and of Mrs. Drack's sensibility, saw even, glittering there in letters of gold and as a part of the whole metallic coruscation, the large figure of her income, largest of all her attributes, and (though perhaps a little more as a luminous blur beside all this) the mingled extasy and agony of Mr. Pitman's hope and Mr. Pitman's fears. (17:515–16)

To this creature Julia "sacrificed her mother on the altar—proclaimed her false and cruel," whereupon "the massive [Mrs. Drack] just spread and spread like a rich fluid a bit helplessly spilt" (17:519). Hence Julia "gave him away in short, up to the hilt, for any use of her own, and should have nothing to clutch at now but the possibility of Murray Brush" (17:518).

Her meeting two days later in Central Park with Brush initiates another Jamesian ironic reversal while it also matches up structurally with her meeting with Pitman, her "quondam stepfather." Of all Julia's prior suitors Murray Brush had been in a sense the most notorious because of his not being sufficiently a "gentleman." Things have been bad enough for her with the likes of Mrs. George Maule, who "loathes" Julia and "poisons the air [Basil French] breathes" with damaging stories to the young man's sisters about Julia and her lineage (17:511). Brush asks her, "What harm, in the sight of God or man, Julia . . . did we ever do?" But Julia retorts: "'Am I talking of *that?* Am I talking of what *we* know? I'm talking of what others feel—of what they *have* to feel; of what it's just enough for them to know not to be able to get over it, once they do really know it. How do they know what *didn't* pass between us, with all the opportunities we had? . . . You see I've no margin,' . . . letting him take it from her flushed face as much as he would that her mother hadn't left her an inch" (17:530).

The rupture here between social pretense and moral truth is so great it at once absorbs and inverts reality itself. Julia is claiming that there is literally no "margin" left her for truth. More than that, she is proposing that reality lies in the stigmatizing of her by others because she herself is marginalized. Only distortion will prevail in her "respectable" world, the kind of extravagant distortion we saw above in James's description of Mrs. Drack—his transmutation, really, of Washington Irving's satirical vision of New York Dutch society and its shallowness.

Julia and Murray, reminiscent of Kate Croy and Merton Densher in *The Wings of the Dove*, apparently once shared an honest affection but had no future, since neither had money. Now the two of them are experienced and jaded; Julia, for instance, "once more fairly emptied her satchel and, quite as if they had been Nancy and the Artful Dodger, or some nefarious pair of that sort, talking things over in the manner of 'Oliver Twist,' revealed to him the fondness of her view that, could she but have produced a cleaner slate, she might by this time have pulled it off with Mr. French" (17:529).

But the next ironic layer, or "twist," is that Brush himself, after a three-year stay in Europe, has now become high-toned, sophisticated, and smooth, very much a part of the New York social landscape. He tells her with condescension, " 'leave it to me a little, won't you?' He had been watching, as in his fumes, the fine growth of his possibilities; and with this he turned on her the large warmth of his charity. It was like a subscription of a half a million. 'I'll take care of you' " (17:531). "'I'll fling over you," he intones, "Well, the biggest *kind* of rose-coloured mantle!" (17:532–33). Brush's profuse, unctuous turn here is merely the prelude to *his* great revelation, one mirroring Mr. Pittman's before. Murray, too, is engaged to one Mary Lindeck, who has the money but not yet the social position. It soon becomes clear that Brush and his intended are avid to be admitted into the "fortress" of Basil French's circle. Julia reflects on Murray's tactics: "She had ceased personally, ceased materially—in respect, as who should say, to any optical or tactile advantage—to exist for him, and the whole office of his manner had been the more piously and gallantly to dress the dead presence with flowers" (17:537).

James's richly abstract language here in counterpoint to the fine metaphor following it emphasizes the way Julia is for Brush an inanimate object, at most an "objective." Such conceptual overtones are also deeply consistent with the imagery of her as "the dead presence." For Julia the full implication of their all being so willing to "work" each other descends on her consciousness, "going down and down before it." Encountering "the great lumps and masses of truth," the young woman "knew inevitable submission, not to say submersion, as she had never known it in her life" (17:534). Profoundly demoralized, Julia dazedly agrees to Brush's proposition of a social entrée to Basil French. However, her abstracted acquiescence is figuratively rendered by James in a powerful and oft-reiterated conceit as a "music-box in which, its lid well down, the most remarkable tunes were sounding"

(17:537). For despite her submission to Brush's plan Julia now sees "as clear as the sun in the sky" that the Murray Brushes "would dish, would ruin, would utterly destroy her" (17:539). She knows of course that all Brush and especially Mary Lindeck desire is "to get at" the Frenches. Yet although she will go through the motions for them and keep to the end "this pretence of owing them salvation," she also knows in her concluding epiphany at home that she is all through. Like John Marcher at the end of "The Beast in the Jungle," she flings herself on her face and

> yielded to the full taste of the bitterness of missing a connexion, missing the man himself, with power to create such a social appetite, such a grab at what might be gained by them. He could make people, even people like these two and whom there were still other people to envy, he could make them push and snatch and scramble like that—and then remain as incapable of taking her from the hands of such patrons as of receiving her straight, say, from those of Mrs. Drack. It was a high note, too, of Julia's wonderful composition that, even in the long lonely moan of her conviction of her now certain ruin, all this grim lucidity, the perfect clearance of passion, but made her supremely proud of him. (17:541–42)

James's conclusion here is obviously meant to be comprehensive, yet it also has the characteristic open-endedness, irony, and ambiguity of his late work; an ambiguity utterly different from, say, "Four Meetings," or any of the tales early in his career. Whereas in "Four Meetings" we were just not privy to Caroline Spencer's inner mind at the end of her story, here we have the "grim lucidity" of Julia Bride's interior consciousness, and the ambiguity resides instead in the various interpretations we might make of it.

Is Julia "supremely proud" of Basil French because he is somehow, somewhere, above and beyond all the social manipulation that, as Julia seems aware, infects her moral being, compromises, in her own words, "the freeborn American girl" (17:532)? Just how "free" is this character? Is Julia convinced of her "certain ruin," because, although she knows Basil and his family will never assent to the Brush/Lindeck maneuver, she herself is hopelessly and helplessly "capable of proposing anything to any one" (17:541)—including, as we and she know, the sacrifice of her own mother, however deserving of censure her mother seems to be? Is Julia in fact her mother's daughter throughout the sequence of the tale, her deputy (an interpretation reinforced by the fact that her mother never appears), and is her "ruin" therefore primarily a social or a moral one? Is there even further irony and pathos to be found in Julia's remnant core of generosity, shown in her spontaneous aid to Mr. Pitman, even at her mother's expense; is this her saving grace, while her participation in the conniving manipulation surrounding her is what has ruined her—and can we readers really disentangle the two? Is Julia's divided psyche even suggested by her own unwillingness to lie, together with her willingness to let others lie for her, and is that precisely why she "saves" Mr. Pitman? But then, is it also possible that Julia blights her possibilities in the second encounter because she feels the guilt of betraying her mother in the first? Is all of this James's measure of the society itself, that Julia's betrayal of her mother just might constitute her honest and most generous moment, yet be an act which in no way purges what is worst in the social order nor has any redeeming value whatever?

If Julia's desperate and hopeless complicity underscores James's view that the "freeborn American girl" is no longer innocent (by the time of this tale he called Daisy Miller in the New York Edition "pure poetry" when measured against the present scene), is it not still significant that the European experience has turned Murray Brush, much like Chad Newsome in *The Ambassadors*, from a somewhat awkward, decent person to a more civilized manipulator—a "gentleman"? In looking over James's admirably "foreshortened" tale with all these questions in mind, one marvels how well its two major scenes interrelate. In the first one, Julia hopes Mr. Pitman will lie to Basil about her mother, and then is surprised first by his engagement and thereupon her willingness to betray her mother for him. In the second, Julia hopes Murray Brush will tell the truth and establish her innocence, then agrees to help him out even though it seals the ruin of her chances. It is as if the soiled and reformulated Daisy Miller figure is still, at some mysterious level, better and more vulnerable than the "gang" that surrounds her, including Basil French.

All but lost in James's wonderful handling of these two matching episodes is the fact that the first with Mr. Pitman and eventually Mrs. Drack takes place in "the Museum" and the second with Murray Brush in "the Park." It suggests figuratively that both art and nature have somehow been enlisted in the corruption of social institutions. Wherever Julia turns in the polluted waters of her situation, the reflecting mirrors of her consciousness reflect and intensify the distortions of a young life "too early old," as Emerson once expressed it. Indeed, the "young person so troubled," as James calls her, is throughout the tale suffused "with the rage of desperation and, as she was afterward to call it to herself, the fascination of the abyss" (17:528). Even the principle of beauty, which Julia together with her absent-present mother continues to embody, is somehow an instrument for retaliation by others. Julia's experience of possessing beauty only constitutes

> the way their prettiness had set them trap after trap, all along—had foredoomed them to awful ineptitude. When you were as pretty as that you could, by the whole idiotic consensus, be nothing *but* pretty; and when you were nothing "but" pretty you could get into nothing but tight places, out of which you could then scramble by nothing but masses of fibs. And there was no one, all the while, who wasn't eager to egg you on, eager to make you pay to the last cent the price of your beauty. (17:498)

Julia Bride, much like Lily Bart in Edith Wharton's *House of Mirth*, is James's narrative "deputy" for a bleak vision of New York society and a reassessment of the purity, innocence, and "pure poetry" of the Daisy Miller phenomenon in American culture. The restricted third-person point of view does not—as with, say, Adela Chart in "The Marriages," with Winterbourne in "Daisy Miller," with John Marcher in "The Beast in the Jungle," or even with Pemberton in "the Pupil"— seem to carry with it that measure of unreliability, greater or lesser, found in so many of James's tales. Rather, the darkness of Julia's consciousness and the disturbance of her conscience seem equal to James's own dark vision. Yet the absence of narrative untrustworthiness does not, in this tale of James's last phase, fail to multiply the ambivalence, extravagance, and complexity of James's moral world. If Julia points directly to Lily Bart's moral and social entrapment, the deeper enigma of her nature suggests far less obviously a character like, say, Ibsen's Hedda Gabler.

"The Bench of Desolation" has frequently been called James's *Winter's Tale*, a comparison that derives from its profound combination of tragic suffering and ultimate reconciliation among its two major characters, Herbert Dodd, the viewpoint "deputy," and Kate Cookham, his antagonist. In this expressionistically poetic yet sad tale set appropriately near England's bleak, rural Land's End in a town called Properley, James weaves a long, melancholy parable of wisdom through pain using both setting and economic class at the opposite extremity from "Julia Bride." Dodd, an antique shopkeeper of "high-class rarities" and would-be gentleman a "trifle over-refined or 'effete'"[39] is threatened by Kate with breach of promise. Recoiling from the "vulgarity" of legal action while filled with smug self-righteousness, he agrees prematurely to pay her £400 over several years, a debt that impoverishes him, leaving him nothing but a lowly clerical job at the Gas Works and leading eventually to the death of his wife, Nan Drury, and their two daughters. Yet the inevitable Maupassant-like twist in this tale is the reappearance of Kate after more than ten years, now astonishingly "oh, yes—a real lady" (*CT,* 390) and even wondrously solicitous of Dodd's welfare. Her "idea" all along has been to prove herself a figure worthy of his regard as well as to bring him back his own money fivefold, money saved and invested as he, with his genteel preciousness, could never begin to accomplish. Although Dodd has been "stranded by tidal action, deposited in the lonely hollow of his fate" and hears the "wail" of his dead family (*CT,* 386), he comes to realize that his and Kate's original rift was a tragic mutual misunderstanding, and that in the intervening years she herself has endured as much as he "the beads, almost all worn smooth, of his rosary of pain" (*CT,* 384).

The sound of Kate's surname, Cookham, insinuates James's grim irony, and she is even compared early in the tale to the witch Meg Merrillies; indeed, Dodd himself feels that her return is "at once a fairy-tale and a nightmare" (*CT,* 411). The reader must consider, then, whether Kate's "idea" is from James's viewpoint still another "violation"; but the answer is not easy, for the original fault and prejudgment of each by the other is shown to have been clearly mutual. Moreover, Dodd through suffering appears to develop spiritually, to lose the egoism and pretentiousness exhibited early in the nouvelle; he even comes to feel that his freedom and wounded pride alike are "the thinnest of vain parades" and "the poorest of hollow heroics" (*CT,* 416).

The bench of the title is one Dodd always frequents on the Marina at Land's End, facing westward into the sea. While on the one hand, the bench has been well described as "an open-air chapel of grief" (Vaid, 181), it seems as well almost the immemorial national artifact of the stoic people with whom James lived, whether in coastal town (like James's own town of Rye) or park within village or city.[40] Sitting on his bench of desolation with Kate, Dodd shares with her the "secret of the dignity of sitting still with one's fate" (*CT,* 388). This tale is not without considerable ambiguity, however, and even in a sense grazes the grotesque in James's poetic extravagance, found especially in several highly extended expressionist conceits along the same lines as the celebrated "pagoda" image in *The Golden Bowl*.[41] But the note of tragic misconception and suffering remains authentic, if also complicated. The story is an unusual blend of forgiveness, suffering, and reconciliation, yet it is also gritty with irony and poetic extravagance—as if James's "tenor" and "vehicle" were, for once, not always at ease together and simulate instead Dodd's own "experiences, in which the unforgettable and the unimaginable were confoundingly mixed" (*CT*, 406).

As powerful and painful as are "Julia Bride" and "The Bench of Desolation," despite their opposite subject matter, "A Round of Visits," James's last published story, is possibly the most extraordinary of all his tales. On the one hand, it is, like "Julia Bride," a reformulation and metamorphosis of his social realism and the tragedy of society. On the other hand, it both epitomizes his poetic extravagance and goes far beyond "Julia Bride" in rendering the ghostly realm, meditative aura, and "field" that distinguish the great quasi-supernatural tales of the major phase, "The Beast in the Jungle" and "the Jolly Corner." In short, it displays a rare convergence of all the major strands of James's late period in one compressed work other than one of the last great novels. Although in general it is, like "Julia Bride," still neglected by comparison with the two tales just mentioned, Nicola Bradbury suggests of it briefly that "the power of the tale depends upon a strict sense of form" (216). My analysis explores carefully that sense of form, which is not nearly so readily apparent as with James's earlier work; but this tale has both the comprehensiveness and concision of a Beethoven quartet, and there are many other issues to address simultaneously with its strict sense of form. It ultimately embodies well "the joy of sovereign *science*"—James's own praise of Shakespeare—which Bradbury attributes to the great novels like *The Golden Bowl* (220). Indeed, "A Round of Visits" is perhaps best described as the nonghostly alter ego of "The Jolly Corner." James's refracted consciousness, penumbra-like aura, "unuttered utterances," and other such features characteristic of his manner are all here in richness and complexity.

The point-of-view character, Mark Monteith, is obsessed fully as much as John Marcher or Spencer Brydon, but the reader is not quite aware of this at first. Like Spencer Brydon, Monteith returns from Europe after many years and finds the entire culture of New York grotesque and phantasmagoric. The Pocahontas Hotel, for example, exhibits "one extraordinary masquerade of expensive objects, one portentous 'period' of decoration, one violent phase of publicity" after another: its "heavy heat, the luxuriance, the extravagance, the quantity, the colour, gave the impression of some wondrous tropical forest, where vociferous, bright-eyed, and feathered creatures, of every variety of size and hue, were half smothered between undergrowths of velvet and tapestry and ramifications of marble and bronze" (*CT,* 431).

Such "fauna and flora" cause Monteith's "bruised spirit" to draw in and "fold its wings" (*CT,* 431). Monteith is bruised in a double sense: first, he is laid up for three days with the grippe after disembarking on Wednesday into a "blinding New York blizzard"; second, his deeper illness or "deep sore inward ache" (*CT,* 427) is itself the cause of his return: the discovery that his distant cousin and early schoolmate, Phil Bloodgood, to whom he entrusted his financial assets, has embezzled money from Mark and several other members of a small Europeanized American circle, and then has absconded ahead of the law. Cloistered in the ugly "Du Barry" hotel and face-to-face with Bloodgood's picture, "Our sufferer . . . would have liked to tell someone; extracting, to the last acid strain of it, the full strength of his sorrow. . . . there was something of his heart's heaviness he wanted so to give out" (*CT,* 429). But the hotel doctor who tends to Monteith's grippe is the first of a series of people who show no interest in his anguish. James's protagonist wishes to blurt out: "Oh *he's* what the matter with me—that, looking after some of my poor dividends, as he for the ten years of my absence had served me by doing, he has simply jockeyed me out of the whole little collection, such as it was . . . to 'sail' ten days ago, for parts unknown and as yet unguessable. . . . it's the horror of *his* having done it, and done it to *me*—without a mitigation or, so to speak, a warning or an excuse" (*CT,* 430). This speech is an "unuttered utterance" characteristic of James's late idiom, for the hotel doctor, who pronounces him well by Saturday, has a manner that precludes such an exchange: "Countless possibilities, making doctors perfunctory, Mark felt, swarmed and seethed at their doors; it showed for an incalculable world" (*CT,* 430). This early statement eventually and unexpectedly penetrates the very thematic core of the tale, and is, although greatly disguised, a case of verbal foreshadowing.

Monteith's first encounter after leaving his sickroom on Sunday is with Mrs. Folliott, a fellow victim of Bloodgood's larceny, whom he has last seen and argued with six months earlier in London, and who wants "to know if he *now* stood up for his swindler" (*CT*, 432). Mrs. Folliott's crudeness epitomizes the "new crowd" and deeply offends Monteith, in part because, unlike himself, he knows she still has considerable money left. Although she recognizes "Monteith's right to loathe" Bloodgood too, she bewails "her wretched money to excess" but does so "with a vulgarity of analysis and an incapacity for the higher criticism, as her listener felt it to be, which made him determine resentfully, almost grimly, that she shouldn't have the benefit of a grain of *his* vision or *his* version of what had befallen them, and of how, in particular, it had come; and should never dream thereby (though much would she suffer from that!) of how interesting he might have been" (*CT*, 433–34).

Such passages alert us to Monteith's own belief in his difference from the rapacious American double-dealing culture he "comes home" to, from the grotesque iconography of that culture presented by the Pocahontas Hotel to Mrs. Folliott and the "hue and cry" of the new crowd. "There was nothing like a crowd, this unfortunate knew, for making one feel lonely" (*CT*, 434)—thus as Monteith moves from place to place James strikes a profoundly modern Prufrockian note; he evokes, as does Eliot's poem itself, a modern equivalent to a Dantesque pilgrim moving through the Bolgias of the underworld, an association also reinforced by innumerable uses of "labyrinth."[42]

Monteith's one hope for the kind of empathetic exchange he seeks is a welcoming note from Florence Ash, whom he has not seen for nine years but who in his Paris days had been the sympathetic recipient of all his troubles, so "innocent" compared "with those of his present hour" (*CT*, 438). At lunch, however, he encounters by sheer chance a "pretty girl" who tells him she is the sister-in-law of Newton Winch, a former friend and schoolmate, who has read of Monteith's arrival in the papers and wonders what could have brought "that shirker" Mark back after such a lapse of years. Monteith is quite surprised, for he has all but forgotten about Winch's existence, since the latter had been so dull and uninteresting. But the young woman presses him to go visit Winch, who is "up there in Fiftieth Street alone" (her sister, Winch's wife, is no longer living), for he has "appeared of late so down." Winch too, it seems, has been shut in with grippe, but "the horrid poison just seemed to have entered into poor Newton's soul" (*CT*, 435–36). This last comment constitutes an acute verbal echo of Monteith's own condition, even though the "pretty girl" apparently speaks it lightly and Monteith himself sees no connection and remains uninterested. "Well then," she urges, "feel for others. Fit him in" (*CT*, 436).

His much anticipated afternoon visit with Florence Ash takes an entirely unexpected turn, for the same woman who nine years past regularly ministered to him in his troubles and to whom he expects to pour out his thoughts and feelings about Bloodgood seizes upon his company to unburden to him "such immensities" of her own recent life, most particularly her separation from her husband, Bob, who is off to Washington and about to "patch up something" with Mrs. Folliott, one of a "regular 'bevy'" (*CT*, 439). As she fills him in and puts "the whole case to him, all her troubles and plans," Monteith soon realizes there "would be no chance for *his* case, though it was so much for his case he had come." Yet he experiences a strange "convulsion, the momentary strain of his substituting, by the turn of a hand, one prospect of interest for another" (*CT*, 440). For now he realizes "he could serve supremely—oh, how he was going to serve!—as the most sympathetic of all pairs of ears" (*CT*, 439).

At this juncture in James's tale a pattern of reverse expectations has been clearly established, although for Monteith himself the case is, on the contrary, one of savoring a new epiphany. After he leaves Florence Ash he returns to the street, and stands alone while "a choked trolley-car . . . howled, as he paused for it, beneath the weight of its human accretions"; there follows "the suffering shriek of another public vehicle and a sudden odd automatic return of his mind to the pretty girl, the flower of Mrs. Folliott's crowd, who had spoken to him of Newton Winch" (*CT*, 442). The violence of such street imagery issues from the rhetoric of James's fiction and hints at some connection to Newton Winch, yet for Mark it is instead the "same remarkable agent of fate" that gives him the memory of Winch's address; and he decides that "the direct intervention of Providence" (*CT*, 442) wishes him to extend sympathy rather than seek it.

> Providence had, on some obscure system, chosen this very ridiculous hour to save him from cultivation of the sin of selfishness, the obsession of egotism, and was breaking him to its will by constantly directing his attention to the claims of others. Who could say what at that critical moment mightn't have become of Mrs. Folliott . . . if she hadn't been able to air to him her grievance and her rage?— just as who could deny that it must have done Florence Ash a world

of good to have put her thoughts about Bob in order by the aid of a person to whom the vision of Bob in the light of those thoughts . . . would mean so delightfully much? It was on the same general lines that poor Newton Winch, bereft, alone, ill, perhaps dying, and with the drawback of a not very sympathetic personality—as Mark remembered it at least—to contend against in almost any conceivable appeal to human furtherance, it was on these lines, very much, that the luckless case in Fiftieth Street was offered him as a source of salutary discipline. (*CT,* 443)

The final visit with Newton Winch, wholly unplanned, is the most fully elaborated of the entire tale and, of course, the very scenic or Jamesian "discriminated occasion" toward which the tale has pointed from the beginning. It consists above all of a series of cascading revelations for both Monteith and the reader, and hence exhibits a set of dramatic stages of consciousness and discovery. The first of these is that Winch is a totally different man from the common, even coarse person Mark remembered from college and some abortive law school years. Even though the apartment shows the same "rich confused complexion of the Pocahontas," Monteith has "never seen anyone so improved," a man who has "been ill, unmistakably," yet has also "undergone since their last meeting some extraordinary process of refinement." He even "presented himself now as if he had suddenly and mysteriously been educated" (*CT,* 444). This transformation, not unlike Murray Brush's in "Julia Bride," is also very reminiscent of Chad Newsome's in *The Ambassadors,* except that this time the mysterious educative process and refinement has, unlike Chad's or Murray's, occurred in America, not Europe, and is visibly associated with illness and ravage. Even more remarkable is that Winch, in marked contrast to the two women and the hotel doctor, divines at once that Monteith himself is deeply troubled. Such unexpected sensitivity from "coarse common" Newton Winch brings tears to Mark's eyes. "Why, how do you know? How *can* you?" Meanwhile James describes Winch as "hover[ing] there . . . considerably restless, shifting from foot to foot, changing his place, beginning and giving up motions"—body movements indicative of "the history of something that had happened to him ever so handsomely shining out" (*CT,* 446).

The crowning touch occurs when Winch tells Mark his coming out is "interesting," the "astonishing note" absent from everyone else in the day's round of visits and the reaction we recognize by now Mark has sought most of all. So grateful is the protagonist that he in turn responds, "There must be, my dear man, something rather wonderful the matter with you!" since Winch, that is, perceives Mark's state; "there *must* be—for you to see! I shouldn't have expected it." "Then you take me for a damned fool?" laughs "wonderful Newton Winch" (*CT,* 447). Monteith's pain and need are utterly apparent, and Mark's assumption is that Winch's pain is high-toned and "interesting" like his own. James's handling of the scene and exchange has already begun to take on the eerie aura of an encounter with an alter ego such as found in the ghost stories. Monteith, for example, reacts to the altered Winch as to "*this* incalculable apparition" and with "the oddest intensity of apprehension, admiration, mystification" (*CT,* 447, 445)—all such language is unmistakably the lexicon and terminology of James's ghost stories.

A part of the enchantment of the new Winch is the play of "his fine fingers—had he anything like fine fingers of old?" (*CT,* 444). Although this detail has no sinister overtones for Mark, it serves for James the function of anticipating the next revelatory stage in the visit, the topic of Phil Bloodgood's treachery and betrayal. This stage actually starts with Monteith's sudden perception that Winch's improvement has resulted among other things from "the removal of what had probably been one of the vulgarest of moustaches," and how once he had noted "the very opposite turn of the experiment for Phil Bloodgood." Part of Newton's "capture of refinement," then, is that he has "shaved and was happily transfigured. Phil Bloodgood had shaved and been well nigh lost; though why should one just now too precipitately drag the reminiscence in?" (*CT,* 447–48). Why indeed, except for the synchronism of James's narrative consciousness or "Central Intelligence," on one hand, and the activity of Monteith's unconscious (and true) association of the two men, on the other. Winch on his side appears equally telepathic in this ghostly nonghostly tale, for he suddenly discerns "the state of [Monteith's] soul" by exclaiming: "I know now why you came back. . . . I *have* it! It can't but have been for poor Phil Bloodgood. He sticks out of you, the brute—as how, with what he has done to you, shouldn't he? . . . What a hog to have played it on *you,* on *you,* of all his friends!" (*CT,* 448–49).

Winch's own business responsibilities "don't differ much" from Bloodgood's (and James invites the attentive reader to hear the verbal echo-pun of Winch's "play" of fingers earlier with his "What a hog to have played it on *you*"). Winch's empathy by now totally disarms Monteith, who in full contrast to his earlier response to Florence Ash now fears he is "too hysterically gushing," for "his wound was to that extent open—he winced at hearing the author of it branded" (*CT,* 449). James's extravagant pun here clearly places Winch with Bloodgood. Nevertheless, Monteith surprises Winch by his reply: "I feel sore, I admit, and it's a horrid sort of thing to have had happen; but when you call him a brute and a hog I rather squirm, for brutes and hogs never live, I guess, in the sort of hell in which he now must be" (*CT,* 450). This is just the sort of perception Mark had wished to share with Florence Ash and earlier with Mrs. Folliott, the sort of "interesting" person he was prepared to be; but really, beneath even that, lies the dominion of his own obsession. Winch, in response, "dangled and swung himself, and threw back his head and laughed" (*CT,* 450)—James's figure here is really of a man hanging, although Monteith does not "see" it, even though he himself (like an alter ego) has just said he "squirms."

Nevertheless, something telepathic does occur, for "our hero found himself on his feet again, under the influence of a sudden failure of everything but horror—a horror determined by some turn of their talk and indeed by the very fact of the freedom of it. It was as if a far-borne sound of the hue and cry, a vision of his old friend hunted and at bay, had suddenly broken in" (*CT,* 450). Once again, Mark's subconsciousness, I would contend, knows that Bloodgood and Winch are at one, and Winch's presence is what ignites the "horror" of the distant presence of a hunted Phil Bloodgood. But Mark can now only gush, to use his own word, what he has desperately wanted to say to the others all day long: "All I'm conscious of now—I give you my word—is that I'd like to see him"; and then: "I'd go to him. Hanged if I wouldn't—anywhere!" (*CT:* 451) We recall it is Newton already "hanging" in the extravagance of James's tacit metaphor, and it is likewise Newton who protests in greater and greater pain: "Don't wish him that, Monteith—don't wish him that!" But Mark now keeps on, finally saying exactly those things he came back to New York to say, verbalizing his obsession. He would go to Bloodgood, he insists, "like a shot"; he would "try and make out with him how, after such things—" as their friendship from far back, Bloodgood could have done this. Mark would go, above all else, "to understand." He can also tell, however, even as he speaks, the "extent of [Newton's] recent ravage. 'You must have been ill indeed'" (*CT,* 451–52). What he does not understand, at least not consciously, is how his statements—again, the very ones the reader senses he came home from abroad to make—are affecting what he observes in Winch's face. He wonders if he should go, but Winch compulsively insists he remain and talk: "You keep me up—and you see how no one else comes near me." Again, Mark misses the possible significance of that statement, but at least he himself no longer rationalizes about "Providence" and ministering fate: "I myself had no one to go to." And Newton grins feverishly, while blurting, "You save my life" (*CT*, 452–53).

All of this initiates the third and climactic stage in the visit with Winch. As before James employs marvelous extended passages on the minute workings of Monteith's consciousness far too intricate to convey here, especially since now, I would suggest, what has hitherto been subconscious is raised by the very pressure of the encounter toward consciousness. Winch wants Mark to sit down, but Mark, absorbed in his own "interesting" sensitivity regarding Bloodgood, prefers to stay standing. Winch then turns from him and "swung off" in an "unnatural manner." Once Monteith sees him from behind his entire "look," so improved before, suddenly takes on a contrasting sinister aspect. Mark divines he is "looking for something," for Mark "caught it . . . with his own sensibility all in vibration"—note again the ghostly, telepathic air of the moment (*CT*, 454).

We have seen already in "The Great Good Place" James's use of an image of a person turned away or perceived from the back to denote the alter ego.[43] In Newton Winch's case, his face turned away seems to call into being his true situation and identity, whereas before the greatly "improved" face in different gaze had somehow eclipsed it— an idea conceptually evocative of *différance* in contemporary Derridian critical theory. For Monteith, "Everything had changed—changed extraordinarily with the mere turning of that gentleman's back"; and now "they were suddenly facing each other across the wide space with a new consciousness" (*CT*, 454–55). Winch has been trying surreptitiously with his leg to conceal a gun, which partially sticks out from the chair on the hearthrug, a gun he meant to hide when Monteith surprised him by arriving. Symbolically, of course, it is clear that this gun, like Winch himself, cannot go unexposed, and that Monteith in a sense is the emblematic cause of its revelation even while he literally espies it. No longer with his veneer of "improvement," Winch implores Monteith "in God's name to talk to me—to *talk* to me!" The pretense is over. "Of course I'm in deep trouble . . . but turning you on was exactly what I wanted." Then most tellingly, "My interest was in your being interesting. For you *are!* And my nerves—!" (*CT*, 456). All day

Monteith had hoped to be "interesting"; Winch's "interest" is in being distracted from the suicide he contemplates; and of course the crimes themselves involve financial "interest." Winch in his "ravage" tells Mark that if he really wants to go to Bloodgood, "I'm such another. . . . Only I've stayed to take it." Mark finally understands "inexpressibly" the "monstrous sense of his friend's 'education.' It had been, in its immeasurable action, the education of business, of which the fruits were all around them" (*CT*, 457).

Winch awaits the arrival of the police, whose "long sharp sound shrilled in from the outer door" (recollecting, for the kind of reader James hopes to have, the piercing sounds of the New York street earlier). Newton tells him, "You've helped me to wait. . . . You've tided me over. My condition has *wanted* somebody or something. Therefore, to complete this service, will you be so good as to open the door?" Mark's eyes return to the revolver under the chair, and he asks Winch with a searching look, "What do you mean to do?" When Winch says, "Nothing," Mark presses him, "On your honour?" "*My* 'honour?'" counters Winch, "with an accent that [Mark] felt even as it sounded he should never forget." "You're wonderful!" says Monteith, and "We *are* wonderful" repeats Winch in a classic Jamesian exchange—yet one that very importantly connects these two men and brings home to us their oneness (*CT*, 458). When Mark lets in the police detective and a "great belted constable," he suddenly hears "the infallible crack of a discharged pistol and, so nearly with it as to make all one violence, the sound of a great fall." Newton is "stretched on his back before the fire; he had held the weapon horribly to his temple, and his upturned face was disfigured." The constable asks Monteith severely, "Don't you think, sir, you might have prevented it?" And Mark—so James ends his tale—"took a hundred things in . . . things of the scene, of the moment, and of all the strange moments before; but one appearance more vividly even than the others stared out at him. 'I really think I must practically have caused it'" (*CT*, 459).

James purposely does not have Monteith identify or name his causative act, and it is more than likely that Monteith himself is only on the threshold of understanding what he means. Is the "one vivid appearance" staring out at him a monstrous act unwittingly committed by himself? Is it perhaps an issue or idea that from the "hundred things" and "strange moments before" rises out and interprets them? Or is the "one appearance" the very ghostly presence itself of Newton Winch, including even the "upturned disfigured face" now unequivocally so different from yet in its deeper way revealing of the changed and "interesting" face that had met him, the face whose shaved moustache had gained so much in contrast with Bloodgood's? It should be recalled that Bloodgood's own face at the Pocahontas Hotel had "stared out" from a photograph at Monteith: "To live thus with his unremoved, undestroyed, engaging, treacherous face, had been . . . to live with all of the felt pang" (*CT,* 429). Therefore the reader is now left to interpret Monteith's final statement of self-accusation—late-Jamesian both in its unexpectedness and in its function as an invitation to that same reader to begin anew, to reconsider what he or she thinks this whole story has meant; in this respect it epitomizes James's claim in "The Art of Fiction" that "experience is never limited, and it is never complete." From a dramatic point of view, however, it presents us with the Jamesian "register" or point-of-view character in the act of just discovering something momentous and unsavory about himself. Although the issue at hand is not of comparable life-and-death magnitude, the ending of James's "Tree of Knowledge" (1900) is another such Jamesian "beginning," as it starts to dawn on Peter Brench that his lifelong assumptions about his secret understanding with Mrs. Mallow and his relationship with the rest of the Mallow family have been self-deceived.[44]

From a broader American philosophical framework, however, the ending of "A Round of Visits" is James's parallel to and refinement of Emerson's profound conception, voiced in his essay "Experience," that "It is very unhappy, but too late to be helped, the discovery we have made that we exist. That discovery is called the Fall of Man"[45]—in other words, the burden of self-consciousness. And in that same framework James continues his lineage also with Hawthorne, for whom self-consciousness seems virtually always to be consciousness of evil and of one's inevitable participation in it whether one wills it or not.

If Monteith's visit made the critical difference between Winch's considering suicide and actually committing it, the reason may be that his guilt doubled and redoubled when Mark expressed compassion for Bloodgood, even the wish to "go like a shot" to him. In so naming the weapon in advance, Monteith is also himself an unwitting instrument of execution. Had he only torn into Bloodgood as "brute" and "hog" the way Winch wished him to, tried hard to make him do, Winch might perhaps have been able to harden himself and withstand his own inward wound, to pull back protectively much like Monteith himself with Mrs. Folliott and Mrs. Ash. What Winch could not endure was the vivid presence and embodiment in Mark Monteith of those people who had trusted him and whose sympathetic pain was manifest. Winch himself, who is knowledgeable of Bloodgood's crimes, is pretty sure that his own are "worse" (*CT,* 457). Mark Monteith's visit was a com410te surprise, the indirect result of an offhand bit of conversation by the pretty sister-in-law at lunch, an agency of fate. And this raises the next boundary or layer of James's stratification of meaning, the issue or idea that emerges from the tale. Monteith during the day gradually comes to think that "Providence" is dictating to him on behalf of ministering to others, yet the result is one of horror and a measure of violence unusual in the canon of James. One wonders momentarily whether James, like Twain in "The Man that Corrupted Hadleyburg," or Crane in "The Blue Hotel," has penned a profoundly dark, even bitter critique on the workings of providence, or whether instead he is more characteristically using it as a "transitional idea," to use again William James's terminology, that exposes reflexively the speciousness of the viewpoint character. This second seems likely, if only because Monteith's apparent epiphany about "Providence" supposedly saves him from the "sin of selfishness" and the "cultivation of egotism"— that sounds just too much like a John Marcher. It actually makes us conscious of how much Monteith has been preoccupied and obsessed with himself, and how that obsession carries over ironically into his visit with Winch. In the earlier sections it is Monteith's self-pity that propels him to others in order to unburden himself of his troubles, and that makes the exchange with Mrs. Folliott so loathsome to him. The high opinion he entertains of Mrs. Ash originates in self-interest, his remembrance of her former ministrations of sympathy; and his disappointment in her lack of sensitivity and refinement is measured purely by her lack of condolence for him. It is therefore, of course, the degree to which Newton Winch offers him consolation that Monteith believes him to have undergone such an "extraordinary process of refinement." Admittedly it is difficult not to think of this tale as exhibiting a terrible and ironic twist of fate, given the sequence of the visits; yet James in his last phase has once again, as with "The Beast in the Jungle," greatly interlaced character and fate. Perhaps the idea that emerges most is the one James lays down so early in the tale in connection with the hotel doctor, that "countless possibilities" are what make "doctors perfunctory" in an "incalculable world." By the end of this extraordinary story we can appreciate all too well why doctors remain perfunctory, and we most assuredly feel the truth of the world's incalculability. Indeed, we remember all too well the later ironic consequences in "The Pupil" after Pemberton assures Morgan Moreen that "I'm your doctor."

We have already seen that the ghostly level of "A Round of Visits" is one of its principal features. In addition to the faces of Newton Winch and Phil Bloodgood, which "stare out" at Monteith, one must keep in mind that Mark himself is, in his own way, a spectral figure and a type of alter ego to both Winch and Bloodgood, a relationship suggested by the very geometry of the story, since Monteith is in search of Bloodgood and ends up with his surrogate in Winch. James's verbal artistry, as we might expect, also supports this: Winch, for example, exclaims that Bloodgood "sticks out of" Monteith. It should be remembered that Monteith, like Spencer Brydon in "The Jolly Corner," is an American expatriate newly returned to a "monstrous" New York from Europe, where he has been removed and protected from American culture. Scholars routinely and legitimately associate the terrible milieu described with James's own reaction and description in *The American Scene*. It cannot be overstressed, however, that both Spencer Brydon and Mark Monteith have lived abroad through incomes that derive directly from American financial holdings. In fact, that is to my mind the fundamental ground of being that qualifies each as an alter ego to the type of ravaged and ravenous American businessman produced by the coarse culture that appalls them, and it is also from a psychoanalytic standpoint why they *are* so appalled. In Monteith's case there is particular sophistry in the notion of his remaining "pure" in Europe through Bloodgood's handling of his affairs; and when Bloodgood's treachery is revealed it sets into motion the obscure process by which Monteith's eventual confrontation with Winch results in the recognition of his own contribution to both Bloodgood's villainy and Winch's suicide. This cannot help but destroy his complacement belief in his victimization by and distance from the culture: his pristine separation of self and other is dissolved first by the telepathic permutations of the encounter with Winch and eventually replaced by the harsh light of a new and more genuine self-awareness—Emerson's "Fall." Hence his final statement is the succinct realization that his "interesting" self is very much a part of the American scene all about him: "I really think I must practically have caused it." Even more than Spencer Brydon, then, Mark Monteith illustrates the point that to the very end Henry James continued to probe and sound the defects of character in Europeanized Americans, even though he shifted his interest away from American cultural innocence symbolized in Daisy

Miller, Caroline Spencer, or Isabel Archer and gave us instead the apparitional New York world of ghostly terror in "The Jolly Corner" and
"A Round of Visits," or the less apparitional but no less sinister and
grotesque world of "Julia Bride."

The formal integrity, too, of "A Round of Visits" is another illustration of just how much James by the end had furthered the development of American short fiction as a work of art in the course of his
career. The seven divisions of the tale are halved by the transitional
fourth section (in which no visit occurs), providing a structural balance
between the first and final three segments. The first three, moreover,
are unified by a repetitive pattern of expectation and rebuff in the encounters with the hotel doctor, Mrs. Folliott, and Mrs. Ash. The transitional section, with Monteith again outside in the street, has him
deciding to reverse his search for sympathy and follow the supposed
"will of Providence." The last three sections, in Winch's apartment,
trace the reversal and twisting of Monteith's expectations and judg-
ments with results even more drastically unexpected than those accu-
mulated in the first three sections. Such structural integrity and
underpinning supports the "loose and baggy monster" thesis, advo-
cated by Richard Blackmur, that James's convoluted idiom and complex elaboration are superimposed on a strict classical foundation.[46] But
it also provides the real basis for James's labyrinthine irony, which
inundates the tale: that is, the repeated reversals with the doctor,
Mrs. Folliott, and Florence Ashe; then Monteith's resignation to
"Providence" to attend to poor Winch; and thereupon, of course, that
resolve reversed again by his seeming to have found in Winch the sympathetic ear he had formerly sought. James's chain of irony is further
compounded and deepened when it turns out Monteith has done the
same to Winch as the earlier friends had done to him, ignore his
weightier problem while talking of their own. Yet by the end he has
come in irony full circle back to victimization, only it is his own as
agent rather than as recipient. In naming the tale "A Round of Visits,"
James surely must mean to allude to a doctor's round, but he also, as
in his finest novels, conceives of "operative irony" in terms of a principle of circularity wherein one ends up where one began for opposite
reasons. In either case, the story is certainly not "innocuously entitled"
(Wagenknecht, 173).

The imagery in the tale, finally, is both extravagant and haunting in
close relation to the theme of the story, and it combines with complex
syntax to provide the same distinct idiom carefully scrutinized by

Nicola Bradbury and so many others in the late novels. The principal imagery revolves around the excessive "heat" and "tropical" jungle of the hotel with its lurid "luxuriance" juxtaposed against the "blinding New York blizzard" and "great white savage storm." Outside in the "intensity" of the cold it is a "jump from the Tropics to the Pole" (*CT*, 437). Such imagery evokes the medium of the Dantesque underworld that runs throughout the tale, but it also reflects Monteith's inner turmoil as well as the cold receptions he finds. It suggests especially the collision of extremes that signifies the turmoil and violence of the culture he returns to and deplores, but from which he ultimately cannot claim to stay aloof and innocent.

With this lengthy examination of "A Round of Visits," James's last published story, I have sought to illustrate the direction, texture, and importance of James's achievement in bringing American short fiction to a maturity and poetic complexity not to be found before him. Like most tales he later came to write, it relies on the "visiting mind" as its locus of reality, and thus fulfills the earlier promise in "The Art of Fiction" of the writer's experience as a "huge spider-web" suspended in "the chamber of consciousness" and conveying "the very atmosphere of the mind." It deals, moreover, with large cultural questions regarding Americans and Europe, with the profound issue of moral complicity, and with the misuse and exploitation of individuals by one another in most unanticipated ways, including the idea, never far from James's fiction, that words can be weapons: this may remind us of Graham Greene's great admiration for the late James's Judas complex, his deep preoccupation with betrayal and pity for the betrayers, an idea also shared by J. A. Ward.[47] The tale shows, furthermore, James's increased sense of the inextricable relationship of character and fate, a relationship on the thematic level that parallels that of "impression and experience" at the level of artistic execution. It shows the way in which the spectral, ghostly medium came to establish itself even in fiction not explicitly ghostly, converging in a distinctive Dickensian reality of poetic extravagance buttressed by verbal puns and extended figurative conceits. It illustrates James's mastery of but great flexibility with the untrustworthy point-of-view character, especially a "register" in third-person narration. And it illustrates unforgettably James's tremendous contribution to the genre of his distinctive "operative irony."

Finally, his last published tale typifies the trajectory of James's later fiction as a medium that seeks to dissolve the objective world and project a "field" in which consciousness is correlative to phenomena, in which subject and object virtually transform each other in the acts of perception and reflection and create what Browning called "prismatic hues" of reality. This means, among other things, his use of what his brother, William James, called "ambulatory relations," the due rendering of all those "intervening parts of experience" that occur when human beings perceive, think, and interact with consciousness. Jamesian epistemology in this respect also establishes an analogy with the broad development in twentieth-century natural science, gradually replacing Cartesian and Newtonian models, wherein the structure of reality is homologous with the structure of consciousness. This view therefore suggests why his rendering, like his brother's late philosophy, anticipates phenomenology. His literary artistry, however, shaped and expanded the tale from the acute, witty, incisive agent of social realism in the early years to the elaborate poetic expressionism and moral density of the last phase, clarifying his influence on modern poetry as well as fiction. In "A Round of Visits," for example, we discover a post-Coleridgean polarity between the incalculability of events, on one hand, and the powerful drive of the subconscious, on the other, to bring to light the dark knowledge of the self and other—and of the other as self. To take the full measure of James's development of the genre we need only recollect that our final story, like one of the earliest discussed at length in this study, is another tale of "Four Meetings."

Notes to Part 1

1. For a discussion of James's "Is There a Life after Death?" and its relationship to William James's *The Varieties of Religious Experience* see my *Henry James and Pragmatistic Thought: A Study in the Relationship between the Philosophy of William James and the Literary Art of Henry James* (Chapel Hill: University of North Carolina Press, 1974), 208–25.

2. *The Art of the Novel: Critical Prefaces*, ed. R. P. Blackmur (New York: Charles Scribner's Sons, 1934), 240, 178; hereafter cited in the text as *AN*.

3. See Percy Lubbock, *The Craft of Fiction* (1921; New York: Viking Press, 1957), 156–202 and passim.

4. "The Art of Fiction," in *Partial Portraits* (London: Macmillan, 1888), 388–89; hereafter cited in the text as *PP*.

5. Sergio Perosa, *Henry James and the Experimental Novel* (Charlottesville: University Press of Virginia, 1978); John Carlos Rowe, *The Theoretical Dimensions of Henry James* (Madison: University of Wisconsin Press, 1984); another

strong argument that James transcends realism, though not as proto-modernist, is Daniel M. Fogel, *Henry James and the Structure of the Romantic Imagination* (Baton Rouge: Louisiana State University Press, 1981).

6. *The Novels and Tales of Henry James*, vol. 13, (New York: Charles Scribner's Sons, 1908), 441–42; hereafter cited in the text by volume and page number (e.g., 13:441–42). The twenty-four volumes of this New York Edition appeared between 1907 and 1909.

7. Christof Wegelin, *The Image of Europe in Henry James* (Dallas: Southern Methodist University Press, 1958), 45–46; hereafter cited in the text. At one point Wegelin calls this 30,000-word story a novel, one instance of the confusion surrounding the nomenclature of James's shorter fiction discussed in my preface.

8. This exchange of places on an opposite shore makes a curious and interesting parallel with the visitations in "The Turn of the Screw" involving the Governess and Miss Jessel.

9. Although James does not actually discuss "Four Meetings" in his Preface to volume 16 of the New York Edition (which is stocked with twelve stories, an unusually large number), he does use that Preface to emphasize what he calls the "Dramatise it, Dramatise it!" principle. This is also the same Preface in which he compares the short story to a sonnet. See *AN*, 232–40.

10. Among those who find some fault with the "Four Meetings" narrator are John A. Clair, *The Ironic Dimension in the Fiction of Henry James* (Pittsburgh: Duquesne University Press, 1965), 1–16; Roger Seamon, "Henry James's 'Four Meetings': A Study in Irritability and Condescension," *Studies in Short Fiction* 15 (1978): 155–63; and W. R. Martin, "The Narrator's 'Retreat' in James's 'Four Meetings," *Studies in Short Fiction* 17 (1980): 497–99. Generally speaking, I believe it is mistaken to read the later James back into the early James, although it is certainly valid to detect anticipations of later James in his earlier work. I myself see neither fault nor unreliability in the narrator of "Four Meetings."

11. See Mark Twain's essay, "William Dean Howells," first published in *Harper's Magazine* (July 1906) in *Major Writers of America*, vol. 2, ed. Perry Miller et al. (New York: Harcourt, Brace & World, 1962), 102–6. Although Mark Twain inevitably becomes creatively comic in the essay, the fact that he signed it S. L. Clemens reflects the seriousness and sincerity of his admiration for Howells and his prose, especially the "stage directions."

12. *Selected Shorter Writings of Mark Twain*, ed. Walter Blair (Boston: Houghton Mifflin Co., 1962), 18.

13. James elaborated this figurative conceit in the New York Edition, still another instance of his fine revision.

14. The length of a James nouvelle extends from about 17,000 to 26,000 words if we include "Daisy Miller" and "The Lesson of the Master" as nouvelles, each about 23,000 and 24,000, respectively. "The Pupil" and "The Bench of Desolation" run from 17,000–18,000 words. "An International Epi-

sode" runs to almost 30,000 words. Is it a "long" nouvelle? What of "A London Life," "The Aspern Papers," "The Siege of London," and "The Turn of the Screw," all in the early thirties or forty thousands? They exceed the length of a nouvelle and, as I indicate in my preface, do not yet qualify as short novels. They are just long tales. So "An International Episode" is one of the "shorter" long tales beyond the length of a nouvelle. Strict, consistent classification of James's shorter fiction is obviously difficult, but this problem bespeaks James's creative productivity and elasticity.

15. A notable exception to this tendency is Wegelin, 48–51, whose comment that "James's impartiality is reflected in the symmetrical structure of the story" is a key signature to his approach to the tale.

16. For James's famous and much reprinted passage from *Hawthorne* on the impoverishment of American culture for an aspiring writer like Hawthorne, see *The Art of Criticism*, ed. William Veeder and Susan M. Griffin (Chicago: University of Chicago Press, 1986), 108–9.

17. For a fuller discussion of "Daisy Miller" along these same lines see my essay "Daisy Miller, Backward into the Past: A Centennial Essay," *Henry James Review* 1 (Winter 1980): 164–79

18. For the view that Tina is Juliana's illegitimate daughter by Aspern see Robert C. McLean, "Poetic Justice in James's *The Aspern Papers*," *Papers on Language & Literature* 3 (1967): 264–66, and James W. Gargano, "'The Aspern Papers': The Untold Story," *Studies in Short Fiction* 10 (1973): 1–10; Rowe, 105–6, argues, however, against this view.

19. Wayne C. Booth, *The Rhetoric of Fiction* (Chicago: University of Chicago Press, 1961), 361–64; hereafter cited in the text.

20. Note, too, James's contention in "The Art of Fiction" that "It is an incident for a woman to stand up with her hand resting on a table and look out at you in a certain way; or if it be not an incident I think it will be hard to say what it is" (*PP*, 393). He also claims that a "psychological reason is, to my imagination, an object adorably pictorial" (*PP*, 402). This whole issue of portraiture versus illustration in James's conception of art can also be seen in his change from the early to the late version of "Daisy Miller": the early version is called "Daisy Miller: A Study," which I take to be analogous to an artist's drawing or illustration. James dropped "A Study" from the New York Edition text.

21. For an extensive reading of "The Real Thing" along these lines see my *Henry James and Pragmatistic Thought*, 120–34.

22. See for instance F. O. Matthiessen's introduction to his edition of *Henry James: Stories of Artists and Writers* (New York: New Directions, n.d.), 2; however, Edward Wagenknecht, *The Tales of Henry James* (New York: Ungar Publishing Co., 1984), 50–54, takes time out from his usual handbook format to read it ambiguously. Krishna Baldev Vaid does not cover it in his *Technique in the Tales of Henry James*.

23. Matthiessen does include "The Middle Years" in his "Stories of Art-

ists and Writers"; Vaid, however, puts it in the "anecdote" classification, yet treats it as a cross between anecdote and parable, though not necessarily an art parable. "The Middle Years" grazes many Jamesian categories but eludes them all, except perhaps the "hard, shining sonnet."

24. A very good discussion of this idea can be found in Christof Wegelin, "Art and Life in James's 'The Middle Years,'" *Modern Fiction Studies* 33 (1987): 639–46.

25. A fine, suggestive essay showing how the telegraphist's role is structured by gender and class and situated within an emerging service economy is Dale M. Bauer and Andrew Lakritz, "Language, Class, and Sexuality in Henry James's 'In the Cage,'" *New Orleans Review* 14, no. 3 (1987): 61–69.

26. The whole idea of a reader's process of discovery mirroring that of James' characters is of course suggestive of "reader-response" criticism, a school of literary analysis associated with Wolfgang Iser and his followers. This fruitful approach to James's work can be found most comprehensively in Nicola Bradbury, *Henry James: The Later Novels* (London: Oxford University Press, 1979).

27. David Eggenschwiler, "James's 'The Pupil': A Moral Tale without a Moral," *Studies in Short Fiction* 15 (1978): 435.

28. The reader may perhaps recall my discussion of part of this passage in my preface to this study as exemplary of James's New York Edition revisions. I hope that my analysis of the larger passage will underscore the value of such changes as "wore" for "had," even though, as explained at the beginning of this book, my practice generally has not been to cite such revision as evidence for my interpretation of a given tale.

29. *Henry James Letters*, vol. 1., ed. Leon Edel (Cambridge: Belknap Press, 1974), 253.

30. Ellen Kimbel, "The American Short Story: 1900–1920," in *The American Short Story, 1900–1945: A Critical History* (Boston: Twayne Publishers, 1984), 35, 41.

31. For the modern scientific view I have in mind, see Michael Polanyi, *Personal Knowledge* (Chicago: University of Chicago Press, 1958) and *Knowing and Being* (Chicago: University of Chicago Press, 1969); see also Fritjof Capra, *The Turning Point: Science, Society and the Rising Culture* (New York: Simon & Schuster, 1982); Owen Barfield, *Saving the Appearances: A Study in Idolatry* (New York: Harcourt Brace & World, 1957); and Roger S. Jones, *Physics as Metaphor* (Minneapolis: University of Minnesota Press, 1982). For James's anticipation of this "matrix of modern thought" see Paul B. Armstrong, *The Phenomenology of Henry James* (Chapel Hill: University of North Carolina Press, 1983); John C. Rowe's *The Theoretical Dimensions of Henry James;* and my *Henry James and Pragmatistic Thought*.

32. Eleanor M. Tilton, foreword to *Henry James: "The Marriages" and Other Stories* (New York: New American Library, 1961), x; Vaid, 193, likewise

calls the tale "simple and uninvolved"; Wegelin, 53–54, however, feels there is more complexity to "Miss Gunton" than its "flicker of the *old* international flame."

33. For a discussion of James's transformation of the Daisy Miller figure into Julia Bride not, however, by way of "Miss Gunton" but "Pandora" (1884), see Peter Buitenhuis, "From Daisy Miller to Julia Bride: 'A Whole Passage of Intellectual History,'" *American Quarterly* 11 (1959): 135–46.

34. A representative sample of the massive "Turn of the Screw" scholarship, especially in recent years, can be found in the bibliography at the end of this study. Even as I write, however, a new book-length attempt to reinstate through copious historical research the supernatural interpretation is Peter G. Beidler, *Ghosts, Demons, and Henry James: The Turn of the Screw at the Turn of the Century* (Columbia: University of Missouri Press, 1989).

35. For the early relation of Freud to criticism see Claudia C. Morrison, *Freud and the Critic* (Chapel Hill: University of North Carolina Press, 1968). For the relation of F. W. H. Meyer to William James and, then, to Henry James see my *Pragmatistic Thought*, 208–14.

36. A fine exposition of this concept is by Donna Przybylowicz, *Desire and Repression: The Dialectic of Self and Other in the Late Works of Henry James* (Tuscaloosa: University of Alabama Press, 1986), 27–31; her immediate context is James's *What Maisie Knew* rather than "The Beast in the Jungle."

37. T. S. Eliot, "Henry James: In Memory," in *The Shock of Recognition*, ed. Edmund Wilson (New York: Modern Library, 1955), 856. Eliot's essay on James first appeared in *The Little Review*, August 1918.

38. In *Henry James and Pragmatistic Thought*, 181–87, 199–208.

39. *The Complete Tales of Henry James*, vol. 12, ed. Leon Edel (New York: J.B. Lippincott, 1964), 372, 375; hereafter cited in the text as *CT.* Both "The Bench of Desolation" and "A Round of Visits" were written and published too late for the New York Edition. Since both tales appear in the twelfth volume of the *Complete Tales*, I cite them by that volume and the page.

40. Despite the great prevalence of such simple benches throughout England and Great Britain, it is coincidental irony that Land's End itself now is in process of being "developed" by a Texan entrepreneur into a tinseled holiday resort. James might be appalled but also, I suspect, equal to it as subject matter for his imagination given his intense preoccupation with economic motivation in his late work.

41. Vaid, 182–183, discusses this imagery well.

42. Contrast this with W. R. Martin and Warren U. Ober, "Dantesque Patterns in Henry James's 'A Round of Visits,'" *A Review of International English Literature* 12 (1981): 45–54; also "Introduction," *The Finer Grain* (New York: Scholars' Facsimiles and Reprints, 1986), xii. Martin and Ober try to establish a rigid, allegorical parallel of the tales and its characters with the *Inferno*. More importantly, they argue that Monteith's surprise visit to Newton

Winch provides the latter a means of "newfound hope" of salvation with "his Creator" by his suicide. That is diametrically opposed to the argument I shall make here, but quite independent of that it is a difficult interpretation to understand, especially theologically.

43. The most extensive use of this idea in James is in *The Sense of the Past* when protagonist Ralph Pendrel gazes at his "other" in a portrait that faces not the looker but the "dark backward." James must have long been interested in this idea: Isabel Archer, for instance, first sees Madame Merle from the back while the latter plays the piano in *The Portrait of a Lady*.

44. Compare Peter Brench's concluding statement: "'I think it must have been—without my quite at the time knowing it—to keep *me*!'" (16:190) Even without the context, one can sense James's interest in ending a tale as the beginning of a character's new consciousness. This imparts the dramatic element to his work, allows him to stress individual psychology, and also to get away from the trite practice of which he complained in " The Art of Fiction": "The 'ending' of a novel is, for many persons, like that of a good dinner, a course of dessert and ices, and the artist in fiction is regarded as a sort of meddlesome doctor who forbids agreeable aftertastes" (*PP*, 382).

45. *Selections from Ralph Waldo Emerson*, ed. Stephen E. Whicher (Boston: Houghton Mifflin Co., 1957), 269.

46. "The Loose and Baggy Monsters of Henry James" in *R. P. Blackmur: Studies in Henry James*, ed. Veronica A. Makowsky (New York: New Directions Publishing Corp., 1983), 125–46. This essay originally appeared in *Accent* 11 (1951): 129–46.

47. See Graham Greene, "The Private Universe," in *Henry James: A Collection of Critical Essays*, ed. Leon Edel (Englewood Cliffs, N.J.: Prentice-Hall, 1963), 120-122; also J. A. Ward, *The Imagination of Disaster: Evil in the Fiction of Henry James* (Lincoln: University of Nebraska Press, 1961), 160.

Part 2

THE WRITER

Introduction

Although Henry James is regarded as having less to say critically about short fiction than about the aesthetics of the novel, the evidence shows clearly his aspiration for and understanding of the distinct artistry of short fiction. The problem is that his overall criticism is so substantial that one must isolate his commentary on this subject to appreciate it. The *Notebooks* are the best place to start, and not only for the usual reason, that they provide us with his many "germs" for novels and tales alike. Like the *Letters*, but more so, the *Notebooks* are especially helpful in showing just how persistently James strives in his "self-talk" to meet the special challenge of short fiction, especially the demand for concision, brevity, and foreshortening (the last two words are simply replete throughout both his *Notebooks* and *Prefaces*). Yet the greater challenge for him is to combine such concision with "development" of character and situation, or "relations." This demanding combination leads him inevitably to the nouvelle and the very long tale, but it never precludes his continued attempt at the "anecdote" or short story proper. James speaks of "short story" as something new because the terminology *was* new (first noted in the *Oxford English Dictionary* for 1898). He rarely achieved the "masterly brevity" he speaks of in his letter to Robert Louis Stevenson; yet he did compose many fine "anecdotes"—short stories—all admirably "foreshortened" like the nouvelles. (*Foreshortening*, incidentally, is one of several critical terms James adapted from painting.)

The *Notebooks* are important for another reason. They illustrate how frequently James's initial "germ" is rethought and ramified by the time the story is actually written—another key to why brevity was so difficult for him. For example, in thinking about his character Pandora, the "rival" to Daisy Miller, he is clearly pleased by the concision he had achieved in "Four Meetings"; yet his entry on "The Lesson of the Master" gives no hint of the special "twist" in having St. George himself marry the woman beloved of the "younger *confrere*." The entry on "Greville Fane" does not prepare us for the extensive moral-cannibalism theme exhibited in both children, but it does show James's preliminary interest in and identification with the "witness" or narrator, whose prose idiom is so dominant in the finished tale. The "Turn of the Screw" entry does not address the psychology of the Governess. James set out to tell a ghost story, not a case history of obsession, hysteria, or hallucination. But as a master of psychological realism he just could not keep it out, and the deep merging of *both* dimensions probably created the celebrated ambiguity and controversy of this famous tale.

The notebook entry on "The Beast in the Jungle" is instructive in two ways: first, James typically starts with what he thinks is an "anecdote" and ends up writing a nouvelle (though one admirably foreshortened); second, he quickly projects himself deeply into the drama and "operative irony" of the situation and idea, much like the "Project of Novel" he wrote to Harper & Brothers in preparation for *The Ambassadors*. His entry on "The Jolly Corner" is little more than the "germ"—a man "turning the tables" on the ghost "otherwise qualified to appall *him*"—but gives no promise of the enriched stratified meaning in the finished work, with levels psychoanalytic, cultural, and mythic. "A Round of Visits" is a much fuller entry, yet here again James was absolutely to transform the initial idea of Monteith's being "healed" by helping others into something infinitely more complex, ironic, and multidimensional.

The *Prefaces* again show James's aspiration for brevity, economy, and foreshortening; he speaks of the "science of control" and of "chemical reductions." He also clarifies publicly the distinction between the "anecdote" and the "nouvelle," the latter providing an elasticity that allows for "developments." In general, James conveys the sense of vastly different lengths of tales depending on the extent of "complications" to be treated. Still, his miscount of the number of words in "The Middle Years" is congenital and symbolic; even though a wonderfully compressed "anecdote," this tale is longer than he thought (although one senses his pleasure with it is not just technical but deeply personal). On the other hand, his perceived "iridescence" in "Julia Bride" for "its whole view of manners and morals" in American society is right on the mark.

If the aspirations in the *Letters* tend appropriately to date from the productive years of 1888 through the 1890s, one also comes back to the *Notebooks* during that same period and notices there James's high praise for both Turgenev and Maupassant. His critical essay on Guy de Maupassant is important for several reasons. First and most obviously, it gives us James's critical assessment of and engagement with a great writer of tales rather than another novelist. Second, we see James in his characteristic mode of mediating between Gallic and Anglo-American sensibilities regarding the question of sensuality and "indecency" in fiction: he gives full credit to French practice but takes ample account of Anglo-American moralism. Third, James's own stories are uncannily Maupassant-like on one level, the "twist" or reversal; he invariably proceeds, however, to introduce extension, complication, and mass to an otherwise Maupassant-like base. We can see this clearly in the notebook entry for "The Real Thing." He wanted to do it "as admirably compact as Maupassant," but he could no more leave out additional "complications" there than avoid introducing psychological content into "The Turn of the Screw." Finally—and closely related to the preceding point—there is James's emphasis in the essay concerning Maupassant's technical excellence yet failure to explore "the reflective side" of humanity. Clearly James wished to provide exactly that reflective side left out by the Frenchman. So he hoped to do it all, the technical brevity together with the reflective side. This set of difficult challenges produced the distinct Jamesian tale of varied lengths with Maupassant-like "twists" and interior reflectors of consciousness.

From James's *Notebooks*

[Short Fiction]

34 De Vere Gardens, May 19, 1889

[Hippolyte Taine] talked about many things, and all well . . . but what I wish especially to note here is his tribute to Turgenieff—to his depth, his variety, his form, the small, full perfect things he has left, which will live through their finished objectivity, etc. He rates T. very high—higher in form even than I have done. But his talk about him has done me a world of good—reviving, refreshing, confirming, consecrating, as it were, the wish and dream that have lately grown stronger than ever in me—the desire that the literary heritage, such as it is, poor thing, that I may leave, shall consist of a large number of perfect *short* things, *nouvelles* and tales, illustrative of ever so many things in life—in the life I see and know and feel—and of all the deep and the delicate—and of London, and of art, and of everything: and that they shall be fine, rare, strong, wise—eventually perhaps even recognized (54).

Kingstown, Ireland, Marine Hotel, July 13, 1891

I must hammer away at the effort to do, successfully and triumphantly, a large number of very short things. I have done ½ a dozen, lately, but it takes time and practice to get into the trick of it. I have never attempted before to deal with such extreme brevity. However, the extreme brevity is a necessary condition only for some of them—the others may be of varying kinds and degrees of shortness. I needn't go into all my reasons and urgencies over again here; suffice it that they are cogent and complete. I must absolutely *not* tie my hands with promised novels if I wish to keep them free for a genuine and sustained attack on the theatre. That is one cogent reason out of many; but the

Excerpted from *The Complete Notebooks of Henry James*, ed. Leon Edel and Lyall H. Powers (New York: Oxford University Press, 1986), 24, 33–34, 43–44, 48–49, 54, 55, 56–57, 88, 94–95, 109, 112, 130, 199, 507. © 1986 by Leon Edel and Lyall H. Powers. Reprinted by permission of Oxford University Press, Inc. Excerpts are sequenced by topic rather than pagination.

116

artistic one would be enough even by itself. What I call *the* artistic one *par excellence* is simply the consideration that by doing short things I can do so many, touch so many subjects, break out in so many places, handle so many of the threads of life. X X X X X (57).

Torquay, Osborne Hotel, September 8, 1895
Try to make use, for the brief treatment, of nothing, absolutely *nothing*, that isn't ONE, as it were—that doesn't begin and end in its little self. X X X X X (130).

["Four Meetings"]

London, January 29, 1884
I don't see why I shouldn't do the "self-made girl," whom I noted here last winter, in a way to make her a rival to D[aisy] M[iller]. I must put her into action, which I am afraid will be difficult in the small compass (16 magazine pages which I now contemplate). But I don't see why I shouldn't make the thing as concise as *Four Meetings*. The concision of *Four Meetings*, with the success of *Daisy M.;* that is what I must aim at! (24).

["The Aspern Papers"]

Florence, January 12, 1887
Certainly there is a little subject there: the picture of the two faded, queer, poor and discredited old English women—living on into a strange generation, in their musty corner of a foreign town—with these illustrious letters their most precious possession. Then the plot of the Shelley fanatic—his watchings and waitings—the way he *couvers* the treasure. . . . It strikes me much. The interest would be in some price that the man has to pay—that the old woman—or the survivor—sets upon the papers. His hesitations—his struggle—for he really would give almost anything.—The Countess Gamba came in while I was there: her husband is a nephew of the Guiccioli—and it was *à propos* of their having a lot of Byron's letters of which they are rather illiberal and dangerous guardians, that H[amilton] told me the above. They won't show them or publish any of them—and the Countess was very angry once on H.'s representing to her that it was her duty—especially to the English public!—to let them at least be seen. *Elle se fiche bien* [she doesn't give a hoot] of the English public. She says the letters—

addressed in Italian to the Guiccioli—are discreditable to Byron; and H. elicited from her that she had *burned* one of them (33–34).

["The Lesson of the Master"]

London, January 5, 1888
Another came to me last night as I was talking with Theodore Child about the effect of marriage on the artist, the man of letters, etc. He mentioned the cases he had seen in Paris in which this effect had been fatal to the quality of the work, etc.—through overproduction, need to meet expenses, make a figure, etc. And I mentioned certain cases here. Child spoke of Daudet . . . as an example in point. "He would never have written that if he hadn't married." So it occurred to me that a very interesting situation would be that of an elder artist or writer, who has been ruined (in his own sight) by his marriage and its forcing him to produce promiscuously and cheaply—his position in regard to a younger *confrère* whom he sees on the brink of the same disaster and whom he endeavours to save, to rescue, by some act of bold interference—breaking off the marriage, annihilating the wife, making trouble between the parties (43–44).

["Greville Fane"]

34 De Vere Gardens, February 27, 1889
There comes back to me with a certain vividness of solicitation, an idea that I noted a long time ago, suggested by something that Annie Thackeray once said or repeated to me. That is, her story of Trollope's having had the plan of bringing up his son to write novels, as a lucrative trade. She added (as Mrs. R. Ritchie) that she and her husband had the same idea with regard to her little girl. They would train her up to it as to a regular profession. . . . The particular drama to be that the girl proves quite useless as a novelist, but grows up, marries a snob on the edge of good society, is worldly and hard and would be smart, and is ashamed of her mother. Thinks her novels are vulgar rubbish—keeps her at a distance—almost ignores her—makes her very unhappy. The poor lady is obliged to go on writing, meanwhile, to meet the demands of her son—whom she has thrown into the world to pick up information for her, and who has simply become idle, selfish, extravagant and vicious. She has all sorts of lurking romanticisms and *naïvetés*—make a very vivid amusing pathetic picture of her mixture of queer qualities, etc. . . . Her love of splendour, of the aristocracy, of high society—the

wealth and beauty which she attributes to her people, etc.—contrasted with the small shabby facts of her own life. She dies at the end, worn out, disappointed, poor. The thing had much best be told by a witness of her life—a friend—a critic, a journalist, etc.: in the 1st person: rapid notes. I speak of the telegram from the editor of one of the big papers when she dies, asking for ½ a column about her. I saw and wrote the ½ column and made it kinder. Then for myself I wrote these other notes—kinder still.—The thing to be called by the *nom de plume* of the poor lady—some rather smart *man's* name (48–49).

["The Real Thing"]

Paris, Hotel Westminster, February 22, 1891
In pursuance of my plan of writing some very short tales—things of from 7000 to 10,000 words, the easiest length to "place," I began yesterday the little story that was suggested to me some time ago by an incident related to me by George Du Maurier—the lady and gentleman who called upon him with a word from Frith, an oldish, faded, ruined pair—he an officer in the army—who unable to turn a penny in any other way, were trying to find employment as models. I was struck with the pathos, the oddity and typicalness of the situation—the little tragedy of good-looking gentlefolk who had been all their life stupid and well-dressed, living, on a fixed income, at country-houses, watering places and clubs, like so many others of their class in England, and were now utterly unable to *do* anything, had no cleverness, no art nor craft to make use of as a *gagne-pain* [livelihood]—could only *show* themselves, clumsily, for the fine, clean, well-groomed animals that they were. . . . It *should* be a little gem of bright, quick, vivid form. I shall get every grain of "action" that the space admits of if I make something, for the artist, hand in the balance—depend on the way he does this particular work. It's when he finds that he shall lose his great opportunity if he keeps on with them, that he has to tell the gentlemanly couple, that, frankly, they won't serve his turn—and make them wander forth into the cold world again. I must keep them the age I've made them—50 and 40—because it's more touching; but I must bring up the age of the 2 real models to almost the same thing. That increases the incomprehensibility (to the amateurs) of their usefulness. Picture the immanence, in the latter, of the idle, provided-for, country-house habit—the blankness of their *manière d'être* [way of life]. But in how tremendously few words I must do it. This is a lesson—a *magnificent*

lesson—if I'm to do a good many. Something as admirably compact and *selected* as Maupassant (55, 56–57).

["The Turn of the Screw"]

34 De Vere Gardens, January 12, 1895
Note here the ghost-story told me at Addington (evening of Thursday 10th), by the Archbishop of Canterbury: the mere vague, undetailed faint sketch of it—being all he had been told (very badly and imperfectly), by a lady who had no art of relation, and no clearness: the story of the young children (indefinite number and age) left to the care of servants in an old country-house, through the death, presumably, of parents. The servants, wicked and depraved, corrupt and deprave the children; the children are bad, full of evil, to a sinister degree. The servants *die* (the story vague about the way of it) and their apparitions, figures, return to haunt the house *and* children, to whom they seem to beckon, whom they invite and solicit, from across dangerous places, the deep ditch of a sunk fence, etc.—so that the children may destroy themselves, lose themselves by responding, by getting into their power. So long as the children are kept from them, they are not lost: but they try and try and try, these evil presences, to get hold of them. It is a question of the children "coming over to where they are." It is all obscure and imperfect, the picture, the story, but there is a suggestion of strangely gruesome effect in it. The story to be told—tolerably obviously—by an outside spectator, observer (109).

["The Beast in the Jungle"]

34 De Vere Gardens, February 5, 1895
What is there in the idea of *Too late*—of some friendship or passion or bond—some affection long desired and waited for, that is formed too late?—I mean too late in life altogether. Isn't there something in the idea that 2 persons may meet (as if they had looked for each other for years) only in time to feel how much it might have meant for them if they had only met earlier? This is vague, nebulous—the mere hint of a hint (112).

Lamb House, August 27, 1901
Meanwhile there is something else—a very tiny *fantaisie* probably—in small notion that comes to me of a man haunted by the fear more and more, throughout life, that *something will happen to him:* he doesn't quite know what. His life *seems* safe and ordered, his liabilities and exposures

(as a *result* of the fear) a good deal curtailed and cut down, so that the years go by and the stroke doesn't fall. Yet "It *will* come, it will still come," he finds himself believing—and indeed saying to some one, some second-consciousness in the anecdote. "It will come before death; I shan't die without it." Finally I think it must be *he* who sees—not the 2d consciousness. Mustn't indeed the "2d consciousness" be some woman, and it be she who *helps* him to see? She has always loved him—yet, *that*, for the story, "pretty," and he, saving, protecting, exempting his life (always, really with and *for* the fear), has never known it. He likes her, talks to her, confides in her, sees her often—*la côtoie* [keeps coming close], as to her hidden passion, but never guesses. She meanwhile, all the time, sees his life as it is. It is to her that he tells his fear—yes, she is the "2d consciousness." At first she *feels* herself, for him, his feeling of his fear, and is tender, reassuring, protective. Then she reads, as I say, his real case, and is, though unexpressedly, *lucid*. The years go by and *she sees the thing not happen*. At last one day they are somehow, some day, face to face over it, and then she speaks. "It *has*, the great thing you've always lived in dread of, had the foreboding of—it *has* happened to you." He wonders—when, how, what? "What is it?—why, it is that *nothing* has happened!" Then, later on, I think, to keep up the prettiness, it must be that HE sees, that he understands. She has loved him always—and *that* might have happened. But it's too late—she's dead. That, I think, at least, he comes to later on, after an interval, after her death. She is dying, or ill, when she says it. He *then* DOESN'T understand, doesn't see—or so far, only, as to agree with her, ruefully, that that very well *may* be it: that nothing has happened. He goes back; she is gone: she is dead. *What* she has said to him has in a way, by its truth, created the need for her, made him want her, *positively* want her, more. But she is gone, he has lost her, and *then* he sees all she has meant. She has loved him. (It must come for the READER thus, at this moment.) With his base safety and shrinkage he never knew. *That* was what might have happened, and what *has* happened is that it didn't (199).   √

["The Jolly Corner"]

November 1914

The most intimate idea of *that* ["The Jolly Corner"] is that my hero's adventure there takes the form so to speak of his turning the tables, as I think I called it, on a "ghost" or whatever, a visiting or haunting apparition otherwise qualified to appal *him;* and thereby winning a sort

121

of victory by the appearance, and the evidence, that this personage or presence was more overwhelmingly affected by him than he by *it* (507).

["A Round of Visits"]

34 De Vere Gardens, February 17, 1894

There came to me a night or two ago the notion of a young man (young, presumably), who has something—some secret sorrow, trouble, fault—to *tell* and can't find the *recipient*. X X X X X (88).

Casa Biondetti, April 21, 1894

There is apparently something worth thinking of in the idea I barely noted, a few weeks ago, of the young man with something on his mind—the young man with a secret, a worry, a misery, a burden, an oppression, that he carries about with him and suffers from the incapacity to tell—from the want of a confidant, a listening ear and answering heart, an intelligent receptacle for. He *tries* to communicate it, in the belief that it will relieve him. He goes from house to house and from person to person, but finds everywhere an indifference, a preoccupation too visible, a preoccupation, on the part of every one, with other things, with their own affairs, troubles, joys, pleasures, interests—an atmosphere that checks, chills, paralyses the possibility of any appeal. . . . So he wanders, so he goes—with his burden only growing heavier—looking vainly for the ideal sympathy, the waiting, expectant, responsive recipient. My little idea has been that he doesn't find it; but that he encounters instead a sudden appeal, an appeal more violent, as it were, more pitiful even than his own has had it in it to be. He meets in a word a *demand* where he had at last been looking for a supply—a demand which embodies the revelation of a trouble which he immediately feels to be greater than his own. In the presence of this communication which he has to receive instead of giving it he forgets his own, ceases to need to make a requisition for it. His own ache, in a word, passes from him in his pity and his sympathy; he is healed by doing himself what he wanted to have done *for* him. Such is the little idea—which is perhaps as pretty as another. The charm and interest of the thing must necessarily be in the picture—the little panorama of his vain contacts and silent appeals, the view of his troubled spirit and of the people, the places, he successively turns to only to find that everywhere his particular grief is a false note. No one says to him—it *occurs* to no one to say: "You've got something very painful on your mind—do tell us if we can help you—and what it is!" (94).

From James's *Letters*

To Charles Eliot Norton
Cambridge, [Mass.,] January 16, 1871

Looking about for myself, I conclude that the face of nature and civilization in this our country is to a certain point a very sufficient literary field. But it will yield its secrets only to a really *grasping* imagination. This I think Howells lacks. (Of course *I* don't!) To write well and worthily of American things one needs even more than elsewhere to be a *master*. But unfortunately one is less! . . . I myself have been scribbling some little tales which in the course of time you will have a chance to read. To write a series of good little tales I deem ample work for a lifetime. I dream that my lifetime shall have done it.

To Robert Louis Stevenson
34 De Vere Gardens W., July 31, 1888

After [*The Tragic Muse*], with God's help, I propose, for a longish period, to do nothing but short lengths. I want to leave a multitude of pictures of my time, projecting my small circular frame upon as many different spots as possible and going in for number as well as quality, so that the number may constitute a total having a certain value as observation and testimony.

To William James
Hôtel de la Ville, Milan, May 16, 1890

The Tragic Muse is to be my last long novel. For the rest of my life I hope to do lots of short things with irresponsible spaces between. I see even a great future (ten years) of such. But they won't make money.

To Robert Louis Stevenson
34 De Vere Gardens W., October 30, 1891

I have written and am still to write a goodish many short tales—but

Excerpted from *Henry James Letters*, vols. 1 and 3, ed. Leon Edel (Cambridge: Harvard University Press, 1974), 1:252–53; 3:240, 360–61, 513. Also *The Letters of Henry James*, vol. 1, ed. Percy Lubbock (New York: Charles Scribner's Sons, 1920), 163.

123

you are not to be troubled with them till they prop each other up in volumes. I mean never to write another novel; I mean I have solemnly dedicated myself to a masterly brevity. I have come back to it as to an early love. . . . "La nouvelle suffit à tous" [the nouvelle is sufficient for everybody]. (That word is nouvelle.)

To William Dean Howells
34 De Vere Gardens W., January 22, 1895

I shall never again write a *long* novel; but I hope to write six immortal short ones—and some tales of the same quality.

From James's *Prefaces*

A short story, to my sense and as the term is used in magazines, has to choose between being either an anecdote or a picture and can but play its part strictly according to its kind. I rejoice in the anecdote, but I revel in the picture; though having doubtless at times to note that a given attempt may place itself near the dividing-line. This is in some degree the case with [my nouvelle], in which, none the less, on the whole, picture ingeniously prevails; picture aiming at those richly summarised and foreshortened effects . . .

I arrive with "The Liar" (1888) and "The Two Faces" (1900) at the first members of the considerable group of shorter, of shortest tales here republished; though I should perhaps place quite in the forefront "The Chaperon" and "The Pupil," at which we have already glanced. I am conscious of much to say of these numerous small productions as a family—a family indeed quite organised as such, with its proper representatives, its "heads," its subdivisions and its branches, its poor relations perhaps not least: . . . Great for me from far back had been the interest of the whole "question of the short story," roundabout which our age has, for lamentable reasons, heard so vain a babble; but I foresee occasions yet to come when it will abundantly waylay me. . . .

. . . I must reserve "The Two Faces" till I come to speak of the thrilling question of the poor painter's tormented acceptance, in advance, of the scanted canvas; of the writer's rueful hopeful assent to the conditions known to him as "too little room to turn round." Of the liveliest interest then—or so at least I could luckily always project the case—to see how he may nevertheless, in the event, effectively manoeuvre. The value of "The Two Faces"—by reason of which I have not hesitated to gather it in—is thus peculiarly an economic one. It may conceal rather than exhale its intense little principle of calculation;

Excerpted from *The Novels and Tales of Henry James*, vols. 10, 12, 13, 15, 16, and 17 (New York: Charles Scribner's Sons, 1908–9), 10:xxiv; 12:xxii–xxiii, xxiv; 13:vi; 15:vii–viii, xviii; 16:v–vi, xii; 17:xxv–xxvi.

but the neat evolution, as I call it, the example of the turn of the *whole* coach and pair in the contracted court, without the "spill" of a single passenger or the derangement of a single parcel, is only in three or four cases (where the coach is fuller still) more appreciable.

The anecdote consists, ever, of something that has oddly happened to some one, and the first of its duties is to point directly to the person whom it so distinguishes. He may be you or I or any one else, but a condition of our interest—perhaps the principal one—is that the anecdote shall know him, and shall accordingly speak of him, as its subject.

Among forms, moreover, we had had, on the dimensional ground—for length and breadth—our ideal, the beautiful and blest *nouvelle;* the generous, the enlightened hour for which appeared thus at last to shine. It was under the star of the *nouvelle* that, in other languages, a hundred interesting and charming results, such studies on the minor scale as the best of Turgenieff's, of Balzac's, of Maupassant's, of Bourget's, and just lately, in our own tongue, of Kipling's, had been, all economically, arrived at—thanks to their authors', as "contributors," having been able to count, right and left, on a wise and liberal support. It had taken the blank misery of our Anglo-Saxon sense of such matters to organise, as might be said, the general indifference to this fine type of composition. In that dull view a "short story" was a "short story," and that was the end of it. Shades and differences, varieties and styles, the value above all of the idea happily *developed*, languished, to extinction, under the hard-and-fast rule of the "from six to eight thousand words"—when, for one's benefit, the rigour was a little relaxed. For myself, I delighted in the shapely *nouvelle*—as, for that matter, I had from time to time and here and there been almost encouraged to show.

. . . A marked example of the possible scope, at once, and the possible neatness of the *nouvelle*, it takes its place for me in a series of which the main merit and sign is the effort to do the complicated thing with a strong brevity and lucidity—to arrive, on behalf of the multiplicity, at a certain science of control. Infinitely attractive—though I risk here again doubtless an effect of reiteration—the question of how to exert this control in accepted conditions and how yet to sacrifice no real value. . . .

What I had lately and most particularly to say of "The Coxon Fund" is no less true of "The Middle Years," first published in *Scribner's Magazine* (1893)—that recollection mainly and most promptly associates with it the number of times I had to do it over to make sure of it. To get it right was to squeeze my subject into the five or six thousand words I had been invited to make it consist of—it consists, in fact, should the curious care to know, of some 5550[1]—and I scarce perhaps recall another case . . . in which my struggle to keep compression rich, if not, better still, to keep accretions compressed, betrayed for me such community with the anxious effort of some warden of the insane engaged at a critical moment in making fast a victim's straitjacket. The form of "The Middle Years" is not that of the *nouvelle,* but that of the concise anecdote; whereas the subject treated would perhaps seem one comparatively demanding "developments"—if indeed, amid these mysteries, distinctions were so absolute. . . . However this may be, it was as an anecdote, an anecdote only, that I was determined my little situation here should figure; to which end my effort was of course to follow it as much as possible from its outer edge in, rather than from its centre outward. That fond formula, I had alas already discovered, may set as many traps in the garden as its opposite may set in the wood; so that after boilings and reboilings of the contents of my small cauldron, after added pounds of salutary sugar, as numerous as those prescribed in the choicest recipe for the thickest jam, I well remember finding the whole process and act (which, to the exclusion of everything else, dragged itself out for a month) one of the most expensive of its sort in which I had ever engaged.

But I recall, by good luck, no less vividly how much finer a sweetness than any mere spooned-out saccharine dwelt in the fascination of the questions involved. Treating a theme that "gave" much in a form that, at the best, would give little, might indeed represent a peck of troubles; yet who, none the less, beforehand, was to pronounce with authority such and such an idea anecdotic and such and such another developmental? . . .

. . . The merit of the [short story] is in the feat, once more, of the transfusion; the receptacle (of form) being so exiguous, the brevity imposed so great. I undertook the brevity, so often undertaken on a like scale before, and again arrived at it by the innumerable repeated chemical reductions and condensations that tend to make of the very short story, as I risk again noting, one of the costliest, even if, like the hard, shining sonnet, one of the most indestructible, forms of composition in general use.

. . . the achieved iridescence from within works, I feel sure, more kinds of magic; and our interest, our decency and our dignity can of course only be to work as many kinds as possible. Such value as may dwell in "Julia Bride," for example, seems to me, on re-perusal, to consist to a high degree in the strength of the flushing through on the part of the subject-matter, and in the mantle of iridescence naturally and logically so produced. Julia is "foreshortened," I admit, to within an inch of her life; but I judge her life still saved and yet at the same time the equal desideratum, its depicted full fusion with other lives that remain undepicted, not lost. The other lives, the rest of the quantity of life, press in, squeeze forward, to the best of their ability; . . . What if [Julia] were the silver key, tiny in itself, that would unlock a treasure?—the treasure of a whole view of manners and morals, a whole range of American social aspects?

Note

1. James is wrong. Though very compressed, "The Middle Years" is over 7,500 words.

From "Guy de Maupassant"

I

The first artists, in any line, are doubtless not those whose general ideas about their art are most often on their lips—those who most abound in precept, apology, and formula and can best tell us the reasons and the philosophy of things. We know the first usually by their energetic practice, the constancy with which they apply their principles, and the serenity with which they leave us to hunt for their secret in the illustration, the concrete example. . . .

. . . what the sincere critic says is, "Make me something fine in the form that shall suit you best, according to your temperament." This seems to me to put into a nutshell the whole question of the different classes of fiction, concerning which there has recently been so much discourse. There are simply as many different kinds as there are persons practising the art, for if a picture, a tale or, a novel be a direct impression of life (and that surely constitutes its interest and value), the impression will vary according to the plate that takes it, the particular structure and mixture of the recipient. . . .

What makes M. de Maupassant salient is two facts: the first of which is that his gifts are remarkably strong and definite, and the second that he writes directly *from* them, as it were: holds the fullest, the most uninterrupted—I scarcely know what to call it—the boldest communication with them. A case is poor when the cluster of the artist's sensibilities is small, or they themselves are wanting in keenness, or else when the personage fails to admit them—either through ignorance, or diffidence, or stupidity, or the error of a false ideal—to what may be called a legitimate share in his attempt. It is, I think, among English and American writers that this latter accident is most liable to occur; more than the French we are apt to be misled by some convention or other as to the sort of feeler we *ought* to put forth, forgetting that the best one will be the one that nature happens to have given us. We have

Excerpted from *Partial Portraits* (London: Macmillan, 1888), 243–87.

doubtless often enough the courage of our opinions (when it befalls
that we have opinions), but we have not so constantly that of our perceptive apparatus that we in fact neglect, and there are probably many
among us who would erect this tendency into a duty. M. de Maupassant neglects nothing that he possesses; he cultivates his garden with
admirable energy; and if there is a flower you miss from the rich par-
terre, you may be sure that it could not possibly have been raised, his
mind not containing the soil for it. He is plainly of the opinion that the
first duty of the artist, and the thing that makes him most useful to his
fellow-men, is to master his instrument, whatever it may happen to
be. . . .

. . . His eye *selects* unerringly, unscrupulously, almost impudently—
catches the particular thing in which the character of the object or the
scene resides, and, by expressing it with the artful brevity of a master,
leaves a convincing, original picture. If he is inveterately synthetic, he
is never more so than in the way he brings this hard, short, intelligent
gaze to bear. His vision of the world is for the most part a vision of
ugliness, and even when it is not, there is in his easy power to gener-
alise a certain absence of love, a sort of bird's-eye-view contempt. He
has none of the superstitions of observation, none of our English indul-
gences, our tender and often imaginative superficialities. . . .

. . . It is easy to exclaim that if he judges life only from the point of
view of the senses, many are the noble and exquisite things that he
must leave out. What he leaves out has no claim to get itself considered
till after we have done justice to what he takes in. It is this positive
side of M. de Maupassant that is most remarkable—the fact that his
literary character is so complete and edifying. "Auteur à peu près ir-
réprochable dans un genre qui ne l'est pas" [an author almost irre-
proachable in a genre that isn't], as that excellent critic M. Jules
Lemaître says of him, he disturbs us by associating a conscience and a
high standard with a temper long synonymous, in our eyes, with an
absence of scruples. The situation would be simpler certainly if he
were a bad writer; but none the less it is possible, I think, on the
whole, to circumvent him, even without attempting to prove that after
all he is one. . . .

. . . M. de Maupassant adds that in his view "psychology should be
hidden in a book, as it is hidden in reality under the facts of existence.
The novel conceived in this manner gains interest, movement, colour,
the bustle of life." When it is a question of an artistic process, we must
always mistrust very sharp distinctions, for there is surely in every

method a little of every other method. It is as difficult to describe an action without glancing at its motive, its moral history, as it is to describe a motive without glancing at its practical consequence. Our history and our fiction are what we do; but it surely is not more easy to determine where what we do begins than to determine where it ends—notoriously a hopeless task. Therefore it would take a very subtle sense to draw a hard and fast line on the borderland of explanation and illustration. If psychology be hidden in life, as, according to M. de Maupassant, it should be in a book; the question immediately comes up, "From whom is it hidden?" From some people, no doubt, but very much less from others; and all depends upon the observer, the nature of one's observation, and one's curiosity. For some people motives, reasons, relations, explanations, are a part of the very surface of the drama, with the footlights beating full upon them. For me an act, an incident, an attitude, may be a sharp, detached, isolated thing, of which I give a full account in saying that in such and such a way it came off. For you it may be hung about with implications, with relations, and conditions as necessary to help you to recognise it as the clothes of your friends are to help you know them in the street. You feel that they would seem strange to you without petticoats and trousers. . . .

. . . The cause we plead is ever pretty sure to be the cause of our idiosyncrasies, and if M. de Maupassant thinks meanly of "explanations," it is, I suspect, that they come to him in no great affluence. His view of the conduct of man is so simple as scarcely to require them; and indeed so far as they are needed he *is*, virtually, explanatory. He deprecates reference to motives, but there is one, covering an immense ground in his horizon, as I have already hinted, to which he perpetually refers. If the sexual impulse be not a moral antecedent, it is none the less the wire that moves almost all M. de Maupassant's puppets, and as he has not hidden it, I cannot see that he has eliminated analysis or made a sacrifice to discretion. His pages are studded with that particular analysis; he is constantly peeping behind the curtain, telling us what he discovers there. The truth is that the admirable system of simplification which makes his tales so rapid and so concise (especially his shorter ones, for his novels in some degree, I think, suffer from it), strikes us as not in the least a conscious intellectual effort, a selective, comparative process. He tells us all he knows, all he suspects, and if these things take no account of the moral nature of man, it is because he has no window looking in that direction, and not because artistic scruples have compelled him to close it up. The very compact mansion in which he dwells presents on that side a perfectly dead wall. . . .

. . . Nothing can exceed the masculine firmness, the quiet force of his own style, in which every phrase is a close sequence, every epithet a paying piece, and the ground is completely cleared of the vague, the ready-made and the second-best. Less than any one to-day does he beat the air; more than any one does he hit out from the shoulder.

II

He has produced a hundred short tales and only four regular novels; but if the tales deserve the first place in any candid appreciation of his talent it is not simply because they are so much the more numerous: they are also more characteristic; they represent him best in his originality, and their brevity, extreme in some cases, does not prevent them from being a collection of masterpieces. (They are very unequal, and I speak of the best.) The little story is but scantily relished in England, where readers take their fiction rather by the volume than by the page, and the novelist's idea is apt to resemble one of those old-fashioned carriages which require a wide court to turn round. In America, where it is associated pre-eminently with Hawthorne's name, with Edgar Poe's, and with that of Mr. Bret Harte, the short tale has had a better fortune. France, however, has been the land of its great prosperity, and M. de Maupassant had from the first the advantage of addressing a public accustomed to catch on, as the modern phrase is, quickly. In some respects, it may be said, he encountered prejudices too friendly, for he found a tradition of indecency ready made to his hand. I say indecency with plainness, though my indication would perhaps please better with another word, for we suffer in English from a lack of roundabout names for the *conte leste* [risqué tale]—that element for which the French, with their *grivois* [cheerily licentious], their *gaillard* [risqué], their *égrillard* [spicy], their *gaudriole* [broadly risqué], have so many convenient synonyms. It is an honoured tradition in France that the little story, in verse or in prose, should be liable to be more or less obscene (I can think only of that alternative epithet), though I hasten to add that among literary forms it does not monopolise the privilege. Our uncleanness is less producible—at any rate it is less produced.

For the last ten years our author has brought forth with regularity these condensed compositions, of which, probably, to an English reader, at a first glance, the most universal sign will be their licentiousness. They really partake of this quality, however, in a very differing degree, and a second glance shows that they may be divided into numerous groups. It is not fair, I think, even to say that what they have most in common is their being extremely *lestes*. What they have most in common is their being extremely strong, and after that their being extremely brutal. A story may be obscene without being brutal, and *vice versâ*, and M. de Maupassant's contempt for those interdictions which are supposed to be made in the interest of good morals is but an incident—a very large one indeed—of his general contempt. . . .

. . . The author fixes a hard eye on some small spot of human life, usually some ugly, dreary, shabby, sordid one, takes up the particle, and squeezes it either till it grimaces or till it bleeds. Sometimes the grimace is very droll, sometimes the wound is very horrible; but in either case the whole thing is real, observed, noted, and represented, not an invention or a castle in the air. M. de Maupassant sees human life as a terribly ugly business relieved by the comical, but even the comedy is for the most part the comedy of misery, of avidity, of ignorance, helplessness, and grossness. When his laugh is not for these things, it is for the little *saletés* [dirty sayings] (to use one of his own favourite words) of luxurious life, which are intended to be prettier, but which can scarcely be said to brighten the picture. . . .

. . . Sometimes there is a sorrow, a misery, or even a littler heroism, that he handles with a certain tenderness (*Une Vie* ["A Life"] is the capital example of this), without insisting on the poor, the ridiculous, or, as he is fond of saying, the bestial side of it. Such an attempt, admirable in its sobriety and delicacy, is the sketch, in *L'Abandonné* ["The Abandonment"], of the old lady and gentleman, Mme. de Cadour and M. d'Apreval, who, staying with the husband of the former at a little watering-place on the Normandy coast, take a long, hot walk on a summer's day, on a straight, white road, into the interior, to catch a clandestine glimpse of a young farmer, their illegitimate son. He has been pensioned, he is ignorant of his origin, and is a commonplace and unconciliatory rustic. They look at him, in his dirty farmyard, and no sign passes between them; then they turn away and crawl back, in melancholy silence, along the dull French road. The manner in which this dreary little occurrence is related makes it as large as a chapter of history. . . .

When Thackeray relates how Arthur Pendennis goes back to take pot-luck with the insolvent Newcomes at Boulogne, and how the dreadful Mrs. Mackenzie receives him, and how she makes a scene, when the frugal repast is served, over the diminished mutton-bone, we feel that the notation of that order of misery goes about as far as we can bear it. But this is child's play to the history of M. and Mme. Caravan and their attempt, after the death (or supposed death) of the husband's mother, to transfer to their apartment before the arrival of the other heirs certain miserable little articles of furniture belonging to the deceased, together with the frustration of the manoeuvre not only by the grim resurrection of the old woman (which is a sufficiently fantastic item), but by the shock of battle when a married daughter and her husband appear. No one gives us like M. de Maupassant the odious words exchanged on such an occasion as that: no one depicts with so just a hand the feelings of small people about small things. These feelings are very apt to be "fury"; that word is of strikingly frequent occurrence in his pages. *L'Héritage* is a drama of private life in the little world of the Ministère de la Marine—a world, according to M. de Maupassant, of dreadful little jealousies and ineptitudes. Readers of a robust complexion should learn how the wretched M. Lesable was handled by his wife and her father on his failing to satisfy their just expectations, and how he comported himself in the singular situation thus prepared for him. The story is a model of narration, but it leaves our poor average humanity dangling like a beaten rag.

Where does M. de Maupassant find the great multitude of his detestable women? or where at least does he find the courage to represent them in such colours? Jeanne de Lamare, in *Une Vie*, receives the outrages of fate with a passive fortitude; and there is something touching in Mme. Roland's *âme tendre de caissière* [tender soul of a cashier], as exhibited in *Pierre et Jean*. But for the most part M. de Maupassant's heroines are a mixture of extreme sensuality and extreme mendacity. They are a large element in that general disfigurement, that *illusion de l'ignoble, qui attire tant d'êtres* [illusion of ignoble things, which attracts so many people], which makes the perverse or the stupid side of things the one which strikes him first, which leads him, if he glances at a group of nurses and children sunning themselves in a Parisian square, to notice primarily the *yeux de brute* [bestial eyes] of the nurses; or if he speaks of the longing for a taste of the country which haunts the shopkeeper fenced in behind his counter, to identify it as the *amour bête de la nature* [brute love of nature]; or if he has occasion to put the boulevards before us on a summer's evening, to seek his effect in these terms. . . .

It may seem that I have claimed little for M. de Maupassant, so far as English readers are concerned with him, in saying that after publishing twenty improper volumes he has at last published a twenty-first, which is neither indecent nor cynical. It is not this circumstance that has led me to dedicate so many pages to him, but the circumstance that in producing all the others he yet remained, for those who are interested in these matters, a writer with whom it was impossible not to reckon. This is why I called him, to begin with, so many ineffectual names: a rarity, a "case," an embarrassment, a lion in the path. He is still in the path as I conclude these observations, but I think that in making them we have discovered a legitimate way round. If he is a master of his art and it is discouraging to find what low views are compatible with mastery, there is satisfaction, on the other hand, in learning on what particular condition he holds his strange success. This condition, it seems to me, is that of having totally omitted one of the items of the problem, an omission which has made the problem so much easier that it may almost be described as a short cut to a solution. The question is whether it be a fair cut. M. de Maupassant has simply skipped the whole reflective part of his men and women—that reflective part which governs conduct and produces character. He may say that he does not see it, does not know it; to which the answer is, "So much the better for you, if you wish to describe life without it. The strings you pull are by so much the less numerous, and you can therefore pull those that remain with greater promptitude, consequently with greater firmness, with a greater air of knowledge." Pierre Roland, I repeat, shows a capacity for reflection, but I cannot think who else does, among the thousand figures who compete with him—I mean for reflection addressed to anything higher than the gratification of an instinct. We have an impression that M. d'Apreval and Madame de Cadour reflect, as they trudge back from their mournful excursion, but that indication is not pushed very far. An aptitude for this exercise is a part of disciplined manhood, and disciplined manhood M. de Maupassant has simply not attempted to represent. I can remember no instance in which he sketches any considerable capacity for conduct, and his women betray that capacity as little as his men. . . .

The erotic element in M. de Maupassant, about which much more might have been said, seems to me to be explained by the same limitation, and explicable in a similar way wherever else its literature occurs in excess. The carnal side of man appears the most characteristic if you look at it a great deal; and you look at it a great deal if you do not look at the other, at the side by which he reacts against his weaknesses, his defeats. The more you look at the other, the less the whole business to which French novelists have ever appeared to English readers to give a disproportionate place—the business, as I may say, of the senses—will strike you as the only typical one. Is not this the most useful reflection to make in regard to the famous question of the morality, the decency, of the novel? It is the only one, it seems to me, that will meet the case as we find the case to-day. Hard and fast rules, *a priori* restrictions, mere interdictions (you shall not speak of this, you shall not look at that), have surely served their time, and will in the nature of the case never strike an energetic talent as anything but arbitrary. A healthy, living and growing art, full of curiosity and fond of exercise, has an indefeasible mistrust of rigid prohibitions. Let us then leave this magnificent art of the novelist to itself and to its perfect freedom, in the faith that one example is as good as another, and that our fiction will always be decent enough if it be sufficiently general. Let us not be alarmed at this prodigy (though prodigies are alarming) of M. de Maupassant, who is at once so licentious and so impeccable, but gird ourselves up with the conviction that another point of view will yield another perfection.

Part 3

THE CRITICS

Introduction

There are few tasks more doomed to inadequacy than representing a selection of academic criticism on the fiction of Henry James. Whole volumes appear constantly—even entire series of volumes such as Harold Bloom's *Modern Critical Interpretations*—and all are but the merest smidgen of pieces reprinted from a pool of possibilities so wide and deep as to be a kind of paralyzing North Sea. Furthermore, such volumes more often than not are devoted to a single novel, or even a single fine tale, so frequently miscalled a "short novel." The reason for this situation is that James and Faulkner equally spark richer and more plentiful criticism year in and year out than any other American author. The reader of this volume can consult the Bibliography to find further analyses of James's tales, but should understand that, although the list may look full, it is but a particle of what it could be—even with respect to the many articles listed there on "Daisy Miller," "The Turn of the Screw," and "The Beast in the Jungle." My choices in the Bibliography are guided by three principles: to present different schools of interpretation; to present examples of excellence and to favor more recent scholarship over older studies; and to provide at least some items, such as various introductions to collections, that will be helpful for the less advanced student of James.

Each of the four essays I have chosen for this section approaches James in an entirely different way, and each does so thoroughly enough to give the reader a genuine sense of the methodology beyond what is possible in a tiny excerpt. These choices are also governed, however, by the constraints of space; there are innumerable fine essays on individual tales that alone could take up virtually this entire section. Many, though not all, of them are listed in the Bibliography.

J. J. Liggera's essay on Peter Bogdanovich's film version of "Daisy Miller" is interesting not only as film criticism per se but for the sophisticated way he interprets Bogdanovich's *Daisy Miller* by way of both James's "Art of Fiction" and the classic film technique of Orson Welles. His essay is worth reading even if one does not agree with his high assessment of the film. Dennis Pahl's epilogue to his *Indeterminate*

Fictions examines "The Aspern Papers" from the point of view of a contemporary deconstructionist. Pahl's ingenious interplay between James's text and the New York Edition's Preface does the very opposite of what is traditional in James studies—it "decenters" James and argues instead for the absence of a unified sensibility. Pahl also makes use of James's "garden walls" metaphor in a creative way opposite to my own in this study.

William R. Goetz's study of the many levels of "framing" in "The Turn of the Screw" is good both for its analysis of oral versus written formulas governing the telling of the tale and also for exhibiting the sort of "Chinese box" approach found in much contemporary criticism, especially structuralism. His brief reference to the Harley Street master-uncle as a "surrogate for the author" reminds me of John C. Rowe's Marxist-feminist approach by way of the "absent" master (*The Theoretical Dimensions of Henry James*). Finally, James W. Gargano's 1986 study of the rich "mosaic" imagery in "The Beast in the Jungle" illustrates the authentic vitality of formalist criticism right in the heart of a time when it is not supposed to be au courant. As always, it depends more on the critic than the "ism." To my knowledge, none of these essays has before been reprinted.

J. J. Liggera

At the end of Peter Bogdanovich's lovely, imaginative, and yet, literal translation of James's *Daisy Miller*, Winterbourne stands atop Daisy's gravesite, the camera backing off further and further as if repelled by his image standing solitary and stiff. In his mind he carries on an interior conversation with his Aunt, Mrs. Costello, containing two shocks of recognition. One is cultural: perhaps, Winterbourne thinks, recalling his Aunt's early warning that he was "booked to make a mistake," "I've lived too long in foreign parts." The other is more critical for it indicts Bogdanovich's—and James's—audience, which, seeing through Winterbourne's eyes, has become as stiff towards Daisy as he has. Dryly he offers, "She would have appreciated one's esteem."[1]

Esteem wasn't so much to ask, but to the snobbish circle of transplanted Americans living in Europe, it was too much to give. This parting insight about the simplicity of Daisy's heart clears the air about her character, and suddenly she becomes for us in retrospect the beautiful, romantic, assertive, young American she was. The headstrong woman who came to a bad end because "she did what she liked" (p. 142) was merely hoping to kindle a receptive flame in a kindred spirit. What she got from Winterbourne was judgment. Instead of finding the entrée into a culture foreign to her that she expected to follow from Winterbourne's romantic attentions, she suffered the literal "cold shoulder"—Bogdanovich has his Mrs. Walker, the social tyrant, turn her daringly exposed shoulders round on Daisy—from the American colony flitting about Europe. The huge priggish image holds for a moment with the mustachioed Winterbourne revealed in splendid isolation. He is pretentiously and awkwardly suited after the European style, an American become a stuffed shirt. The image then bleaches out in a soft gold, a stinging conviction of Winterbourne, whose lovelessness proved lethal.

Excerpted from "'She Would Have Appreciated One's Esteem': Peter Bogdanovich's *Daisy Miller*," *Literature/Film Quarterly* 9 (1981): 15–21. Reprinted by permission of *Literature/Film Quarterly*.

141

For a similar want of affection, Bogdanovich's film, like Daisy, lies moldering in its grave. Too bad, for this rueful haunting film of an equally haunting and alluring small novel is among the most artistic and successful ventures of literature into film. Bogdanovich grasped the core of *Daisy Miller* as "a love story about missed opportunities, it's about class differences, it's about an unwillingness to commit oneself emotionally to something that is alien or different" (p. 8). In his mind, Winterbourne was clearly the villain for judging rather than supporting Daisy. As he puts it, "Why shouldn't she do what she likes?" (p. 25) He had to drop an original script and found that he must submit his usual film talents, culled from and dependent on film history and nostalgia, to a Jamesian, pre-filmic world. He was able to do so because he felt that *Daisy Miller* was left unfinished by James. Thus like one of those novelists James describes in "The Art of Fiction," Bogdanovich used his artistic imagination to portray what was "unseen" but guessed from James's "seen."[2] He was truly an author or auteur willing to go through James's spiderweb of consciousness and become one on "whom nothing is lost."

His method was to take a hint from Orson Welles and start his film with the boy, Randolph, a device he extended throughout the film to its dramatic conclusion in which Randolph silently glares at Winterbourne.[3] The vocabulary recalls much from Welles: rapid-fire dialogue to indicate Daisy's innocent but seemingly boorish self-assertion, minimal use of close-ups in order to place characters within their environment, dramatic camera angles. Bogdanovich's technique establishes Winterbourne as the film's "central consciousness." His imagery is "painterly"; music is used to reveal emotion and character, particularly as Daisy and Mr. Giovanelli sing; James's dialogue replaces Bogdanovich's; and film histrionics are pared to produce a style which gives the feel of James's era and art.

Bogdanovich was particularly aware in making *Daisy Miller* that, "This is the first movie I've made in which the time period of the story exists prior to the invention of movies" (p. 20). He thought he would have to recreate the story but decided to stick to the basic line, realizing that, "It was a fragile tale, and if I was going to change it in any way, it had to be done in terms of interpretation rather than in the actual sequence of events" (p. 10). What motivated Bogdanovich to interpret was that he felt the tale a "sketch," and not a "finished canvas" (p. 11). So he set himself the task of fleshing out this short work. James himself seems to have suspected the unfinished quality of this novel. In his 1909 "Preface," coming thirty-one years after the initial writing, he says that the book is a "study" for reasons that he can't recall. He feels that Daisy has a certain "flatness" (p. 31), which becomes for Bogdanovich the opening wedge for his imagination to play, to create without changing. . . .

James the theorist defined the novel as Hawthorne before him by emphasizing detail and what might loosely be called realism. James's realism, however, is not photographic or limited to what we see. He gives as an example the woman who passes a barracks and gets only a glimpse. From the impression that quick look made on her mind she can write a novel on barracks life.[4] To James, an author with an observer's eye for detail is apt to have any impression call into play his storehouse of information to give solidity and background to that impression. The same theory is operative to Bogdanovich as author in his translation of James, although he had to work hard to create circumstances nearly a hundred years gone. But he did so using talents, old and new, to create an era in which the real thing was never quite done or said, but hinted. When Daisy proclaims, "I prefer weak tea" to Winterbourne's company, he seems not to react. Bogdanovich drew the scene that way for his observation is, "People never react in normal conversation. I may say something that shocks the hell out of you, but you wouldn't show it on your face at all" (p. 12). Winterbourne's reaction, or failure to give a reaction, is his overall response to Daisy. He now knows when she upbraids him rather more pointedly than his proprieties permit that she knows more than he thought she did. The scene works not because James says Winterbourne doesn't react—James, in fact, doesn't register his reaction—but because Bogdanovich guesses from his own experience that Winterbourne would once again refuse to show his emotions.

James's standard serves as a gloss on Bogdanovich's method in re-creating an era far in the past in a time before the world dreamed in black-and-white film images. He wrote: "The power to guess the unseen from the seen, to trace the implication of things, to judge the whole piece by the pattern, the condition of feeling life in general so completely that you are well on your way to knowing any particular corner of it—this cluster of gifts may almost be said to constitute experience" ("Fiction," p. 203). Bogdanovich's biggest gamble or guess is to characterize Daisy with fast talk, so fast that only bits and pieces flutter to the top, although they are often meaningful bits. James reports that upon first meeting Daisy, Winterbourne is struck that "It was many years since he had heard a young girl talk so much." In fact, she "chattered." This chatter is part of her charm to the rapidly becoming foppish Winterbourne, and James adds in almost paradoxical fashion, "she was quiet, she sat in a charming tranquil attitude" (p. 45). Bogdanovich adds to this Jamesian richness by filming Daisy in a series of stunning images. Her costumes set her off from everyone else. In the Castle of Chillon, the lightbeams filter through the melancholy pile to fall softly on a radiant Daisy; even in the Colosseum, shot in an ominous Picasso-like blue, Bogdanovich dresses her in a white near-bridal gown clutching one red, red rose, the flower representing passion and innocence, the feminine contradiction that defeats Winterbourne. Even in the grayness, she is radiant. Bogdanovich is more than accurate in translating James: he is remolding his own talents, incorporating Wellesian technique, and sketching his own images to conjure for our modern age an era of paintings rather than photography. His colors are so varied and gay that the world represented cannot allow the thought of the kind of black and white that colors his two best known films, *The Last Picture Show* and *Paper Moon*. James is open to experimentation; for him, the success of an author's form depends on "the test of execution . . . it is what is most personal to him" ("Fiction," p. 201). Again Bogdanovich is like Welles in that his sensibility is more European than American; his painterly style comes largely from his father's love of the French Impressionists.[5] He notes that his background creates a dualism in him that confuses critics: "I was brought up in a household that was completely European rather than American . . . I do have an artistic background which is totally European—my father being a Serbian painter, and my mother a Viennese" (p. 22). Yet it is that very background that allows him to see Daisy's problem and also to supply images to represent it: in short, to create a new form to represent a woman from a bygone time caught in a cultural trap. In the midst of European luxury, little brother, Randolph, says that at least his father is "in a better place." Winterbourne thinks Randolph means "the realm of celestial rewards," but what Randolph means is Schenectady, New York. The little Miller adds, "My father's rich, you bet" (pp. 43–44).

The film then is a creative mix in which Bogdanovich makes a new style for himself by utilizing several techniques, especially Wellesian, and a personal structure in order to bend to James's art. The opening shot of the film recalls Welles; it is a slow extended single camera movement from the top of the ornate hotel that houses the Millers to the main floor, a reverse of *Kane*'s trick shot at the opera which sweeps continuously up until it reaches the workmen on the scaffolding. In the Castle a contorted up shot reminiscent of Welles comes from the dungeon floor and perches Daisy and Winterbourne precariously on the edge while he calmly explains to her the term "oubliette." The picture is one of the few extreme shots in the film, but it is appropriate to give a look at the would-be lovers' relationship and its potential for danger. Bogdanovich flavors the scene to capture Winterbourne's estrangement from things of the heart, or, as James suggests, things American, by having him recite from Byron's "Prisoner of Chillon," more from erudition than passion. It is apparent that in choosing to be the scholar, Winterbourne is missing a chance for his own romantic involvement, a transgression Daisy, in her not too subtle way, does not let slip by.

As the scene ends, Daisy is in a huff at Winterbourne. They ride back in a carriage as the refrain of a melancholy harmonica is heard in the distance, the same music that opened the couple's happy entrance into the Castle. When they had entered, potential for adventure was rife. Winterbourne in a silent scene seemed to be paying off the aged guard so that he could be alone with Daisy. All the time the music rather romantically hinted that such moments of beauty cannot last. As the carriage hurries away, in one of the few scenes in which Daisy ever looks back, that is to say does not push forward, she steals a lingering glimpse of the Castle through the small carriage window, a picture of fading romantic possibility. Now the music sounds, not for passing romance, but for not having seized the moment. Without the backing of Winterbourne's affection, the liberation of Daisy Miller, the woman who "did what she liked"—even in foreign lands and in 1878—was lost. She seems to know it.

Bogdanovich uses music also to define both Daisy and Giovanelli. He portrays the Italian as a sprightly but decidedly silly figure rather than the brilliant opportunist James gives us, the change quickly showing us Daisy's innocence in mistaking such a man for a gentleman and also allowing us to think that she might indeed see Giovanelli as he is and still want his companionship, especially in the absence of Winterbourne's declaration of love. At Mrs. Walker's party he sings to the upper crust's polite boredom. Later, in an evocative scene in her hotel sitting room, Daisy prompts Giovanelli to sing "Pop Goes the Weasel," a song whose phrasing is too demanding for his accent to bear. He becomes a comic figure in front of Winterbourne, come calling, who is forced to sit and listen in Daisy's parlor. Unlike her faux pas at Mrs.

Walker's she is clearly in control, saying in effect to Winterbourne that she prefers him. Then under Giovanelli's polite urging, Daisy rises to sing "Maggie." Here Bogdanovich defines Daisy as perhaps not even James has been able to do. Cybill Shepherd, roundly cursed for this film, rises and sings beautifully; by that I mean, flawlessly. She stands with her hands in her lap, the picture of girlish charm, a bit flirtatious, but innocent, incredibly blonde and pretty, but not sensual. She shines. It is a moment, one of those impressions by which James defines his concept of experience, that also radiates her whole being as a gift. Even Winterbourne is not immune. He smiles.

The image of Daisy singing contains her paradoxically robust yet fragile nature. The image is the product of the kind of "fine" intelligence that James calls for in order that a novel or its "picture . . . partake of . . . beauty and truth" ("Fiction," p. 213). James is abundantly generous inputting the responsibility for artistic form not in rules but in the mind and personal sensibility of the artist. Bogdanovich in this film is an artist; again like Welles he is no slave to form, even when translating from literary masters. He uses everything within reach to grasp for those two costly abstractions, beauty and truth, and gives us *Daisy Miller* in its completeness as both novel and film.

Thus in the Pincio, Bogdanovich creates a moment in which Daisy and Winterbourne stop to view a Punch and Judy show; the scene is not in the novel and Bogdanovich is guessing that such shows took place. Daisy is buoyant and Winterbourne's stiffness melts a bit. Out of the corner of his eye, he catches sight of a woman in a white dress much like Daisy's. She is an older, more mature woman, a knowing woman. She meets his glance momentarily. The camera records Winterbourne's look and then records Daisy's high-spirited reaction to the brawling puppets. She, too, catches Winterbourne's eye but there is a world of difference in these looks. One is flirtatious; the other is lustful. But Winterbourne can respond to neither. He is too caught between cultures to advance toward either European decadence or American innocence. The effect of this vignette is that we see James's hero as effete. Yet we see him so subtly and quickly that we remain dependent upon his view of things to the end, failing to withdraw from him until too late. The secret of James's novel is brought home: the reader—or viewer—doesn't really care about the frivolous Daisy until he himself learns, also too late, what a suspicious prig he has been and how he has betrayed his best instincts for love, as well as his culture, for acquired standards, acquired from the rather cowardly Winterbourne.

In the most melancholy rueful moment of the film Winterbourne comes jauntily along with a bouquet of flowers to Daisy's hotel. Music plays gaily but we hear no dialogue. We are being deliberately held back from Winterbourne and forced to view him. He opens the hotel door and we see through lace on the window pane. He jogs up the stairs, at long last following his instincts and about to rescue Daisy. He is happy, and we who have followed him so long are happy, too, but then we notice there is a shadow on the lace curtain as the door closes. Winterbourne is stopped half-way up the first set of stairs by the voice of the concierge, though we don't hear it. The flowers droop; he descends the stairs and passes out through the door again as the lace turns from brightness to gray. Daisy is dead. We know that Winterbourne has irrevocably lost the best and freshest part of his future.

What then can finally be said of Bogdanovich's film? What thousands of words can be worth pictures unseen? A Wellesian vocabulary and a Jamesian structure mixed with a very personal response have produced a gem-like film whose time did not, and perhaps has not come.

Notes

1. Henry James, *Daisy Miller* (New York: Warner Paperback, 1974), p. 43, contains an interview with Peter Bogdanovich and notes changes between James's 1878 and 1909 editions, especially useful as Bogdanovich constantly made choices between the two; hereafter cited by page references.

2. A useful introduction to James's theories of realism as well as the essay "The Art of Fiction" is included in Jane Benardete, ed., *American Realism* (New York: Capricorn, 1972), pp. 177–225; hereafter cited as "Fiction."

3. "Well, Orson Welles once said to me, 'If I were doing that picture, I'd begin with the boy'" (p. 14).

4. In his novel *The End of the Affair* (Harmondsworth, Middlesex: Penguin, 1962), p. 10, Graham Greene rejoins, "I think at some stage of her book she would have found it necessary to go to bed with a guardsman if only in order to check on the details."

5. Andrew Sarris' introduction to an interview with Welles in *Interviews With Directors* (New York: Avon, 1967), pp. 528–29, comments, "Welles' films are now less American than European in outlook"; "from the beginning, Welles imposed a European temperament on the American cinema."

Dennis Pahl

The sort of centrality that James as a creative artist proposes for himself—as he not only stands behind and lends "assistance" to the central character but also comes to possess him completely—seems clear enough. Yet at this point, let us understand that for all of the claims that James makes in his prefaces for a center of consciousness that would control his fiction, that would serve as an interpretive and metaphysical base for it, James still, perhaps unwittingly, succeeds only in undermining the very notion of this "center," and of himself as a self-possessed, all-commanding critic of his own text. We may take as an illustrative example of James's ironization of the central interpretive consciousness (of the whole idea of "mastery") a short novel that deals explicitly with the problem of the literary critic—*The Aspern Papers*, first published in 1888 and later revised for the New York edition in 1908.

The "center of consciousness" that James employs in this narrative is a nameless critic who tries through devious means to obtain the private letters of a long-deceased American expatriate, the poet Jeffrey Aspern, the objective here being one that is typical of certain forms of literary scholarship: to "lay bare the truth" while still trying to preserve the sanctity of the god-like artist.[1] But just how possible is it for this critic-narrator to discover the truth of Jeffrey Aspern? And what exactly is the cost of such an interpretive venture? The loss of the letters at the end of the narrative—when Miss Tina, rejected in love, decides to destroy them—surely bespeaks the ultimate failure on the critic's part to "read" his beloved poet; yet we should be aware that even before this crucial moment, James's text is bent on dramatizing how the act of reading (criticism) becomes problematic from its outset, doomed as it is to subvert its own intentions toward making a full disclosure of the

Excerpted from "James's Unintentioned 'Decentering' in the Text of *The Aspern Papers*," in *Architects of the Abyss: The Indeterminate Fictions of Poe, Hawthorne, and Melville* by Dennis Pahl (Columbia: University of Missouri Press, 1989), 107–14. Reprinted by permission of the University of Missouri Press. © 1989 by the Curators of the University of Missouri.

truth. Indeed, all of the vehicles and passageways that the critic hopes to use to acquire the prized Aspern papers (and thus "read" the poet) become as well the very obstacles that make impossible the success of his interpretive quest. . . .

The critic originally hopes to "get a footing" (11)—to establish himself firmly within reach of Aspern's "literary remains" (12)—by becoming a lodger in Juliana and her niece's old and dilapidated Venetian palace, whose attached garden, as he tells Miss Tina, is indispensable to his comfort and his literary pursuits. It soon becomes obvious that the garden that the critic feels compelled to "work" (15) and that he "*must* have" (17) functions as what Susanne Kappeler sees as a "metonymic displacement" of the obsessively sought-after papers.[2] Instead of drawing him closer to the object of his desire, that is, to the "treasure" (43) that would reveal the true Jeffrey Aspern, the critic's "working the garden" only moves him further away; it constantly operates as a displacing of the "truth." Indeed, since the garden is positioned next to, or *before*, the part of the house that contains the well-hidden Aspern papers, it thus becomes both literally and figuratively what the critic calls a "pretext" (11).

Here in the garden the critic "cultivates" his "plot" and in so doing turns what we might ordinarily think of as a natural place into the site of art and deception, a place where the critic can practice his fiction. Besides being the locale where he initiates his devilish attempts to seduce the innocent Miss Tina into obtaining for him the precious documents, the garden also becomes a sort of library, furnished with the critic's low table and armchair, with his "books and portfolios," with all that would be required to carry on his usual "business of writing" (45). And though he does spend much of his time here musing on his covert "campaign," he likewise finds amid his newly blossomed flowers an atmosphere ripe for hatching romances and "spinning theories" (48), if not about Jeffrey Aspern then about the poet's primary source of inspiration, his mistress Juliana. Thus the arbour in which the critic has succeeded in installing himself becomes the place where Aspern's life (as well as that life—Juliana's—inextricably bound to it) is not so much comprehended as it is invented, "spun" out or fictionalized, to complete that idealized portrait of the poet that the critic most desires to see. Like the "horrible green shade" (23) that Juliana wears over her failing eyes and like the green box (105) in which Aspern's papers are concealed—both, in their greenness, symbolizing what is "natural" and hence what is "true"—the garden of the Misses Bordereau serves less as a vehicle for knowing the truth about Aspern than as a barrier or, more precisely, as a border that would permanently separate the critic from any "inside" knowledge—or from any knowledge that is inside the house (in this sense the name of the two spinsters, *Bordereau*, is suggestive of the critic's problem).

Because the critic's desire to "read" Jeffrey Aspern can result only in his own invention of the poet's life—a fictionalization—we can thus say that the Aspern papers that he tries to obtain are precisely those papers he has come to compose, *The Aspern Papers*, the narrative that we are now reading. This suggests that the narrator-critic has been, all along, placing himself in the position of Aspern, in effect attempting to identify with him to the extent of usurping the poet's life or, let us say, of trying to repeat it. Our first indication that such is the case is when the critic, conjecturing on how Aspern may have treated some of his more unreasonable women admirers, tries to imagine himself "in his [Aspern's] place—if I could imagine myself in any such a box" (7), thus calling attention to the box of letters that contains the poet's "essence." Later on, the critic admits to feeling the spirit of Aspern, which keeps "perpetual company" with him and assumes the role of his "prompter":

> I had invoked him and he had come; he hovered before me half the time; it was as if his bright ghost had returned to earth to assure me he regarded the affair [of obtaining the letters] as his own no less than as mine and that we should see it fraternally and fondly to a conclusion. (42)

Sensing a "mystic companionship, a moral fraternity with all those who in the past had been in the service of art," the critic clearly sees himself as a kind of artist figure whose muse is Jeffrey Aspern; and so now, longing to have his life be continuous with Aspern's, he is determined to share in "the general romance and the general glory" (43) that was once the domain of that most illustrious expatriated American poet. In a virtual playing out of the scenario of Aspern's life, the critic becomes an American man of letters who has gone abroad and who is now making love to—or, more accurately, seducing—Juliana's more innocent counterpart, Miss Tina (who could well be not Juliana's niece but rather her illegitimate daughter by Aspern). That the critic, throughout the course of his Venetian sojourn, consistently deceives and finally spurns Miss Tina does not necessarily undermine the parallel with Aspern's love affair with Juliana, as we learn early that according to certain "impressions" (none of which the critic can allow himself to believe, so inclined is he to idealize Aspern), the esteemed poet had "treated her [Juliana] badly, just as . . . he had 'served' . . . several other ladies in the same masterful way" (7).

The attempt on the critic-narrator's part to "get into the skin" of his beloved poet may well suggest to us the sort of subjective reading by a central consciousness that James characteristically insists on. But, we may ask, what possibility exists for the critic to be metaphysically *present*—that is, a subject—when his life is so bound up in his other, Jeffrey Aspern (someone whom he has for the most part invented in the first place)? In this world of literature to which he devotes himself, it becomes apparent that while displacing the object of his study he cannot help but displace himself as well, distancing himself as he does from what he would like to know as his own subjective center, his "critical heart."

His loss of a stable position for himself may be said to be emblematized toward the end of the narrative, when, floating aimlessly along the Venetian canals in his gondola, he begins to view the city as "an immense collective apartment," a "splendid common domicile, familiar domestic and resonant." In the Piazza San Marco he envisions an "ornamental corner" and in the palaces and churches "divans of repose" (140). Though such images appear to convey a sense of security, one must realize that the critic here is, more importantly, losing his "ground," experiencing as he does the uncanny collapse of those territorial boundaries that might otherwise be recognizable, that is, the inside and the outside (apartment interiors and city "streets").[3] Moreover, what makes his "position" doubly bizarre is the fact that the seemingly "familiar" and "domestic" landscape in which he finds himself *simultaneously* takes on the unreal, the fictive, aspect of a "theatre with its actors clicking over the bridges," the footways that edge the canals assuming "the importance of a stage." Indeed, by the end of his visionary voyage through the "streets" of Venice, the critic's "home" of a city is shown to strangely transform itself into "little houses of comedy" (140). Such a lack of a sense of place, of a sense of centeredness, may remind us that the old palace in which the critic tries to center himself—and which also becomes his center of interest—is said to be, in Juliana's very first, consequential words, "very far from the centre" (25). Neither can the critic "get a footing" with respect to Aspern or with respect to his own "self."

As the critic in James's story fails to establish himself as a subject, as a center of consciousness, we may now wonder how James himself can maintain a "central" position, can hold his ground as a critical consciousness that would have mastery over, as well as bring unity to, the text. It is in the critical preface to *The Aspern Papers* that James tries to represent himself as an authorial presence or an originating consciousness. Here, as in many of his prefaces, he attempts to locate the "germ" of his narrative, that special moment or set of circumstances in the past that gave rise to the story. Thus he begins his preface: "I not only recover with ease, but I delight to recall, the first impulse given to the idea of 'The Aspern Papers'" (*AN*, 159).

The origin of the story, James argues, is related not to any situation that he might have "'found'" but to one that he was able to recognize once it presented itself to him, as if "'literary history' . . . had in an out-of-the-way corner of the great garden of life thrown off a curious flower that I was to feel worth gathering as soon as I saw it. I got wind of my positive fact, I followed the scent" (*AN*, 159). In a certain way we are reminded here of how Hawthorne claims to have come upon his story of *The Scarlet Letter* in a rag of scarlet cloth that, in availing itself to his sympathetic understanding, communicated "some deep meaning." For James, the "positive fact" whose scent he follows is not an object of cloth but a woman named Jane Clairmont, who was once Byron's mistress. Clairmont, in the "mere strong fact" of her still living and thus of her testifying for "the reality and the closeness of our relation to the past" (*AN*, 162), provides James with the essential ingredient for his story concerning the reclusive mistress of that "American Byron" (*AN*, 166) Jeffrey Aspern.[4]

But if the presence of Jane Clairmont in Florence (where James was residing at the time) is supposed to provide the perceived origin of his story, we might do well to notice how James succeeds only in ironizing this "origin" by making it completely imperceptible, by placing it at such a distance that for it ever to be "perceived" it must first be *invented*. For James it becomes important to keep this vestige of the "Byronic age" (*AN*, 165)—Miss Clairmont—"preciously unseen" in order not to run the risk of "depreciating that romance-value" that her long survival assures. Indeed, her potential for being rendered into artistic form becomes all the greater if she is left unapproached and unread, for as James believes, he would have little to gain by "pretending to read meanings into things [i.e., Miss Clairmont] absolutely sealed and beyond test or proof—to tap a fount of waters that couldn't possibly not have run dry" (*AN*, 161–62). Interested less in accumulating facts than in what he shall "add to them" and how he shall "turn them" (*AN*, 163), James thus keeps himself at a far remove from his story's most original "fact."

When at one moment in the text James speaks of the "palpable imaginable *visitable* past," he seems to be referring to the way in which Miss Clairmont's presence signals a continuity with a previous historic period; but his language, as we notice, is general enough that it may relate as well to his own desire to establish, here in the preface, a continuity with the *story's* past, with *its* origins. Here he draws the analogy between trying to appreciate, or know, the past at too many removes and looking over a garden wall:

> With more moves back the element of the appreciable shrinks—just as the charm of looking over a garden-wall into another garden breaks down when successions of walls appear. The other gardens, those still beyond, may be there, but even by use of our longest ladder we are baffled and bewildered—the view is mainly a view of barriers. (*AN*, 164)

What James is describing here is the difficulty of ever recovering the origin of his narrative, of ever laying bare the secret truth of his story; for as it is suggested early in the preface, there is nothing but barriers, one after another, to subvert whatever "revisiting, re-appropriating impulse" James may have. Seeking that "general impression" of Florence that was supposed to help give rise to his story, James compares the entertaining of this impression to "the fashion of our intercourse with Iberians or Orientals" whose form of courtesy is such that "we peep at most into two or three of the chambers of their hospitality, with the rest of the case stretching beyond our ken and escaping our penetration" (*AN*, 160). The sense that multiple barriers stand in the way of making palpable or visitable that past wherein the story was born is further emphasized when James, envisioning past settings, sees "in too thick and rich a retrospect . . . my old Venice of 'The Aspern Papers,' . . . the still earlier one of Jeffrey Aspern himself, and . . . even the comparatively recent Florence that was to drop into my ear the solicitation of these things" (*AN*, 161). Each of these remembrances simply serves as another "wall" that obscures James's view of that "garden" in which his story truly began.[5]

The final barrier that James must confront is, ironically enough, the very preface that he is writing; for instead of acting as a kind of critical-historic foundation for his narrative, it becomes but another fiction, in some ways no different from the story it is supposed to introduce. James seems in his preface almost to repeat the quest of his narrator-critic in the story, searching as he does for the truth of his "papers," trying to link them with some previous moment in history. The images of garden walls and impenetrable chambers, all of which play such an important role in the narrator's plight, reappear in the preface, serving James in the same way as they do the narrator-critic: as representations of the obstacles that would prevent one from ever determining the truth of the text. Because James imports the basic elements of his fictional discourse into his own critical preface, it is no longer possible to discern where the boundaries between fiction and criticism properly lie. Decentering himself as a "center of consciousness," as a self-same critical mind that stands *before* the book (originating and dominating it), James thus reduces to a fairy tale the notion that—as he says in another preface—"to criticise is to appreciate, to appropriate, to take intellectual possession, to establish in fine a relation with the criticised thing and make it one's own" (*AN*, 155).

Notes

1. Henry James, *The Aspern Papers*, New York Edition of *The Novels and Tales of Henry James* (New York: Charles Scribner's Sons, 1908), p. 90. All future references to *The Aspern Papers* pertain to this edition. All references to James's prefaces are to *The Art of the Novel*, ed. R. P. Blackmur; hereafter cited in the text as *AN*.

2. Susanne Kappeler, *Writing and Reading in Henry James*, London: MacMillan Press, 1980, p. 34.

3. For a discussion of "territories" in the novel, see Rosemary F. Franklin, "The Military Metaphors and the Organic Structure of Henry James's 'The Aspern Papers'." *Arizona Quarterly* 32, no. 4 (Winter 1976):327–40. I would argue, against Franklin, that the military metaphors call attention not to formal unity but to violence, rupture, and difference in James's text.

4. Though James cites Miss Clairmont's presence in Italy as the most essential "fact," he also points out that two additional items were important to his story, one having to do with an "ardent Shelleyite" who failed to obtain certain Shelley documents from Miss Clairmont and the other concerning "a younger female relative of the ancient woman" (*AN*, 162–63).

5. We may well view Jeffrey Aspern here as a barrier to truth if we consider that "behind him" stands the poet Byron and behind Byron probably a long line of romantics that includes even such fictitious lovers as Shakespeare's Italian, Romeo (52).

William R. Goetz

It would seem that by now critics must have studied every facet of *The Turn of the Screw*, but one of the most problematic parts of the text, the short "frame" section that precedes the governess's narrative, has been examined in a rather limited way. Almost invariably it has been treated as a sort of prolongation of the story, which introduces us to the setting and characters (especially the young heroine) and perhaps furnishes us with some clues for judging the reliability of the narrative that follows. The pursuit of such clues is certainly valid, but I would like to propose a different use for the "frame," and consider it not so much as an informative background to the principal narrative but as an exemplary scene by means of which James tells us how to read his tale. In this light, these opening pages of the text can be regarded as establishing a protocol for reading. This protocol will not tell us how to choose between the well-known interpretations of the tale—how to break through the deadlock produced by the Freudian and the literalist (or fantom) readings[1]—but it may well tell us why we *cannot* choose, why James's story has proved so intractable to any definitive exegesis. This resistance of the tale does not derive, I believe, from any vague "richness" of content but from the deliberately complex hermeneutic structure it embodies. This structure is revealed largely through the "frame" (a term I shall continue to use until its inadequacy can be shown) and the special questions it raises, questions about the different types of narrative that exist, and about the kinds of meaning and authority that these different narrative types entail.

One of the most evident features of the "frame" is that it consists of an *oral* story-telling scene which introduces a *written* narrative. In itself, it consists of two parts: the "frame" proper, mainly direct report describing the fireside scene with Douglas and his listeners, and then a couple of pages of "prologue" (the narrator's own term) cast largely as

Excerpted from "The 'Frame' of *The Turn of the Screw:* Framing the Reader In," *Studies in Short Fiction* 18 (1981): 71–74. Reprinted by permission of *Studies in Short Fiction*.

indirect report informing us about the governess's visits to the uncle of Miles and Flora in London and about the conditions of her contract. We also learn here about the provenance of the long written text that will follow. We are told that this text will be the anonymous first-person narrator's own "exact transcript" of the governess's manuscript, which he has received from Douglas, who in turn had it directly from the authoress.

In terms of narrative strategy, then, the main function of the opening section is to present an oral situation which explains and motivates the written text that follows. This function conforms to a long novelistic tradition and does not seem to provide any special reason for questioning the authenticity of the text that Douglas will read. The pertinent question these pages raise is not the reliability of this text in particular so much as the difference between oral stories and written texts in general. What traits of the oral story-telling scene are brought to special attention, and thereby implicitly contrasted with the traits of the written narrative that comes after it?

As one might expect, James's characterization of the oral audience is ambiguous. On the one hand, the rapid evocation of an atmosphere conducive to ghost-stories seems to be a serious setting of mood, a way of molding the generic expectations of *us*, the literary audience. On the other hand, we cannot help noticing that our counterparts within the fiction, the chiefly female audience (as it seems) gathered around the fire, are depicted as frivolous and fatuous. They indeed seem like those "merely witless" readers whom James mentions, only to dismiss them, in his Preface to the tale.[2] Their fatuity is recorded in the comments and questions they put to Douglas, in their way of trying to force his story to yield us answers to questions that are either premature or simply—the wrong questions. To an inquiry about the mode of Miss Jessell's death, Douglas replies: "'That will come out: I don't anticipate.'"[3] Even the narrator, who seems at times to be the privileged member of Douglas's audience, the one whom Douglas himself deems to be most apt to understand the story, is capable of making the wrong inference. When the narrator hastily assures the others that "the story will tell" with whom the governess was in love, Douglas pulls him up short: "'The story *won't* tell . . . not in any literal vulgar way'" (italics in original).

This last response reveals the limits, as well as the privileges, of oral narrative. The oral audience is privileged precisely because it can ask these questions, can indulge in an actual dialogue with the author (or here the transmitter) of the story, and force him to suggest the way in which it should be understood. But, try as they may, they cannot get him to reveal its secret. On the contrary, he tells them that the text will never reveal its secret in the "literal vulgar way" they demand. If their curiosity about the text is vulgar, that is *because* it is literal. Any successful interpretation, Douglas is implying, is going to have to go beyond the letter of the text. But Douglas stops far short of endorsing any particular "deep" or symbolic reading, the Freudian one or any other. The protocol for reading (or listening) that he intimates here is almost entirely negative, consisting only of caveats.

The final striking thing about this introductory oral scene is that it breaks off here, for good. When we speak by analogy of the picture "frame," we think of a border that sets off the fictional work from reality on all sides, continuously. But the "frame" of *The Turn of the Screw* is asymmetrical: it does not return at the end. Its absence at the end may seem natural to us, since we are so immersed by that point in the governess's voice that we have likely forgotten that any other voices preceded it. In fact, however, the governess does not exist as a voice at all but pre-eminently as a written text, one that cannot be questioned, one that is both a court of final appeal and (as generations of critical debate have now proved) an unsatisfying, incomplete testament. That the governess's narrative is, taken by itself, incomplete and even incomprehensible is something that the narrator has taken pains to tell us. He introduces his "prologue" with the following: "It appeared that the narrative he [Douglas] had promised to read us really required for a proper intelligence a few words of prologue." One is tempted to add that for a truly "proper intelligence" the tale would also have required a few words of epilogue. But such an epilogue, in the form of an open dialogue between oral teller and audience, is exactly what is missing. At the end both Douglas and the governess are inaccessible, and interpretations of the text must remain undecidable. Either they must run beyond the given text (as the Freudian reading does), trying to complete the governess's narrative by saying for her what she did not quite say, or they remain within her text, or short of it (the literalist reading), overlooking many signals that the text is clearly giving off.

The problem is that the governess cannot simply be circumvented; she is not merely a narrator within the tale, reliable or unreliable, whose vision can be put into proper perspective by some adjustment on the reader's part. The "frame" shows us through its incompleteness that there is no easy recourse to an author, whether implied or real, just as for the governess herself there is to be no recourse to the master, her employer. Douglas describes the "main condition" of the girl's employment in these terms: " 'That she should never trouble him [her employer]—but never, never: neither appeal nor complain nor write about anything. . . .' " Thus before the governess's narrative begins we witness a shift of authority from the master's shoulders to her own, with the master clearly acting here as a surrogate for the author, James. Like the Duke in *Measure for Measure,* this Jamesian master arranges his players, instructs them in their roles, sets them in motion, and disappears. Only, unlike Shakespeare's Duke, he will never return.

The governess's memory of her employer, however, remains with her throughout her story, and she continually yearns for a renewed contact with him, for a repetition of that primal *oral* scene of her interview with him. But, being caught now within her own literary text, she can only *write* letters to him, and even these she can scarcely bear to send. To the finish she remains a victim of a disabling paradox, which is that she can prove herself worthy of the master only by allowing him to forget about her. The text becomes the prison within which she is entrapped, along with the other characters. The governess and Mrs. Grose, Miles and Flora, even Peter and Miss Jessel: it is tempting to see them as six characters vainly in search of an author.[4]

The dilemma of the governess is a paradigm for our dilemma, as the tale's readers. In imitation of the governess, critics have always felt the need to go to an outside authority for help: not to the master of Bly but to James himself (in his Prefaces and letters, for example) or to Freud. In a way these appeals are encouraged, even demanded, by the enticing incompletion of the text, but at the same time the text is demonstrating that these appeals cannot really cut the Gordian knot of the story's interpretation. On the other hand, if we are tacitly told, as the governess is told explicitly, that we cannot write for outside help, this does not mean that we are given complete license to arrive at our own subjective conclusions. If *The Turn of the Screw* is an exemplary fiction for hermeneutic problems, this is not because it will support radically divergent, even mutually exclusive, readings, but because it obliges the reader to choose one reading and at the same time to see the inadequacy of his choice. The governess's choice has been to believe in the ghosts. Her dilemma, which is also ours, is that of being given an authority of which she is not really capable, but which she cannot shake off either. The result is the continual tension between her longing to escape from the text by returning to the master and her constant fall back into her imprisonment. *The Turn of the Screw* is indeed, as James said, "an *amusette* to catch those not easily caught,"[5] but this is a riddle that teaches us something essential about the necessary dangers of interpretation.

Notes

1. I am in agreement with Walter Benn Michael's recent statement that no real solution has yet been offered to the "horns of this dilemma." In general, Michael's essay is the one I have found to be most compatible with my own reading of *The Turn of the Screw*. See Michael, "Writers Reading: James and Eliot," in *Modern Language Notes* 91 (October 1976): 827–49.

2. In *The Art of the Novel: Critical Prefaces*, ed. R. P. Blackmur (New York: Scribner's, 1934), p. 172.

3. *The Turn of the Screw* (New York: W.W. Norton, 1966). This, the Norton Critical Edition, follows the text of the New York Edition. If no chapter number is given, the quotation comes from the novella's opening section.

4. For the characters' general obsession with getting in touch with the master, see for instance chapters 12, 13, 16, 17, and 18.

5. *The Art of the Novel*, p. 172.

James W. Gargano

In "The Beast in the Jungle," Henry James attempts to make a formidable dramatic action out of what he calls in one of his most interesting prefaces "a great negative adventure."[1] The point of the story is the pointlessness of John Marcher's subordination of reality to his belief that a unique and possibly terrible destiny awaits him. Marcher's special fate (to be "*the* man, to whom nothing on earth was to have happened") is made vivid by his involvement or noninvolvement with May Bartram, a devoted companion who represents the possibility of a more fruitful life. In essence, "The Beast in the Jungle" traces Marcher's tortuous route to total negation through a series of episodes in which he fails to perceive, or, as James puts it, "is afraid to recognise what he incidentally misses" (p. xi). Appropriately, Marcher's death-like withdrawal from life reaches its climax at May's grave where his adventure is completed not in a traditional physical ordeal, but in his shrinking from a monster created by his own psychic urgencies and imagination.

James faced the technical problem inherent in dramatizing nonlife by shifting his artistic focus from narrative incidents to clusters of images that mark the stages of his protagonist's psychological evasions. By filling the void resulting from Marcher's inaction, imagery itself becomes a kind of dominant action, an adumbration of the subconscious energies of Marcher's inner life. The inventiveness that most fiction writers expend on plot James thus invests in interrelated images and symbols that tell a tense story of omissions and possibilities rather than accomplished deeds. What emerges is an engrossing tapestry or mosaic made up of roads not taken, wrong turns fearfully followed, and chances missed. Ultimately, all the withdrawals, denials, and suppressions gather paradoxically into a symbol of startling emotional violence.

Both clear and suggestive, James's imagery possesses sharp immediacy and almost endless radiation. Even the most perfunctory reader

Excerpted from "Imagery as Action in 'The Beast in the Jungle,'" *Arizona Quarterly* 42 (1986): 351–67. Reprinted by permission of *Arizona Quarterly*.

will grasp the author's purport in naming his contrasting characters Marcher and May. More careful readers, however, will see ramifications of meaning in other examples of seasonal imagery: the opening incident at Weatherend with its faint lure of October light; May and Marcher's comedy of terror in April; and the graveyard denouement in the fall that revives, with stunning variation, the April fiasco. The same mixture of obviousness and allusiveness controls most of the images in "The Beast in the Jungle" and keeps the novella from hardening into allegory or evaporating into supersubtle implications. . . .

An examination of James's imagery as the major vehicle of his thought in "The Beast in the Jungle" will reveal its pervasiveness, its closely woven texture, and its function in designating the phases of Marcher's fascinating psychological disintegration. Clearly, James's art depends most heavily on images associated with seasons, links or connections, light, and burial.[2] With metaphysical subtlety, he also employs a complex of sibyl-seeress-sphinx images to elaborate May Bartram's role as a counterintelligence whose glimpses into Marcher's mind date many of the crises of his inner history. Finally, to achieve his almost surrealistic climax, James relies on violent beast imagery to conclude Marcher's negative, actionless adventure. . . .

Because seasonal imagery pervades almost every facet and nuance of the six sections of "The Beast in the Jungle," it deserves special attention. James employs it in naming and defining his characters, setting his scenes, stressing motivation, and giving poetic coloration and resonance to his theme of the unlived life. It is so sensitively stitched into the texture of the work that it might be called the figure in the carpet.

The overall purpose of the seasonal imagery is to contrast the unnatural "law" of Marcher's life with the law governing natural processes. James, of course, associates Marcher with the end of winter and the possibility of spring, but unlike the month of March, the protagonist possesses no new or creative energies. Time passes and he remains immovably constant. James allows him occasional stirrings of life, but these stirrings occur in the depths of his being and are—until the end of the novella—overruled by an emotional rigidity stemming from his view of himself as someone mysteriously placed outside the context of ordinary humanity. Whereas the seasons flow into one another and are part of a changing order, James's main character is first seen at Weatherend, an English country house where natural fluidity seems to end and a kind of stasis prevails. Even May Bartram, who should symbolize growth, typifies pallid possibilities and has little energizing power for

Marcher. She affects him as a faded memory to which he can attach no importance: having fully blotted out his past life because in a real sense it has not happened, he cannot even recall that he had met her in his youth and confided his obsession to her. Indeed, James shows him as pathetically desiring "to invent something, to get her to make-believe with him that some passage of a romantic or critical kind *had* originally occurred. He was really reaching out in imagination—as against time" (p. 67).

As the interval between March and May, April has a sinister importance in James's novella. It looms as the cruelest month not because, as in T. S. Eliot's wasteland, it compels new growth, but because it acts as an unnatural, permanent barrier. For James, April does not serve as a bridge but as a lacuna, a gap never successfully spanned. It represents the germinal vigor almost entirely absent from Marcher's makeup. It represents the unruly and agitated time of the beast which in healthy lives must be lived through and thus accommodated to the procession of the months. To bypass it is to miss the initiating forces that stimulate and assure efflorescence and harvest. Predictably, then, what doesn't happen in "The Beast in the Jungle" actually does and does not take place in April: James shows that, though Marcher is physically present at his unique destiny, he witnesses no action as the beast springs. With his story beginning and ending in the fall, Marcher has more symbolic affinity with that season than with either April or May.

James places his climactic April scene with great care in the fourth section of "The Beast in the Jungle." It therefore begins the second half of the novella with the tragic assurance that the protagonist will never discover in May Bartram the quickening force of the month for which she is named. This conclusion is reached, however, only after three preparatory sections in which highly dramatic images establish the characters' identities, their relations to each other, and their reactions to seasonal change and time. . . .

Light imagery . . . affords a clue throughout the novella of the characters' clarity of perception and their fund of vitality. It is indicative of Marcher's original state of mind that he "recalls" the smallest detail of his earlier meeting with May and figuratively sees the dark past suddenly lit. In an artful use of light to give action and movement to his narrative, James compares Marcher's confidence in his memory to an "impression operating like the torch of a lamplighter who touches into flame . . . a long row of gas-jets" (p. 64). Imagery shapes the scene into a neat drama of Marcher's psychic ineptitude and his need to believe he shared a past with May. His brilliant illumination, which should prove a transforming acuteness, only proves to be a trick of his imagination as she refutes his version of their original encounter, leaving him comically in the dark. Imagery continues to function actively when May informs him of his earlier confession and "a light broke for him." Already preparing for later developments, James characterizes the light coming from Marcher's unaided sight as weak and misleading and that coming from May as genuine and revelatory. Her perceptions are, and continue to be, trustworthy and illuminating; before the end of the first section, Marcher himself comes to place implicit faith in "the light in her eyes."

Like his imagery of links and light, James's burial imagery offers a slight hint that Marcher may emerge from his privacy and adopt a creative interest in life. For example, Marcher's conjectures about his first encounter with May turn on the possibility that what happened then may be "too deeply buried—too deeply (didn't it seem?) to sprout after so many years" (p. 66). Yet, sprout it does as May attaches herself to a man whom she has a right to treat as a lunatic. It might not even be extravagant to propose, as some critics have, that James consciously staged one of the initial meetings between the ill-sorted pair "at Pompeii, on an occasion when they had been present there at an important find"—when the past came unexpectedly to light in the present (p. 65).[3] Marcher, with May's necessary assistance, unearths something precious—a past confidence, a spontaneous approach to a shared life— that had been buried, if not for centuries, at least for ten round years. The vexing question inherent in the burial imagery is, however, whether he will use his knowledge to foster a new relationship or to serve his old monomania. Obviously, May's freedom to attach herself to him derives from her roots in reality—her roots, if it is not too much of a conceit, in April. Will Marcher, James appears to tease his readers into asking, improve upon the one generous act of his early life and be worthy of May's proferred aid? . . .

The second section, however, moves from the emergence of opportunity to near fatalism as James dramatizes May's certainty that Marcher will never outgrow the fatuity that makes him incapable of change. The section is framed by the opening declaration of May's knowledge ("The fact that she 'knew'") and her closing reliance on his inveterate blindness ("You'll never find out"). Unpromisingly, the goodly bond slackens into a loveless avoidance if not parody of marriage supported by the plausible argument, masking a fear of commitment, that a gentleman cannot ask a lady to accompany him on a "tiger-hunt." James's image patterns make it clear that as May desires the reality rather than the semblance of closeness, Marcher's sensibility narrows and his openness to the world's charm decreases; he retains his "dissimulation" toward the "people in London whose invitations he accepted and repaid," and, worst of all, he values his connection with May only because she supplies him with another pair of eyes with which to scrutinize his obsession. Link and bonding imagery paradoxically convicts Marcher of the cardinal Jamesian sin of exploiting a human being as if he or she were a means or tool to further egotistic ends.

In a little drama all its own, burial imagery also undergoes a radical change in the second section of "The Beast in the Jungle." James presents Marcher as at first buoyed up by the discovery that May is privy to his secret, which figures as "the buried treasure of her knowledge." Almost exuberantly, Marcher savors the good fortune of his new companionship: "He had with his own hands dug up this little hoard, brought to light . . . the object of value the hiding-place of which he had, after putting it into the ground himself, so strangely, so long forgotten" (p. 76). By the end of the section, however, James's imagery exposes Marcher's mismanagement of his excavated treasure. Moreover, in possibly the major twist of the second section, May now assumes importance as the possessor of a secret of her own, the closely guarded perception that by ceasing to respond to human vibrations Marcher is well on his way toward his destiny. This second secret, earned by shrewd observation and deeply hidden until the graveyard scene at the end of the novella, extends the burial imagery and serves as the dramatic center of Marcher's curiosity as he seeks to know what she knows. Still, he will pathologically fail to see that May and not any secret is the real treasure that might liberate him from his fate.

In perhaps the most audacious image in the second section, James begins to transform May into a Cassandra figure, one of the most penetrating of his uncommonly penetrating women. With a metaphysical élan worthy of John Donne, he ascribes to her an "indescribable" art which consists in the "feat of at once—or perhaps it was only alternately—meeting the [Marcher's] eyes from in front and mingling her own vision, as from over his shoulder, with their peep through the apertures" (p. 82). Obviously, May's vision has assumed an almost prophetesslike acuteness enabling her to formulate the law of Marcher's being: in possession of a light denied him, she penetrates his masks and hollow relationships and beholds him changeless and immovable in the flux of time. Indeed, as "they grew older together," her genuine attachment to him helps her to believe that he will never feel enough sympathy with another human being to "find out" what she has learned about him.

In the second section, James's skillful blurring of the time scheme of his novella emphasizes that for his protagonist the years accomplish nothing but their own passing. Though the beast crouches in "the twists and turns of the months and the years," Marcher exists physically *in* time while psychically *out* of it, sinking deeper and deeper into a temporal void, a constant autumn. No action takes place, but James's imagery invests his characters' inaction with developing drama. Unable to see that May comes to him like a new spring, Marcher is a striking example of what Henry Adams, in "The Dynamo and the Virgin," thought of as modern man's insensitivity to woman as a generative and dynamic force. By looking outside of time and beyond his own and May's innate energies, he perverts nature's laws instead of attuning himself to their rhythm. May, in contrast, achieves a kind of consummation through a life of effort and love even though she already assumes the burden of the sphinxlike intelligence who, in the fourth section, ponders the riddle of life and lost opportunities.

In the short third section, James's imagery pushes his vivid drama of consciousness toward its fatal turning point by intensifying the emptiness of the Marcher-May relationship and May's sibyllike clairvoyance. All is artful preparation for the April scene in which the "negative adventure" reaches its climax of inaction, imperceptiveness, and unfulfillment. With acuteness couched in a wry tone of social satire, James presents May and Marcher almost jesting about the meaning of their long-standing tie. With a levity with undercurrents of mordant irony, she states that in the eyes of the world she seems a woman who has had her man (which she hasn't) while he passes for a man like another (which he isn't). Still, May's secret knowledge makes her sensitive to the double entendre in their banter: her language implies the truth and yet guards her secret, salves his doubts, and still gives him enough encouragement to make a closer and more binding approach. With subtle indirection, she addresses her words to his inner ear or to some recess in him uncontaminated by his obsession. Nevertheless, despite the tactful ministry of her love, he clings to his mock link with her and maintains his separateness under the guise of nearness. There is little likelihood that he will be capable of making use of his approaching April opportunity.

The seasonal imagery in this section, however, indicates that March-er's sensibility is not impermeable. Although he fails to pick up May's subliminal messages, he begins to heed the increasingly overt lesson of time. He worries that the fleeting months and years will leave him "no margin" for his adventure. He discovers time's predatoriness in May's illness and aging: "She looked older because, inevitably, after so many years, she *was* old, or almost; which was of course true in still greater measure of her companion" (p. 95). He is frightened by the bleak possibility that May will die unprivileged to see the enactment of his doom, and he is appalled that as a victim of time he may have been "sold." Indeed, he almost achieves real feeling and knowledge when he experiences the "dread of losing her by some catastrophe": ultimately, though, his brooding and fear are only new forms of his vast emotional expenditure on the road to inaction.

Nevertheless, the time imagery of the third section marks an important milestone on Marcher's journey. After the first chapter launches him on a fresh start and the second, with a countermovement, exposes that start as false, the third chapter reveals an incompatibility between his rationalizations about himself and his deeper, subconscious stresses. James ingeniously suspends Marcher in an inconclusive state of semiapprehension. May's subtle innuendos, the rapacity of the seasons, and the imminence of May's death have so upset his equilibrium that though his mind clings from habit to his own concerns, it is invaded by ambivalences and a new appreciation of May's humanity. He praises her for being "kind" and "beautiful"; he feels "sorry for her"; and he wonders before dismissing the thought, whether her death could be the fatality he has so long expected. He so identifies with her plight that as her health deteriorates, he imagines himself as suffering from "some disfigurement of his outer person." The train of surprises set in motion by her helplessness before time causes him to dread existence without her as an empty prospect.

Clearly, James complicates Marcher's psychological state by showing him as a man of divided sensibility who knows that he does not know what his subconscious is trying to reveal to him; he cannot convert into thought what May has begun to make him grope toward. Marcher thus acts according to earlier, fixed assumptions no longer relevant to his altered situation. He cannot quite grasp the idea that May embodies the primal creativity operating with inevitability in nature but capable of being rejected by narcissistic man. With a greater than usual emphasis, James makes his heroine suggest both a season and a woman, a natural and a human impulse: she affirms an eternal principle of growth and fruition, but as a mere woman, she can only urge by gesture and circumlocution that Marcher break out of himself and live to the fullest reaches of his humanity. Her physical breakdown signals that Marcher is approaching his last chance to "save" himself through her. At the conclusion of the third chapter, however, with her secret intact and her light fading, he appears an unlikely candidate to restore her and himself to health.

With a heavy reliance on light and linkage imagery, James places his climactic April scene in the fourth section of "The Beast in the Jungle." The strange couple meet on an April day whose "light" inauspiciously produces a "sadness sharper than the greyest hours of autumn." The fireplace in May's house has no fire or light, and James declares that "it would never see a fire again" (p. 98). The cold fireplace corresponds to the "cold light" in May's eyes and both prefigure a fundamental loss of spirit as Marcher imagines that "her light might at any instant go out." With little light at her disposal (and with the "perfect old French clock" ticking time away), May still sees April as a possible saving link between herself and Marcher. Insisting that "It's never too late," she makes a last effort toward union (as she had made the first) and walks toward him "with a gliding step" that "diminishes the distance between them." The reverberations which James's imagery has by this time achieved lend a special emotional power to her desperate effort at connection: her movement brings her "nearer" and "close" to Marcher and all but speaks, with a language all its own, with "some finer emphasis" (p. 105). Nevertheless, he remains frozen in self-concern and, wondering what she has to give him, maintains his separateness.

The ingenuity of the April scene consists in James's creation of an episode of simultaneous action and nonaction, tragic recognition and comic blindness, springtime possibilities and autumnal bleakness. Marcher, who keeps waiting for the answer to his question, seals his doom on that crucial April day. For May, with her "face shining at him, her contact imponderably pressing," the negative adventure has been all too positive. His climax has the chill of anticlimax, but as he "gape[s] . . . for her revelation," she closes her eyes as if she has seen too much and then gives way to "a slow fine shudder" (p. 106). Although James does not belabor his point, any reader responsive to the pressure of the novella's imagery can interpret the quiet melodrama of May's "slow fine shudder" and Marcher's "fear that she might die

167

without giving him light" (p. 106). She has seen the beast leap while Marcher innocently and expectantly questions the vacancy. In her resultant collapse, she surrenders her function and all hope for him, and when he explicitly asks what has happened, she makes a sphinxlike pronouncement on his doom: "What *was* to." The light she brought to their affair has been extinguished and her bold experiment at linking him to life has been frustrated.

May's dual role as discerning intelligence and as the rejected spirit of spring culminates in two seemingly strained but entirely successful images. The first, May as sphinx, reveals her possession of the secret to the riddle that has puzzled Marcher since the end of the novella's opening pages; aged, and her face marked with innumerable "fine lines" that might have been "etched by a needle," she resembles a "serene and exquisite but impenetrable sphinx" who has attained ultimate wisdom. But the clue to her helpless sagacity is contained in the image almost implausibly intertwined with that of the sphinx.[4] May's faded "green scarf, her wax-white face, and her soft white draperies" make her look like a lily: "She was a sphinx, yet with her white petals and green fronds she might have been a lily too—only an artificial lily, wonderfully imitated and constantly kept, without dust or stain, though not exempt from a slight droop and a complexity of faint creases, under some clear glass bell" (pp. 98–99).

James's imagistic language resolves itself into a more compelling and intellectual drama than is usually conveyed by crude physical action. It leaves no doubt that Marcher has turned the natural woman into an artificial being preserved in an inviolate, inhuman state. Far from being the free germinal impulse she should naturally be, May is an object in a glass cage, a perfect victim of a monstrous egotist afraid to respond to her unspoken pleas.

The fifth section of "The Beast in the Jungle" begins with a variation on the sphinx motif and ends with Marcher's obsession with the buried secret (no longer likely to prove a treasure) that he must now exhume without May's help. James also weaves light imagery into his expanding psychological mosaic. However, the most moving motif in the special pathos of this section is that of the goodly bond established in the first section as Marcher's link to new possibilities is now permanently dissolved.

First, however, James refines upon the sphinx image and presents May, in her last conversation with Marcher, as a tender sibyl who speaks in riddles and mysteries. Although James describes her as communicating "with the perfect straightness of a sibyl," Marcher feels that her words are "all beyond him" (pp.110–11). The scene takes on structure, intellectual play, and emotional density from the energy of its controlling image. May tells Marcher strange and bewildering things that he believes without understanding: for instance, she convinces him that, despite his unawareness of it, he has met his fate; she assures him that he has crossed an unseen line and is now firmly established on "the other side" of his experience. She troubles him by warning him away from the knowledge of what has happened because "it's too much"; yet, she minimizes it by declaring it safely past. Her sibylline utterances leave him with the mournful sense of having had his ordeal and, at the same time, having been cheated of it. He suspects her of telling him that "his light has failed" but he ambivalently feels that as she speaks, "some light, hitherto hidden, had shimmered across his vision" (p. 113).

May's death functions as an ironic climax of the linking imagery by leaving Marcher stranded like some Hawthornian outcast of the universe. As if to emphasize the consequences of his mock hero's insensitivity to May's appeals, James shows him as having less claim to be one of her mourners than "the stupidest fourth cousin"; he is bereft, without the dignity of being able to claim any relationship with the woman who has been his mainstay. In terms of hard, practical reality, he and May had had no bond, no real intimacy. So Marcher deplores his outcast state, his banishment to the jungle that has grown more "spacious," stilled, and vacant. Even his visit to May's grave does not change his condition: it is as if the woman who offered him a link with life at Weatherend has broken all connection with him as "her two names [on the tombstone] became a pair of eyes that didn't know him" (p. 118).

The fifth section concludes with intermingled light and burial images that have the ring of a final verdict—Marcher beats "his forehead against the fact of the secret" kept in the grave and, in a bitter echo of May's Weatherend confession when a "light broke for him," now "no palest light broke" (p. 118). Nevertheless, James plants clues that these negative images will be replaced by unnaturally active ones: that his protagonist will see a lurid light, make an unexpected and cata-strophic connection, and unearth a new and terrible "treasure." Before her death, May had been distressed that Marcher might be close to seeing his own folly and had put him off with kind ruses. But the accumulating data of his subconscious life will belatedly force him to see what she has seen. In fact, in his final colloquy with May, a "light . . . shimmered across his vision" only to be lost in darkness. Before it vanished, however, "the gleam had already become for him an idea" that would take the shape of a beastly nemesis (p. 113).

In the last section, James arrives at his psychological climax by re-capitulating the major motifs of his novella: The fall day of the con-cluding graveyard scene recalls the dim October light at Weatherend, where Marcher's alliance with May began; light, however, returns with phantasmagoric effect; the riddle of the buried, sphinxlike woman is spelled out with brutal distinctness; and the April horror Marcher had once failed to see weirdly returns in the deadness of the autumn.

James sets the scene of his protagonist's epiphany in a "garden of death," where Marcher rests "on the low stone table that bore May Bartram's name." Having severed all connection with the world and even with himself, Marcher revisits the cemetery to renew his tie with "the creature beneath the sod" and to get "back into his own pres-ence"; he is ready for the shock given him by a grief-stricken man at a nearby grave, a man whose "ravaged" face expresses the full meaning of the goodly bond. What the sphinxlike woman had tried to tell Marcher becomes manifest: "The sight that had just met his eyes named to him, as in letters of quick flame, something he had utterly, insanely missed" (p. 124). Obviously an alter ego who is blest in spite of his affliction, the mourner conveys a message that Marcher might have learned from Pompeii, from May's constant movement toward him, and from her once bright and then failing light. Significantly, Marcher's enlightenment comes as images of light succeed one another with ghastly coruscations: James refers to "a train of fire," a meaning which "flared," a "smoky torch," an "illumination" that "blazed to the zenith" (p. 125).

As already noted, the opening scene at Weatherend, like the final episode, takes place in the fall of the year "when the leaves were thick in the alleys." The major difference between the two scenes, however, is the difference between a promising prospect and a bitter harvest. May, the original light-bringer and spirit of the "goodly bond," is dead, and the fate she could not save Marcher from has been realized. The last incident also resembles and contrasts with the earlier April scene in section four: April, the symbol of possible connection and actual separation, returns as a surrogate for May and functions as the law of retribution. Moreover, Marcher's imaginary re-creation of the April day ironically completes James's book of hours and seasons with the conversion of a negative adventure into charged sensation. In direct contrast to the earlier April scene, the concluding fall-April episode contains an outburst of melodramatic imagery. The hush becomes a rush, Marcher's avoidances end in confrontation, and his deferred expectations shape themselves into an abnormal reality. In describing the "horror of awakening," James does not sentimentally grant his protagonist a reprieve or allow the violated May to make a redemptive speech from the grave: sickened with self-knowledge, Marcher experiences the full measure of his fate, and the beast, thwarted once, makes his destined leap.

Notes

1. *The Novels and Tales of Henry James*, the New York Edition, vol. 17 (New York: Charles Scribner's Sons, 1909), x. All future references to "The Beast in the Jungle" will be to this edition; pagination will be indicated in the text.

2. Martha Banta deals sensitively with such "value" images as "gain" and "loss," and she incidentally touches upon burial imagery in *Henry James and the Occult: The Great Extension* (Bloomington: Indiana University Press, 1972), 194–212.

3. Cf. James Ellis, "The Archaeology of Ancient Rome: Sexual Metaphor in 'The Beast in the Jungle,'" *The Henry James Review* 6 (Fall 1984): 27–31 ("Pompeii then serves as a metaphor not for hollowness or death but rather for life rediscovered," p. 29.)

4. William Nance relates the sphinxian imagery to the Oedipus myth: "'The Beast in the Jungle': Two Versions of Oedipus," *Studies in Short Fiction* 13 (1976): 433–40.

Chronology

1843   Henry James born 15 April at 21 Washington Place, New York City.

1843–44   Taken abroad by parents.

1845–55   Spends childhood in Albany and New York City.

1855–58   Attends schools in Geneva, London, and Paris and is privately tutored.

1858   Lives in Newport, Rhode Island.

1859   Attends school in Geneva; studies in Bonn.

1862–63   Studies at Harvard Law School.

1864   Family settles in Boston and then in Cambridge. Early book reviews published.

1865   First story in *Atlantic Monthly.*

1869–70   Travels in England, France, and Italy. His cousin, Minny Temple, dies.

1870   Returns to Cambridge, publishes first novel, *Watch and Ward,* in serialized form in *Atlantic Monthly.*

1874–75   Tries New York City, writing literary journalism for *Transatlantic Nation.* First three books published: *Transatlantic Sketches, A Passionate Pilgrim and Other Tales,* and *Roderick Hudson.*

1875–76   Spends year in Paris with Turgenev, Flaubert, Edmond de Goncourt, Zola, Daudet.

1877   *The American.*

1878   "Daisy Miller," first published in *Cornhill Magazine,* establishes his fame on both sides of the Atlantic. *French Poets and Novelists. The Europeans.*

1879   *Daisy Miller: A Study / An International Episode / Four Meetings. The Madonna of the Future and Other Tales.*

1880   *Confidence.*

1881	*The Portrait of a Lady. Washington Square / The Pension Beaurepas / A Bundle of Letters.*
1882–83	Revisits America, death of parents. *The Siege of London / The Pension Beaurepas / The Point of View.*
1884	*Tales of Three Cities.*
1884–86	Resumes residence in London; sister Alice comes to live near him.
1885	*Stories Revived* (tales).
1886	Takes flat in De Vere Gardens, Kensington. *The Bostonians. The Princess Casamassima.*
1887	Long stay in Italy. Friendship with Constance Fenimore Woolson.
1888	*Partial Portraits. The Reverberator. The Aspern Papers / Louisa Pallant / The Modern Warning.*
1889–90	*A London Life / The Patagonia / The Liar / Mrs. Pemperley. The Tragic Muse.*
1890–92	"Dramatic years." Seeks to win a place in the theater. Dramatizes *The American*, which has short run.
1892	Alice James dies.
1893	*The Real Thing and Other Tales.*
1894	Constance Woolson commits suicide in Venice. James journeys to Italy and visits her grave in Rome.
1895	He is booed at first night of his play *Guy Domville*. Abandons theater. *Terminations* (tales).
1896	*Embarrassments* (tales).
1897	*The Spoils of Poynton. What Maisie Knew.*
1897–98	Settles in Lamb House, Rye, Sussex. *The Two Magics: The Turn of the Screw / Covering End.*
1899–1900	*The Awkward Age. The Sacred Fount.*
1900	*The Soft Side* (tales).
1902–1904	*The Ambassadors. The Wings of the Dove. The Golden Bowl.*
1903	*The Bettter Sort* (tales).
1905	Revisits United States after twenty-year absence, lectures on Balzac.

1907   *The American Scene.*

1907–09   Edits New York Edition, published in twenty-four volumes.

1910   William James dies. *The Finer Grain* (tales).

1913   Writes his autobiographies, *A Small Boy and Others, Notes of a Son and Brother.*

1914   *Notes on Novelists.* Begins war work.

1915   Becomes British subject.

1916   Receives the Order of Merit. Dies 28 February in Chelsea, two months before his seventy-third birthday. His ashes are buried in a Cambridge, Massachusetts, cemetery.

Selected Bibliography

Primary Works

The Aspern Papers / Louisa Pallant / The Modern Warning. 2 volumes. London and New York: Macmillan, 1888.

The Author of Beltraffio / Pandora / Georgina's Reasons / The Path of Duty / Four Meetings. Boston: James R. Osgood and Co., 1885.

The Better Sort. New York: Charles Scribner's Sons; London: Methuen, 1903. "Broken Wings," "The Beldonald Holbein," "The Two Faces," "The Tone of Time," "The Special Type," "Mrs. Medwin," "Flickerbridge," "The Story in It," "The Beast in the Jungle," "The Birthplace," "The Papers."

Daisy Miller: A Study / An International Episode / Four Meetings. 2 volumes. London: Macmillan, 1879.

The Diary of a Man of Fifty and A Bundle of Letters. New York: Harper & Brothers, 1880.

Embarrassments. New York: Macmillan; London: Heinemann, 1896. "The Figure in the Carpet," "Glasses," "The Next Time," "The Way It Came."

The Finer Grain. New York: Scribner's; London: Methuen, 1910. "The Velvet Gloves," "Mora Montravers," "A Round of Visits," "Crapy Cornelia," "The Bench of Desolation."

In the Cage. Chicago and New York: Herbert S. Stone & Co., 1898.

The Lesson of the Master / The Marriages / The Pupil / Brooksmith / The Solution / Sir Edmund Orme. New York and London: Macmillan, 1892.

A London Life / The Patagonia / The Liar / Mrs. Temperley. London and New York: Macmillan, 1889.

The Madonna of the Future and Other Tales. 2 volumes. London: Macmillan, 1879. "The Madonna of the Future," "Longstaff's Marriage," "Madamme de Mauves," "Eugene Pickering," "The Diary of a Man of Fifty," "Benvolio."

A Passionate Pilgrim and Other Tales. Boston: James R.Osgood & Co., 1875. "A Passionate Pilgrim," "The Last of the Valerii," "Eugene Pickering," "The Madonna of the Future," "The Romance of Certain Old Clothes," "Madame de Mauves."

The Private Life / Lord Beaupré / The Visits. New York: Harper & Brothers, 1893.

The Private Life / The Wheel of Time / Lord Beaupré / The Visits / Collaboration / Owen Wingrave. London: James R. Osgood, McIlvaine & Co., 1893.

The Real Thing and Other Tales. New York and London: Macmillan, 1893. "The Real Thing," "Sir Dominick Ferrand," "Nona Vincent," " The Chaperon," "Greville Fane."

The Siege of London, The Pension Beaurepas, and The Point of View. Boston: James R. Osgood and Co., 1883.

The Soft Side. New York: Macmillan; London: Methuen & Co., 1900. "The Great Good Place," "Europe," "Paste," "The Real Right Thing," "The Great Condition," "The Tree of Knowledge," "The Abasement of the Northmores," "The Given Case," "John Delavoy," "The Third Person," "Maud-Evelyn," "Miss Gunton of Poughkeepsie."

Stories Revived. 3 volumes. London: Macmillan, 1885. "The Author of Beltraffio," "Pandora," "The Path of Duty," "A Light Man," "A Day of Days," "Georgina's Reasons," "A Passionate Pilgrim," "A Landscape Painter," "Rose-Agathe," "Poor Richard," "The Last of the Valerii," "Master Eustace," "The Romance of Certain Old Clothes," "A Most Extraordinary Case."

Tales of Three Cities. Boston: Osgood; London: Macmillan, 1884. "The Impressions of a Cousin," "Lady Barberina," "A New England Winter."

Terminations: The Death of the Lion / The Coxon Fund / The Middle Years / The Altar of the Dead. New York: Harper & Brothers; London: Heinemann, 1895.

The Two Magics: The Turn of the Screw / Covering End. New York: Macmillan; London: Heinemann, 1898.

Washington Square / The Pension Beaurepas / A Bundle of Letters. 2 volumes. London: Macmillan, 1881.

The Wheel of Time / Collaboration / Owen Wingrave. New York: Harper & Brothers, 1893.

The Complete Notebooks of Henry James. Edited by Leon Edel and Lyall H. Powers. New York: Oxford University Press, 1986.

The Complete Tales of Henry James. Edited by Leon Edel. 12 volumes. Philadelphia and New York: J. B. Lippincott Co., 1961–64.

Henry James Letters. Edited by Leon Edel. 4 volumes. Cambridge, Mass.: Belknap Press, 1974–84.

The Letters of Henry James. Edited by Percy Lubbock. 2 volumes. New York: Charles Scribner's Sons, 1920.

The Novels and Tales of Henry James. Volumes 10–18. New York Edition. New York: Charles Scribner's Sons, 1908–9.

The Tales of Henry James. Edited by M. Aziz. 3 volumes (continuing). Oxford: Clarenden Press, 1974–.

Secondary Works

Armstrong, Paul B. "History and Epistemology: The Example of *The Turn of the Screw.*" *New Literary History* 19 (1988): 693–712.

Banta, Martha. "Artists, Models, Real Things, and Recognizable Types." *Studies in the Literary Imagination* 16 (1984): 7–34.

Barnett, Louise K. "Jamesian Feminism: Women in 'Daisy Miller.'" *Studies in Short Fiction* 16 (1979): 281–87.

Barry, P. T. "Physical Descriptions in the International Tales of Henry James." *Orbis Litterarum* 35 (1980): 47–58.

Barry, Peter. "In Fairness to the Master's Wife: A Re-Interpretation of 'The Lesson of the Master.'" *Studies in Short Fiction* 15 (1978): 385–89.

Bauer, Dale M., and Andrew Lakritz. "Language, Class, and Sexuality in Henry James's 'In the Cage.'" *New Orleans Review* 14, no. 3 (1987): 61–69.

Bell, Barbara Currier. "Beyond Irony in Henry James: 'The Aspern Papers.'" *Studies in the Novel* 13 (1981): 282–93.

Bell, Milicent. "'The Turn of the Screw' and the *recherche de l'absolu.*" *Delta* 15 (1982): 34–48.

Berkson, Dorothy. "Tender-Minded Idealism and Erotic Repression in James's 'Madame de Mauves' and 'The Last of the Valerii.'" *Henry James Review* 2 (1981): 78–86.

Berthold, Michael Coulson. "The Idea of 'Too Late' in James's 'The Beast in the Jungle.'" *Henry James Review* 4 (1983): 128–39.

Betsky-Zweig, S. "From Pleached Garden to Jungle and Waste Land: Henry James's Beast." In *From Cooper to Philip Roth: Essays on American Literature*, edited by J. Bakker and D. R. M. Wilkinson, 45–55. Amsterdam: Rodopi, 1980.

Biedler, Peter G. *Ghosts, Demons, and Henry James: "The Turn of the Screw" at the Turn of the Century.* Columbia: University of Missouri Press, 1989.

Bier, Jesse. "Henry James's 'The Jolly Corner': The Writer's Fable and the Deeper Matter." *Arizona Quarterly* 35 (1979): 321–34.

Bishop, George. "Addressing 'A Bundle of Letters': Henry James and the Hazard of Authority." *Henry James Review* 8 (1987): 91–103.

———. *When the Master Relents: The Neglected Short Fictions of Henry James.* Ann Arbor, Mich.: UMI Research Press, 1988.

Booth, Wayne. *The Rhetoric of Fiction.* Chicago and London: University of Chicago Press, 1961.

Bradbury, Nicola. *An Annotated Critical Bibliography of Henry James.* New York: St. Martin's Press, 1987.

———. *Henry James: The Later Novels.* London: Oxford University Press, 1979.

Buitenhuis, Peter. "From Daisy Miller to Julia Bride: 'A Whole Passage of Intellectual History.'" *American Quarterly* 11 (1959): 136–46.

————. *The Grasping Imagination: The American Writings of Henry James.* Toronto: University of Toronto Press, 1970.

Caramello, Charles. "The Author's Taste, or, Unturning the Screw." *Dalhousie Review* 64 (1984): 36–45.

Chapman, Sara S. "The 'Obsession of Egotism' in Henry James's 'A Round of Visits.'" *Arizona Quarterly* 29 (1973): 130–38.

Cohen, Paula Marantz. "Freud's *Dora* and James's *Turn of the Screw:* Two Treatments of the Female 'Case.'" *Criticism* 28 (1986): 73–87.

Crowe, M. Karen. "The Tapestry of Henry James's 'The Turn of the Screw.'" *The Nassau Review* 4 (1982): 37–48.

Dahl, Curtin. "Lord Lambeth's America: Architecture in James's 'An International Episode.'" *Henry James Review* 5 (1984): 80–95.

Deakin, Motley. "Two Studies of 'Daisy Miller.'" *Henry James Review* 5 (1983): 2–28.

Draper, R. P. "Death of a Hero? Winterbourne and Daisy Miller." *Studies in Short Fiction* 6 (1959): 601–8.

Dunbar, Viola R. "The Revision of 'Daisy Miller.'" *Modern Language Notes* 65 (1950): 311–17.

Dyson, J. Peter. "Perfection, Beauty and Suffering in 'The Two Faces.'" *Henry James Review* 2 (1981): 116–25.

Eaton, Marcia. "James's Turn of the Speech-Act." *British Journal of Aesthetics* 23 (1983): 333–45.

Edel, Leon. Introduction to *The Ghostly Tales of Henry James*, edited by Leon Edel, v–xxxii. New Brunswick, N.J.: Rutgers University Press, 1948.

————. Introduction to *The Complete Tales of Henry James*, edited by Leon Edel, 17–22. Philadelphia: J. B. Lippincott, 1961.

————. *Henry James: A Life.* New York: Harper & Row, 1985.

Edel, Leon, Dan H. Lawrence, and James Rambeau. *A Bibliography of Henry James.* 3rd ed. Oxford: Clarendon Press, 1982.

Edel, Leon, and Adeline R. Tintner. "The Private Life of Peter Quin[t]: Origins of 'The Turn of the Screw.'" *Henry James Review* 7 (1986): 2–4.

Eggenschwiler, David. "James's 'The Pupil': A Moral Tale without a Moral." *Studies in Short Fiction* 15 (1978): 435–44.

Ellis, James. "The Archaeology of Ancient Rome: Sexual Metaphor in 'The Beast in the Jungle.'" *Henry James Review* 6 (1984): 27–31.

Esch, Deborah. "A Jamesian About-Face: Notes on 'The Jolly Corner.'" *English Literary History* 50 (1983): 587–605.

Fadiman, Clifton. Introduction to *The Short Stories of Henry James*, edited by Clifton Fadiman, ix–xx. New York: Random House, 1945.

Faulkner, Howard. "Text as Pretext in *The Turn of the Screw.*" *Studies in Short Fiction* 20 (1983): 87–94.

Felman, Shoshana. "Turning the Screw of Interpretation." In *Literature and*

Psychoanalysis: The Question of Reading: Otherwise, edited by Shoshana Felman, 94–207. Baltimore: Johns Hopkins University Press, 1982.

Fogel, Daniel Mark. *Henry James and the Structure of the Romantic Imagination.* Baton Rouge: Louisiana State University Press, 1981.

———. "A New Reading of Henry James's 'The Jolly Corner.'" In *Critical Essays on Henry James: The Late Novels*, edited by James W. Gargano, 190–203. Boston: G.K. Hall & Co., 1987.

Fogelman, Bruce. "John Marcher's Journey for Knowledge: The Heroic Background of 'The Beast in the Jungle.'" *Henry James Review* 10 (1989): 68–73.

Freundlieb, Dieter. "Explaining Interpretation: The Case of Henry James's *The Turn of the Screw*." *Poetics Today* 5 (1984): 79–85.

Gage, Richard P. *Order and Design: Henry James' Titled Story Sequences.* New York: Peter Lang, 1988.

Gale, Robert L. *The Caught Image: Figurative Language in the Fiction of Henry James.* Chapel Hill: University of North Carolina Press, 1964.

Gargano, James W. "'Daisy Miller': An Abortive Quest for Innocence." *South Atlantic Quarterly* 59 (1960): 114–20.

Gerlach, John. "Closure in Henry James's Short Fiction." *Journal of Narrative Technique* 14 (1984): 60–67.

Griffith, John. "James's 'The Pupil' as Whodunit: The Question of Moral Responsibility." *Studies in Short Fiction* 9 (1972): 257–68.

Halter, Peter. "Is Henry James's 'The Figure in the Carpet' 'Unreadable'?" In *Continental Approaches to Narrative*, edited by Anthony Mortimer, 25–37. Tübingen, West Germany: Gunter Narr, 1984.

Harris, Janice H. "Bushes, Bears, and 'The Beast in the Jungle.'" *Studies in Short Fiction* 18 (1981): 147–54.

Harvath, Brooke K. "The Life of Art, the Art of Life: The Ascetic Aesthetics of Defeat in James's Stories of Writers and Artists." *Modern Fiction Studies* 28 (1982): 93–107.

Hill, Robert W. "A Counterclockwise Turn in James's 'The Turn of the Screw.'" *Twentieth-Century Literature* 27 (1981): 53–71.

Hocks, Richard A. "'Daisy Miller,' Backward into the Past: A Centennial Essay." *Henry James Review* 1 (1980): 164–78.

Jacobs, J. U. "The Alter Ego: The Artist as American in 'The Jolly Corner.'" *Theoria* 58 (1983): 51–60.

Jensen-Osinski, Barbara. "The Key to the Palpable Past: A Study of Miss Tina in 'The Aspern Papers.'" *Henry James Review* 3 (1981): 4–10.

Jones, O. P. "The Cold World of London in 'The Beast in the Jungle.'" *Studies in American Fiction* 6 (1978): 227–35.

Kauffman, Linda S. "The Author of Our Woe: Virtue Recorded in 'The Turn of the Screw.'" *Nineteenth-Century Fiction* 36 (1981): 176–92.

Kenny, William. "The Death of Morgan in James's 'The Pupil.'" *Studies in Short Fiction* 8 (1971): 317–22.

Kimbel, Ellen. "The American Short Story: 1900–1920." In *The American Short Story 1900–1945: A Critical History*, edited by Philip Stevick, 33–69. Boston: Twayne Publishers, 1984.

Kimbrough, Robert, ed. *Henry James: The Turn of the Screw*. Norton Critical Edition. New York: W.W. Norton, 1966.

Koprince, Susan. "The Clue from *Manfred* in 'Daisy Miller.'" *Arizona Quarterly* 42 (1986): 293–304.

Kraft, James. *The Early Tales of Henry James*. Carbondale: Southern Illinois University Press, 1969.

Lester, Pauline. "James's Use of Comedy in 'The Real Thing.'" *Studies in Short Fiction* 15 (1978): 33–38.

Levine, Robert T. "A Failure of Reading: 'The Aspern Papers' and the Ennobling Force of Literature." *Essays in Arts and Sciences* 12 (1983): 87–98.

Lock, Peter W. "'The Figure in the Carpet': The Text as Riddle and Force." *Nineteenth-Century Fiction* 36 (1981): 157–75.

McMaster, Juliet. "The Turn of the Screw." In *The Novel from Sterne to James: Essays on the Relation of Literature to Life*, by Juliet McMaster and Rowland McMaster, 188–94. Totowa, N.J.: Barnes & Noble, 1981.

Martin, W. R. "The Narrator's 'Retreat' in James's 'Four Meetings.'" *Studies in Short Fiction* 17 (1980): 497–99.

Martin, W. R., and Warren U. Ober. "Dantesque Patterns in Henry James's 'A Round of Visits.'" *Ariel: A Review of International English Literature* 12 (1981): 45–54.

———. Introduction to *The Finer Grain*, edited by W. R. Martin and Warren U. Ober, v–xxii. Delmar, N. Y.: Scholars' Facsimiles & Reprints, 1986.

Matthiessen, F. O. Introduction to *Stories of Writers and Artists*, edited by F. O. Matthiessen, 1–17. New York: New Directions, n.d.

Meyers, Jeffrey. "Velazquez and 'Daisy Miller.'" *Studies in Short Fiction* 16 (1979): 170–78.

Miall, David. "Designed Horror: James' Vision of Evil in 'The Turn of the Screw.'" *Nineteenth-Century Literature* 39 (1984): 305–27.

Milicia, Joseph. "Henry James's *Winter's Tale*: 'The Bench of Desolation.'" *Studies in American Fiction* 6 (1978) 141–56.

Miller, J. Hillis. "The Figure in the Carpet." *Poetics Today* 1 (1971): 107–18.

Monteiro, George. "'He Do the Police in Different Voices': James's 'The Point of View.'" *Topic* 37 (1983): 3–9.

Moon, Heath. "A Freudian Boondoggle: The Case of James's 'The Marriages.'" *Arizona Quarterly* 40 (1984): 35–48.

Ohmann, Carol. "'Daisy Miller': A Study of Changing Intentions." *American Literature* 36 (1964): 1–11.

Peinovich, Michael P., and Richard F. Patteson. "The Cognitive Beast in the Syntactic Jungle: A Study of James's Language." *Language & Style: An International Journal* 11 (1978): 82–93.

Perosa, Sergio. "Henry James's 'The Aspern Papers.'" In *Leon Edel and Literary Art*, edited by Lyall H. Powers, 125–33. Ann Arbor, Mich.: UMI Research Press, 1988.

Person, Leland S. "Eroticism and Creativity in 'The Aspern Papers.'" *Literature and Psychology* 32 (1986): 20–31.

Powers, Lyall H. "James's 'Maud-Evelyn.'" in *Leon Edel and Literary Art*, edited by Lyall H. Powers, 117–24. Ann Arbor, Mich.: UMI Research Press, 1988.

Purdy, Strother B. "Conversation and Awareness in Henry James's 'A Round of Visits.'" *Studies in Short Fiction* 6 (1969): 421–32.

Putt, S. Gorley. *Henry James: A Reader's Guide*. Ithaca, N.Y.: Cornell University Press, 1966.

Rimmon-Kenan, Shlomith. *The Concept of Ambiguity: The Example of James*. Chicago: University of Chicago Press, 1977.

Robbins, Bruce. "Shooting Off James's Blanks: Theory, Politics, and 'The Turn of the Screw.'" *Henry James Review* 5 (1984): 192–99.

Ron, Moshe. "A Reading of 'The Real Thing.'" *Yale French Studies* 58 (1979): 190–212.

Rowe, John Carlos. "Screwball: The Use and Abuse of Uncertainty in Henry James's 'The Turn of the Screw.'" *Delta* 15 (1982): 1–31.

———. *The Theoretical Dimensions of Henry James*. Madison: University of Wisconsin Press, 1984.

Safranek, William P. "Longmore in 'Madame de Mauves': The Making of a Pragmatist." *Arizona Quarterly* 35 (1979): 293–302.

Salmon, Rachel. "A Marriage of Opposites: Henry James's 'The Figure in the Carpet.'" *English Literary History* 47 (1980): 788–803.

———. "Naming and Knowing in Henry James's 'The Beast in the Jungle': The Hermeneutics of a Sacred Text." *Orbis Litterarum* 36 (1981): 302–22.

Salzberg, Joel. "Mr. Mudge as Redemptive Fate: Juxtaposition in James's 'In the Cage.'" *Studies in the Novel* 11 (1979): 63–76.

Schrero, Elliot M. "Exposure in 'The Turn of the Screw.'" *Modern Philology* 78 (1981): 261–74.

Seamon, Roger. "Henry James's 'Four Meetings': A Study in Irritability and Condescension." *Studies in Short Fiction* 15 (1978): 155–63.

Sedgwick, Eve Kosofsky, "The Beast in the Closet: James and the Writing of Homosexual Panic." *Sex, Politics and Science in the Nineteenth-Century Novel*, edited by Ruth Bernard Yeazell, 148–86. Baltimore: Johns Hopkins University Press, 1986.

Shapland, Elizabeth. "Duration and Frequency: Prominent Aspects of Time in Henry James' 'The Beast in the Jungle.'" *Papers on Language and Literature* 17 (1981): 33–47.

Siebers, Tobin. "Hesitation, History, and Reading: Henry James's 'The Turn of the Screw.'" *Texas Studies in Literature and Language* 25 (1983): 558–73.

Smit, David. "The Leap of the Beast: The Dramatic Style of Henry James's 'The Beast in the Jungle.'" *Henry James Review* 4 (1983): 219–30.

Stafford, William T. *James's "Daisy Miller": The Story, the Play, the Critics.* New York: Charles Scribner's Sons, 1963.

Sweeney, Gerard. "The Deadly Figure in James's Carpet." *Modern Language Studies* 13 (1983): 79–85.

———. "The Illness of the Passionate Pilgrim." *American Literary Realism* 21 (1988): 3–18.

Taylor, Linda J. *Henry James, 1866–1916: A Reference Guide.* Boston: G.K. Hall, 1982.

Tierce, Mike. "The Governess's 'White Face of Damnation.'" *American Notes and Queries* 21 (1983): 137–38.

Tintner, Adeline R. *The Book World of Henry James: Appropriating the Classics.* Ann Arbor, Mich.: UMI Research Press, 1987.

———. "An Interlude in Hell: Henry James's 'A Round of Visits' and *Paradise Lost.*" *Notes on Modern American Literature* 5 (1981): no 12.

———. *The Museum World of Henry James.* Ann Arbor, Mich.: UMI Research Press, 1986.

———. *The Pop World of Henry James.* Ann Arbor, Mich.: UMI Research Press, 1989.

Tuttleton, James W. "Propriety and Fine Perceptions: James's 'The Europeans.'" *Modern Language Review* 73 (1978): 481–96.

Vaid, Krishna Baldev. *Technique in the Tales of Henry James.* Cambridge: Harvard University Press, 1964.

Vanderbilt, Kermit. "Notes Largely Musical on Henry James's 'Four Meetings.'" *Sewanee Review* 81 (1973): 739–52.

Volpe, Edmond L. "The Reception of 'Daisy Miller.'" *Boston Public Library Quarterly* 10 (1958): 55–59.

Wagenknecht, Edward. *The Tales of Henry James.* New York: Ungar Publishing Co., 1984.

Waldmeir, Joseph J. "Miss Tina Did It: A Fresh Look at 'The Aspern Papers.'" *The Centennial Review* 26 (1982): 256–67.

Ward, J. A. *The Imagination of Disaster: Evil in the Fiction of Henry James.* Lincoln: University of Nebraska Press, 1961.

———. "Silence, Realism, and 'The Great Good Place.'" *Henry James Review* 3 (1982): 129–32.

Wegelin, Christof. "Art and Life in James's 'The Middle Years.'" *Modern Fiction Studies* 33 (1987): 639–46.

————. *The Image of Europe in Henry James*. Dallas: Southern Methodist University Press, 1958.

Willen, Gerald, ed. *A Casebook on Henry James's "The Turn of the Screw."* 2d ed. New York: Thomas Y. Crowell Co., 1969.

Williams, M. A. "Reading 'The Figure in the Carpet': Henry James and Wolfgang Iser." *English Studies in Africa* 27 (1984): 107–21.

Wilt, Napier, and John Lucas. Introduction to *Americans and Europe: Selected Tales of Henry James*, edited by Napier Wilt and John Lucas. vii–xx. Boston: Houghton Mifflin, 1965.

Wirth-Nesher, Hana. "The Thematics of Interpretation: James's Artistic Tales." *Henry James Review* 5 (1984): 117–27.

Yacobi, Tamar. "Hero or Heroine? 'Daisy Miller' and the Focus of Interest in Narrative." *Style* 19 (1985): 1–35.

Zabel, Morton Dauwen. Introduction to *Fifteen Short Stories*, edited by Morton Dauwen Zabel, vii–xxx. New York: Bantam Books, 1961.

————. Introduction to *The Portable Henry James*, edited by Morton Dauwen Zabel, 1–29. New York: Viking Press, 1951.

Index

The Author

Richard A. Hocks is professor of English at the University of Missouri, Columbia, where he teaches courses in American literature and the two-year interdisciplinary humanities sequence. His *Henry James and Pragmatistic Thought: A Study in the Relationship between the Philosophy of William James and the Literary Art of Henry James* was nominated for the National Book Award in 1974. He has written also on Thoreau, Coleridge, Emerson, Defoe, T. S. Eliot, Owen Barfield, and Michael Polanyi, and has coedited the Norton Critical Edition of *The Wings of the Dove*. He currently writes the Henry James chapter for *American Literary Scholarship* as well as the Analytic Bibliographical Essays for the *Henry James Review*.

The Editor

Gordon Weaver earned his Ph.D. in English and creative writing at the University of Denver in 1970. He is professor of English at Oklahoma State University. He is the author of several novels, including *Count a Lonely Cadence, Give Him a Stone, Circling Byzantium,* and most recently *The Eight Corners of the World.* His short stories are collected in *The Entombed Man of Thule, Such Waltzing Was Not Easy, Getting Serious, Morality Play,* and *A World Quite Round.* Recognition of his fiction includes the St. Lawrence Award for Fiction (1973), two National Endowment for the Arts fellowships (1974 and 1989), and the O. Henry First Prize (1979). He edited *The American Short Story, 1945–1980: A Critical History* and is currently editor of the *Cimarron Review.* Married and the father of three daughters, he lives in Stillwater, Oklahoma.